Economic Agglomeration and the Development of Cities in China

Economic Agglomeration and the Development of Cities in China

Hong Gao
Fudan University, China

World Scientific

NEW JERSEY • LONDON • SINGAPORE • BEIJING • SHANGHAI • HONG KONG • TAIPEI • CHENNAI • TOKYO

Published by

World Scientific Publishing Co. Pte. Ltd.
5 Toh Tuck Link, Singapore 596224
USA office: 27 Warren Street, Suite 401-402, Hackensack, NJ 07601
UK office: 57 Shelton Street, Covent Garden, London WC2H 9HE

Library of Congress Cataloging-in-Publication Data
Names: Gao, Hong, 1986 September– author.
Title: Economic agglomeration and the development of cities in China /
Hong Gao, Fudan University, China.
Description: Hackensack, NJ : World Scientific, [2023] |
Includes bibliographical references and index.
Identifiers: LCCN 2021061613 | ISBN 9789811251559 (hardcover) |
ISBN 9789811251566 (ebook) | ISBN 9789811251573 (ebook other)
Subjects: LCSH: China--Economic policy--2000– | China--Economic conditions--2000– |
Regional planning--China. | Cities and towns--Growth.
Classification: LCC HC427.95 .G3536 2023 | DDC 330.951--dc23/eng/20220207
LC record available at https://lccn.loc.gov/2021061613

British Library Cataloguing-in-Publication Data
A catalogue record for this book is available from the British Library.

The book is sponsored by Fudan University and the Shanghai Institute of International Economics and Finance.

《经济集聚和中国城市发展》
Originally published in Chinese by Fudan University Press Co., Ltd.

For any available supplementary material, please visit
https://www.worldscientific.com/worldscibooks/10.1142/12704#t=suppl

Desk Editors: Balamurugan Rajendran/Nicole Ong

Typeset by Stallion Press
Email: enquiries@stallionpress.com

About the Author

GAO Hong is an Assistant Professor at the School of Economics, Fudan University. Her research covers the fields of urban economics and labor economics. In particular, her work has focused on urbanization, city development, and labor market performance in China. Her current research focuses on understanding the sources of growth and structural changes in Chinese cities.

Contents

About the Author v

Chapter 1 Introduction 1
1.1 Controversies of the Transformation of China's Economic Growth and Urban Development Path 3
1.2 Economic Agglomeration and the Urban Labor Market Performance 7
1.3 Research Framework and Chapters Arranged 13
1.4 Main Contributions 19

Chapter 2 Why Do Big Cities Rise: A Literature Review 23
2.1 Economic Agglomeration Effect: A Review 24
2.2 Urban Labor Market Effect of Economic Agglomeration 33
2.3 Economic Agglomeration and Place-based Policies 39

Chapter 3 Spatial Distribution of the Manufacturing Industry in China since the Reform and Opening Up: Roles of Globalization, Economic Agglomeration, and Economic Policy 51
3.1 Spatial Distribution of Economic Activities: Agglomeration Effect vs. Dispersing Effect 53
3.2 Features and Changes of the Spatial Distribution of China's Manufacturing Industry since the Reform and Opening Up 56

3.3 Knowledge Spillovers and Changes in Spatial Distribution of Manufacturing Industries 65
3.4 Summary 70

Chapter 4 Economic Agglomeration and the Employment of Urban Workers 73
4.1 City Size and Employment: Theory 75
4.2 Economic Agglomeration and the Employment of Workers: Baseline Regression Results 77
4.3 Looking for the Instrumental Variable of City Size 81
4.4 Does Economic Agglomeration Harm Equity: Heterogeneous Influences of City Size on Employment 91
4.5 Summary 104

Chapter 5 Economic Agglomeration and the Income of Urban Residents 105
5.1 City Size and the Income of Workers: A Theoretical Analysis 106
5.2 Economic Agglomeration and the Income of Labors: Baseline Regression Results 109
5.3 The Heterogeneous Influence of City Size on the Income of Workers 118
5.4 Summary 125

Chapter 6 Manufacturing Industry Clusters in China: Data, Method, and Spatial Distribution Characteristics 129
6.1 Inter-industry Linkages, Agglomeration Effects, and Industrial Clusters 131
6.2 Data and Method Used in the Chapter 134
6.3 Defining Clusters of Manufacturing Industries in China 136
6.4 Spatial Distribution Patterns of Manufacturing Clusters in China 144
6.5 Summary 153

Chapter 7 Economic Agglomeration and Cluster Effects in Urban China 155
7.1 Why are Clusters of Manufacturing Industries Important? 156
7.2 Industrial Clusters and Employment Growth 160
7.3 Clusters and Industry Development: Quantity Effect vs. Quality Effect 167

7.4 Industry Value Chain Positions and Heterogeneous Cluster Effects 170
7.5 Summary 175

Chapter 8 Urbanization, Urban Development, and Structural Transformation 179
8.1 Place-Based Policies and Employment Multiplier Effect 183
8.2 Data and Model Specification 185
8.3 Employment Multiplier Effect in the Local Labor Market: Empirical Results 187
8.4 Model Extensions: Urbanization, Economic Agglomeration and Heterogeneous Employment Multiplier Effect 194
8.5 Summary 199

Chapter 9 Conclusions 201
9.1 Main Conclusions 201
9.2 Inclusive Growth and Coordinated Development among Regions 205
9.3 Prospects for Future Researches 208

References 211
Index 223

Chapter 1

Introduction

Cities are places where modern economic activities are concentrated, and the important driving force for the continuous development of economy and society. Cities keep developing along with the great abundance of human material life and the great prosperity of culture. The history of human society is the history of sustained development of cities and constant advance of urbanization. With the development of cities, economic activities tend to be highly concentrated spatially. The data show that the distribution of economic activities is not only imbalanced among countries but also highly concentrated within the same country, with large cities and metropolitan areas getting increasingly more important. The *World Development Report 2009* published by the World Bank begins by noting that about half of the world's economic activities are concentrated in 1.5% of the land areas. Cairo generates more than half of Egypt's GDP, though it covers only 0.5% of the country's total land area. Similarly, the three south-central states of Brazil account for more than half of the total production activities of the country, but their area of land only accounts for 15% of the total land area of the country (World Bank, 2008). With the rise in a number of international metropolises and advances of globalization, resources are less allocated by national power, and the freer flow of production factors across countries makes cities break through the constraints of the national power and occupy the center of the stage of world economy. The mode of global competition changes from inter-country competition to inter-city competition. The competitiveness of a country depends on the competitiveness of its cities to a large extent.

The process of urbanization reflects the process of continuous development and changes of production, social organization, and political structure in different historical development stages of humans. Urbanization started in the industrial revolution, and accelerated in the 20th century. Before the 20th century, urbanization, especially the development of large cities, were merely scattered in parts of countries. According to Ades and Glaeser (1995), in the 16th century, Beijing, with a population of about 600,000, was the largest megacity in the world. Beijing had been keeping the record till the year 1830, when it was surpassed by London. In about 1700, each of such megacities as London, Paris, and Tokyo had a population of only about 500,000. Urbanization accelerated in the 20th century, and some supersized cities emerged. According to the sixth census of the People's Republic of China, Beijing's number of permanent residents reached 19.612 million in 2010. Similarly, megacities such as Paris, London, and Tokyo had seen remarkable increases in population. In 2014, as the largest cities in the world, Tokyo saw its population reach 37.19 million, the population of Paris reached 10.764 million, and that of London reached 10.189 million, far larger than the population before the 20th century (United Nations, 2015). Urbanization, as an international trend, will be going on in the future. According to the estimation of the UN, the world's urban population will increase by 2.8 billion between 2018 and 2050, from 4.2 billion in 2018 to 7 billion in 2050, and 90% of the increase will occur in Asia and Africa. Urban population growth will cover most of the world's population growth over the next three decades, with the world's urbanization rate increasing from 55% in 2018 to 68% in 2050. Among them, the urban population growth of India, China, and Nigeria will account for 35% of the global urban population growth from 2018 to 2050, and China's urban population is expected to increase by 250 million (United Nations, 2018).

Similar to the global trend of urbanization, the economic development of China keeps pacing up with rapid advancements of urbanization. Urbanization in China has accelerated since the reform and opening up in 1978. According to the National Bureau of Statistics, China's total urban population increased from 57.65 million at the end of 1949 to 792.98 million at the end of 2016. The proportion of urban population in the total population, or the urbanization rate, also rose from 10.64% in 1949 to 57.35% at the end of 2016. China's urbanization is so remarkable that Joseph E. Stiglitz, former chief economist of the World Bank, ranks China's urbanization and technological progress in the United States as the two major events affecting human society in the 21st century. In the context of the macroeconomy in which labor and capital's contributions to economic growth tend to decline, the growth of total factor productivity (TFP) will be crucial for China's sustainable economic growth in the future, and accelerating urbanization is an important way for China's economic transformation and upgrading (Wan and Cai, 2012). So, what way of urbanization should China take?

From the perspective of the development concept, cities should make life better. The urban development pattern aiming at improving people's well-being is not only important for maintaining and improving urban competitiveness and sustaining urban growth but also consistent with the concept of inclusive economic growth. Inclusive economic growth not only focuses on the speed of a country's economic growth but also emphasizes the mode of economic growth. It requires that the vast majority of the labor force of a country be included in the process of economic growth to benefit it broadly (World Bank, 2006). Only when economic growth of a country actually enhances its welfare by improving individual's labor market performance, will it be "inclusive" and meaningful. Whether economic growth can be inclusive depends on the pattern of growth and the choice of policies, and urbanization and urban development patterns are crucial. However, at present there is still a controversy on what kind of urbanization path facilitates inclusive growth, and more theoretical and empirical studies are needed. The book hopes to summarize the experience of urban development in China from the perspective of labor market and provide a reference for the choice of the urbanization pattern.

1.1 Controversies of the Transformation of China's Economic Growth and Urban Development Path

Since the reform and opening up in 1978, China has gone through several conversions of economic growth momentum. For a long period of time after the founding of the People's Republic of China, the basic mode of China's macroeconomic operation was the planned economy. China strived to achieve material balance, fiscal balance, foreign trade balance, and price balance when making and implementing plans. At that time, the major objective of macroeconomic planning was to increase the accumulation rate and speed up industrialization. By means of planning, that is, by controlling the prices of agricultural products and the living costs of urban and rural residents, surpluses can be handed over to the country in the form of profits of industrial enterprises as much as possible, so that the accumulation rate of the whole country and investment needed for industrialization can be increased. Although the growth mode at the expense of agriculture and household consumption can realize industrialization quickly in a short term, it is inefficient and unsustainable in the long run, resulting in distorted industrial structure. Shortages, recessive unemployment, and repressed inflation are distinguishing characteristics of macroeconomic operation in the era of planned economy.

Since the reform and opening up in 1978, the rural and urban micro-organizations have been reorganized and price controls have been removed. Furthermore, agricultural and industrial outputs have been mushrooming. Under the background of the reform and opening up, business-friendly policies have seen great success in the context of acceleration of globalization. More than 20 million workers migrated from the central and western regions to east regions, and FDI from the developed countries benefited greatly from abundant labor supply, which facilitates fast industrial growth and the presence of the "factory of the world". The rapid growth of capital and labor input, the institutional dividends brought by institutional reform, the "catch-up effect" of learning from the advanced and structural transformation have all contributed to the rapid growth of TFP in China. Integration into the global value chain since the mid-1990s promoted the development of export-oriented manufacturing industries in China, and export has become the most important economic growth driver.

For more than 30 years, China has maintained an annual GDP growth rate of nearly 10%, which is undoubtedly a miracle in the world economic history. However, after entering the 21st century, the fundamental advantages of China's manufacturing industry have gradually reversed. Li *et al.* (2012) found that the average wage of manufacturing workers in China has been rising continuously in recent years. By the end of 2008, it was higher than most emerging Asian economies such as Indonesia, India, and Thailand, only lower than the Philippines. The loss of the advantages of low labor costs made China face a severe pressure of export growth and FDI relocation. There are certainly reasons behind the rising cost of manufacturing industry, such as rising returns to education and population age structure transformation, but the significant rise of marginal cost of migration under the restriction of the household registration system (*Hukou* system), as well as the resulting slowdown in the growth of urban migrating population and shrinking labor supply cannot be ignored.

The export-oriented development strategy has not only contributed to the miracle of China's economic growth but also resulted in the double imbalance of China's internal and external economy and reduced economic efficiency. The internal imbalance — reflected in the decreasing share of consumption in GDP relative to investment and export-driven growth — is basically linked to China's widening income inequality. The external imbalance is results of low labor costs and an undervalued currency, which established China's comparative advantage on overseas markets and have resulted in China's rising exports and huge foreign currency reserves. Before 2008, the double imbalance of both internal and external economy was masked by the rapid economic growth, while the outbreak of the global financial crisis in 2008 and the shrinking external demand, as well as the fading of demographic dividends under the background of aging, forced China to seek new growth drivers. Due to the gradual disappearance of demographic dividends, gradual decline in the rate of capital accumulation, and the decline in the contribution of TFP to economic growth, China's long-term potential growth rate tends to decline (Yuan Zhigang and Yu Yuxin, 2012; Perkins and Rawski, 2008). Since 2015, China's economy has entered a state of "new normal", where the growth shifted from high speed to medium-high speed. China needs to transform its economic growth pattern as soon as possible.

The first stage of China's economic growth, the stage of high economic growth driven by investment and exports, has come to an end. The Chinese economy is entering the second stage of growth, and urbanization and the development of the service sector will become new drivers of economic growth. The key lies in the expansion of domestic demand. Since the reform and opening up, the achievements of China's urbanization have attracted worldwide attention. The urbanization rate has been increased from 17.92% in 1978 to 57.35% in 2016, with an average annual increase of 1.04 percentage points. However, compared with the urbanization rate of countries with similar income levels or with China's own industrialization rate, the urbanization rate in China is obviously low, and the urbanization process lags greatly behind the industrialization process. Therefore, in the coming decades, China's urbanization should not only continue to advance but also accelerate, in order to reduce the adverse impact on economic growth caused by the rising production cost caused by the lack of urban labor supply under institutional constraints.

Urbanization and urban system optimization will play significant roles in raising productivity. There is a consensus among scholars and policy-makers that China will continue to push forward its urbanization. However, there are still different opinions among scholars as to which way China should take to push urbanization ahead, how to construct the most efficient urban system, and whether large cities or small and medium-sized towns should be given priority in the process of urbanization. According to Zhu Xuangong (2000), China should give priority to the development of small towns as the breakthrough of urbanization promotion at the present stage. This is mainly because the transportation and psychological costs are low for migrant workers from the rural area. In addition, the cost of building small towns is relatively low. Similarly, Qin Daijian (2008) believes that small towns can serve as a link between cities and rural areas by limiting the size and dispersing the functions of large cities. Urban and rural economic development will both be promoted by accelerating the upgrading of urban industries, reducing pollutions in the urban area, and raising agricultural subsidies from the industry sector. Moreover, small towns will also play an important role in stimulating domestic demand and absorbing surplus rural labor force.

Meanwhile, some scholars argue that China should give priority to promoting the development of large cities in order to maximize the economic agglomeration effect and improve economic efficiency. Wang Xiaolu (2010) believes that the number of big cities in China is small. Although small towns will become an important link to absorb rural labor force, they are not attractive to industrial investment and cannot create enough jobs to attract the inflow of population. Furthermore, the efficiency of land use in small towns is significantly lower than that in large cities, and it is difficult for small towns to provide the infrastructure and public services necessary for high-quality life under such small economic scales. Wang Xiaolu believes that the proportion of the population living in big cities in China will keep rising in the next 20 years, and it is expected to reach 39% by 2030. The number of big cities with a population of more than one million will also continue to increase. Similarly, Henderson (2007) believes that due to the long-term restriction of the *Hukou* system on urban expansion, China's urbanization is too localized and small in scale to give play to the advantages of scale economy, which limits the improvement of urban labor productivity and economic growth. Au and Henderson (2006) estimates that 51–62% of the cities in China are insufficient in scales, which has seriously damaged the efficiency of

China's economic growth. In China, output losses caused by under agglomeration account for about 17% of the average output of employees. In fact, the development of large cities and small towns is not mutually exclusive. Xu Zheng *et al.* (2010) believes that the development of small and medium-sized towns should base on the development of large cities. Their empirical results show that the development of small cities shares the benefits brought by the economic agglomeration of large cities, and the closer they are to regional big cities, the more rapidly they are to grow.

What is more, a common misunderstanding about urban and regional development is to equate "inter-regional coordinated development" with "inter-regional synchronized development" and to further contrast "economic agglomeration" with "inter-regional coordinated development". As shown in policies, the development gap between different regions and cities of different sizes is attempted to be narrowed in order to balance the welfares of residents in different regions and cities. The optimal urbanization way, or which should be given priority in the process of development, large cities or small and medium-sized towns, has always been an important issue in the process of urbanization in all countries. Japan, South Korea, and other countries have implemented measures to limit population growth in large cities during their development. The choice of ways of urbanization actually depends on the understanding of optimal city size. Nowadays, in China, policies tend to restrict the development of large cities due to concerns about "congestion costs" such as traffic congestion and environmental pollution. Urban residents also support the policies restricting the inflow of labor force for the sake of their own interests. The advantages of economic agglomeration are neglected to a great extent. In addition, the inflow of low-skilled workers is inhibited by the *Hukou* system in China which is biased toward high-skilled workers. However, there is no final conclusion to the issues mentioned above, and city development patterns are different in different cities and at different stages of development. More empirical evidence are needed.

1.2 Economic Agglomeration and the Urban Labor Market Performance

Theoretically, the optimal size of a city is decided by balancing the agglomeration effect against the crowding-out effect of urban expansion. City agglomeration effect comes from the benefits brought by the concentration of economic activities, which will bring about the increases in labor productivity. Literature on new economic geography points out that due to the increasing returns to scale in production, consumers' preference of consumption diversity, and lower transportation costs, manufacturers will choose regions with relatively large market demands to do business, resulting in larger production scales and higher factor prices in agglomeration areas. In equilibrium, higher factor prices in the agglomeration area must be compensated by higher labor productivity, otherwise, manufacturers aiming at profit maximization will choose other areas with relatively lower factor prices for production (such as Krugman, 1980, 1991a; Davis and Weinstein, 1996, 1999; Krugman and Venables, 1995; Fujita *et al.*, 2001). The relatively higher labor productivity in agglomeration areas mainly comes from three mechanisms: wider input sharing, better matching of production factors and more learning opportunities (Duranton and Puga, 2004). It has been confirmed in empirical studies that economic agglomeration raises productivity (see the review article of Redding, 2009). The crowding-out effect mainly comes from rising prices, production costs, pollution, increased traffic congestion, and relatively higher crime rates in the agglomeration area.

Due to the insufficient understanding of economic agglomeration effect, government policies in big cities tend to limit the expansion of urban population. Urban residents also tend to reject the entry of migrant workers, and oppose the expansion of the urban population. As a result, compared with the level of industrialization and the concentration of economic production activities, the degree of population concentration in China is too low (Lu Ming, 2010; Cai and Zhang, 2012). In addition, it is also found that the concentration of population in China is significantly lower than that in the United States, the United Kingdom, Japan, Indonesia, and other countries with different development levels (Li and Fan, 2003). The lack of population concentration hinders economic agglomeration effect and brings huge efficiency loss to China's economy. Therefore, in the early stage of urbanization when the scale economy effect brought by urban development is stronger than the crowding-out effect, blindly restricting urban development and focusing on developing small and medium-sized cities will bring huge efficiency loss.

Another concern about economic agglomeration is that the expansion of the urban population may intensify competition in the urban labor market, thus increasing unemployment rate and reducing incomes of urban residents. On the one hand, people worry that as urban population grows, cities may not provide enough job opportunities, which will aggravate unemployment. In particular, it is often argued that low-skilled workers face a greater risk of unemployment as cities expand. On the other hand, more intense labor market competition may exert downward pressure on labor wages, thus lowering nominal wages. The rise in the price of non-tradable goods caused by population concentration will further depress the real wages of residents in big cities and harm the welfare of workers.

So is it as feared? We believe a better understanding of the effects of economic agglomeration may help to ease concerns. Economic agglomeration promotes labor productivity through sharing, matching, and learning, and the wage of workers is mainly determined by their marginal output in the production process. In the case of free capital flow, the increase of urban labor supply will not reduce the marginal output of workers. On the contrary, due to the existence of economic agglomeration effect, the rise of labor productivity will increase the marginal output of workers, thus promoting the wage income of them. Economic agglomeration may also increase the non-wage income of workers by encouraging entrepreneurship and facilitating the exchange of information. In addition, the concentration of population and the inflow of workers in big cities do not necessarily increase the unemployment rate in cities. Existing empirical studies have found that migrant workers going to work in cities has little impact on the unemployment rate of local residents (Liu Xuejun and Zhao Yaohui, 2009).

In theory, the employment rate in the local labor market is mainly determined by both demand and supply. On the one hand, the inflow of workers will certainly increase the labor supply in cities. On the other hand, due to the existence of economies of scale in urban development, the increase of urban population will constantly create new job opportunities and push the labor demand curve to move outward. Other things being equal, if jobs were to be created faster than cities were to expand, urban employment rate would rise. However, there is a lack of micro evidence on how the expansion of cities and the effects of economic agglomeration affect the functioning of labor markets, particularly workers' incomes and employment rates. Due to the lack of understanding of economic agglomeration effect, people have incomplete judgment on the result of urban expansion, which further affects the formulation of urbanization and urban development policies. Basing on the micro survey data from the individual workers, Chapters 4 and 5 hope to directly investigate the impact of economic agglomeration (mainly the expansion of cities) on the employment probability and the income of workers, to provide the evidence from China for economic agglomeration effect from the perspective of the labor market, and to provide empirical basis for the establishment of urbanization and urban development policies.

To fully analyze the urban labor market effect of economic agglomeration, we need not only evidence from individual workers but also an understanding of the employment status of urban industries at the overall economic level, which mainly includes the development of manufacturing industry and service industry. Industrial development is the source of urban competitiveness. Only with the continuous improvement of urban competitiveness can a city attract and retain talents. The development of the manufacturing sector is crucial to inclusive economic growth, both in terms of economic growth and employment. Although some people believe that the improvement of China's international competitiveness and the expansion of domestic demand will largely depend on the development of high-end producer services, the development of service industry isolated from manufacturing industry will be like a tree without roots. Premature deindustrialization and the transformation and upgrading toward high-end services will not only harm the growth rate of the economy but also harm the economy's ability to create jobs. In general, faster-growing countries tend to have relatively large manufacturing sector (Rodrik, 2006). As the manufacturing sector absorbs a large number of medium-skilled workers, the contraction of the manufacturing sector may not only lead to the loss of jobs but also lead to the widening of the income gap. Manufacturing, the most important component of the tradable goods sector in China, is the key to absorbing and creating jobs. In view of the important role of manufacturing industry in economic development and employment creation, industrial policies and place-based policies aiming at promoting the development of manufacturing industry have become the common choices of both developed and developing countries. However, there is no final conclusion on whether the place-based policies are effective or not both theoretically and empirically, therefore, more evidence are needed.

In addition, local governments often face different policy choices in promoting local economic growth. There is still a debate about whether local governments should give priority to high-tech and high-value-added industries, or should promote the development of related industries and give play to the complementary effects among industries based on local industrial structure and comparative advantages. Compared with the "one-size-fits-all" introduction and development of high-tech industries, whether cluster-based industrial development and policies to promote the development of industries with stronger spillover effects are more effective needs to be tested empirically. Theoretically, the key to the success of place-based policies lies in the playing of economic agglomeration effect and the resulting increasing returns to scale. Kline (2010) introduced agglomeration effect to the spatial general equilibrium model for analyzing place-based policies and found that when agglomeration effects exist and are strong enough, regional place-based policies will promote local economic growth, thus transforming the local economy from a low-level equilibrium with low employment and low wages to a high-level equilibrium with relatively higher wages and employment. However, some studies believe that local governments often distort the market mechanism and factor allocation by attracting firms to enter a certain place through preferential policies to increase jobs, resulting in the inefficiency of local production and deadweight losses of residents' welfare. This is especially true if the place-based policies are carried out by local government officials in pursuit of personal benefits (Wilson, 1999; Glaeser, 2001). In addition, the increase of local wages brought by job increase of manufacturing industry will also suppress the labor demand of other industries and crowd out jobs of other industries, thus weakening the positive impact of place-based policies on local economy (Moretti, 2011). Therefore, the key to the success of place-based policies is how to promote the agglomeration effect and improve policy efficiency through reasonable industrial selection. It depends on the judgment of local industrial structure and the relatedness between industries, and the industrial cluster is a useful starting point for analysis. Therefore, in Chapters 6 and 7, the classification of industrial clusters will be discussed and their spatial distribution characteristics be described by taking China's manufacturing industrial clusters as the entry point to empirically estimate the labor market effect of industrial clusters.

In addition to the development of the manufacturing industry, the development and employment of the service industry should also become an important perspective to evaluate the agglomeration effect. Over the past four decades, China's economic growth has been highly dependent on investment and exports, and the domestic demand has been weak. This is a serious structural problem facing the Chinese economy. The lag of the service industry is an important factor restraining the growth of the domestic demand in China. Compared with other countries, development of the service sector in China is relatively lagged, and its employment share is low. A typical feature of post-industrialization economy is that the development of service economy plays an important role in modern economic growth. Since the beginning of the 21st century, all developed countries in the world have entered or already entered the service economy without exception, and the employment proportion of the service industry has been increasing, with almost all of the increase of new jobs coming from the service industry (Schettkat and Yocarini, 2003). With the completion of industrialization, China's future job creation, especially the employment of low-skilled workers, will increasingly rely on the development of the service industry. The report to the 19th National Congress of the CPC also made accelerating the development of modern service industries and enhancing service by aiming at making the international standards the strategic priority for supply-side structural reform. Existing literature has confirmed the trend of high concentration of China's manufacturing industry (Barbieri *et al*., 2012; He and Wang, 2012). Therefore, it is of great significance to think about how to promote the development of China's service industry and other issues by studying whether the development of manufacturing industry will have spillover effect on the employment growth of the tertiary industry from the overall level of the city, especially how the spillover effect is affected by the agglomeration effect. Chapter 8 is to study the spillover effect of the employment of manufacturing industry on that of different types of service industry, and further analyze how economic agglomeration effect will affect the ability of the employment of manufacturing industry creating that of the service industry using city-industry level employment data, in order to perfect the analysis on urban labor market effect of the economic agglomeration from the view of the employment of overall industries of cities, and to provide empirical basis for establishing China's regional economic development policies with the support of other packages of labor market policies.

The new way of people-oriented urbanization needs to pay attention to the labor market performance of individuals and industrial development in the process of urbanization. In reality, crowding-out effects such as traffic congestion and ecological environment deterioration are related to people's daily life, so they are more likely to be sensed by government departments and workers. The benefits of economic agglomeration are not easily observed and are therefore largely ignored. For example, it is often feared that a large increase in migrant workers will intensify competition in the urban labor market, thus aggravating unemployment in the urban labor market. Although there is no lack of rationality in this concern, it hinders the process of economic agglomeration to a large extent, hinders the improvement of labor productivity, and violates the original intention of urban development.

1.3 Research Framework and Chapters Arranged

In the process of economic development, economic agglomeration not only influences individual's labor market performance but also influences industrial development macroscopically. Based on a systematic review of relevant literature, this book uses data from individuals, firms, and prefecture-level cities to describe the spatial distribution characteristics and trends of manufacturing industries and industrial clusters, and empirically estimates the impact of agglomeration effect on labor market and industrial development.

Chapter 1 "Introduction" mainly introduces the background, chapters arranged, and summarizes the contribution of it. The chapter is divided into four sections. In Section 1.1, the research background of the book is explained by focusing on the debate about urbanization patterns and the public's neglect of the economic agglomeration effect. Section 1.2 generally discusses the theoretical mechanism of the impact of industrial cluster development and economic agglomeration effect on urban labor market. Section 1.3 outlines the framework and chapters of the book, and the final section outlines the contributions of the book.

Chapter 2 is "Literature Review". The theoretical and empirical literature of new economic geography is systematically reviewed, and their logic is linked with the running of the labor market and industrial development, in order to analyze the causes and mechanism of economic agglomeration effect. Section 2.1 reviews the theoretical and empirical literature of new economic geography as a whole, summarizes theoretical models studying economic agglomeration's role in promoting labor productivity through three kinds of micro-mechanism including sharing, matching, and learning. On this basis, the section reviews empirical literature providing evidence that agglomeration effects may promote labor productivity. Section 2.2 combines literature of new economic geography with the research of labor economics to analyze mechanisms that economic agglomeration effect may affect labor employment and income. Section

2.3 discusses agglomeration effect on the influences of place-based policies, and explores the role of agglomeration effect in the development of manufacturing industries and its spillover into service industries in combination with China's industrial development pattern and macroeconomic structural transformation.

Chapter 3 analyzes the spatial distribution characteristics and their determinants of China's manufacturing industry in the overall context, and explores the influence of economic geography, new economic geography, and economic policy factors on the economic map of China's manufacturing industry. Section 3.1 theoretically discusses the interaction between agglomeration and dispersing forces and their effects on the spatial distribution of economic activities at first. In Section 3.2, based on the theoretical analysis and the economic policy changes since China's reform and opening up, characteristics and changes of the regional distribution of China's manufacturing industry are described with data. It is found that the concentration of economic activities is driven toward eastern China under economic geographical and new economic geographical forces. China's manufacturing employment is mainly concentrated in the eastern regions, descending from the east to the central part and to the west of China. However, in recent years, with the rise of crowding-out effect and the effects of policies balancing regional development, the spatial distribution of manufacturing industry shows a slightly dispersed trend. Section 3.3 explores the spatial distribution characteristics and changes of different types of manufacturing industries, and reveals the role of knowledge spillovers. It is found that there are significant differences in the growth and spatial distribution pattern changes of industries with different skill levels. Job growth in high-skilled industries is relatively faster than that in low-skilled manufacturing industries, and the trend of concentrating toward the eastern regions is clearer. Industries with higher skill levels have lower trend of employment reallocation among regions.

Chapters 4 and 5 construct theoretical and empirical models studying determinants of individual's employment and income, and on this basis, empirically estimate the impact of economic agglomeration on the labor market. Chapter 4 mainly tests the impact of economic agglomeration on the employment of workers. Section 4.1 summarizes the mechanism with which economic agglomeration may affect the employment probability of workers. Although the urban expansion will increase labor supply, it will also improve labor productivity and expand labor demand due to the agglomeration effect. If employment in the area expands more rapidly than population, the employment probability of workers will rise. Section 4.2 introduces the data and empirical model used in this chapter, and tests the impact of urban expansion on workers' employment probability based on the Probit model. Considering the problem of missing variables and reverse causality, Section 4.3 uses the urban population growth from 1953 to 1982 as the instrumental variable of the current urban population, and estimates the model using instrumental variable regression. The positive effect of urban expansion on the employment of workers is confirmed. Section 4.4 further analyzes heterogeneous effect of economic agglomeration on workers with different skill levels by grouping all workers according to their years of education. It is found that workers with lowest skills benefit relatively the most as the urban population expands. This is mainly because big cities have relatively higher demand for low-skilled services.

After confirming the effect of agglomeration on employment, we would like to learn further whether better job opportunities come with the cost of lower incomes. Chapter 5 focuses on the impact of urban expansion on the income of workers. It is believed that urban expansion will bring about economic agglomeration effect, thus improving labor productivity, and the rise of labor productivity will increase the wages of workers. In addition, economic agglomeration can also increase workers' non-wage income by encouraging entrepreneurship and improving the efficiency of information transmission. Section 5.1 constructs the theoretical model of the impact of urban sizes on the income of workers. Section 5.2 describes data and empirical models used in this chapter, and empirically estimates the impact of changes in city size on workers' income. The empirical results show that the impact of city size on the nominal income of workers is significantly positive. In addition, with the improvement of economic agglomeration, the prices of non-tradable goods in the agglomeration area tend to rise, and the real income adjusted by local price levels is a better measure of the welfare of workers. To this end, two different methods are used to construct the price index in prefecture-level cities, and the impact of urban expansion on the real income of workers is further examined. It is found that the effect of city size on workers' real income is significantly positive even after taking into account of prices. The finding also shows indirectly that China's urban system has not yet reached the state of spatial general equilibrium due to such factors as the *Hukou* system which hinders the flow of labors. As an extension of the model,

Section 5.3 uses the method of quantile regression to analyze the heterogeneity of the economic agglomeration effect across workers with different incomes. It is found that although workers with all levels of income benefit from urban expansion significantly, generally speaking, workers at the lowest income quantile benefit the least. It is mainly because jobs of workers with low incomes are usually concentrated in low-skilled service sectors, and compared with other sectors, productivities in low-skilled service industries grow the most slowly. Research in Chapter 5 provides a perspective of income in thinking about the labor market effect of economic agglomeration, and serves as references for analyzing city system and spatial general equilibrium of China.

From Chapters 6–8, our vision expands from individuals to the industrial development of the city as a whole. Chapters 6 and 7 focus on manufacturing development and Chapter 8 focuses on the expansion of service sector employment.

In Chapter 6, based on enterprise and input–output data, 480 four-digit level manufacturing industries in China are classified into clusters, and the spatial distribution characteristics of different industrial clusters are described. It is believed that a good industrial cluster classification should show the following characteristics: regional comparability, comprehensive reflection of various forms of relations among industries, strong industrial relatedness within the cluster, and weak industrial correlation between clusters. Section 6.1 elaborates on the concept of industrial cluster and tries to clarify the differences and connections between industrial cluster, inter-industry linkage, and agglomeration effect. Section 6.2 provides an overview of the data and cluster classification methods used in this chapter, as detailed in Section 6.3. Based on Delgado *et al.* (2014, 2016), various forms of correlation matrices of 480 industries are constructed, and relevant industries are classified into clusters by using the method of clustering analysis. Based on different industry correlation matrix and clustering analysis, a total of 500 different alternative industrial clusters are provided. Then, based on the standards of strong industry correlation within the cluster, large industry differentiation among clusters, and robust cluster classification results, different cluster classifications are scored and relatively optimal industrial cluster classifications are screened out. Finally, the optimal cluster classification alternatives are amended to reduce the abnormal results of some industrial clusters due to data limitations. Based on the results of industrial cluster classification, Section 6.4 further describes the spatial distribution pattern of China's manufacturing industrial clusters. The data show that because of lacking industry diversity, the strength of the industrial clusters of the central and western regions in China is often higher than that of cities in the eastern regions. However, in comparison, there are more strong clusters in the eastern regions and the distribution of manufacturing industry clusters is more diversified. In addition, compared with the eastern regions, the manufacturing industry in the inland regions is located in a relatively upstream industrial chain, and is dominated by resource-intensive industrial clusters.

Then, what kind of influence will clusters have on the industrial development? In theory, cluster development may improve the labor productivity of the industry through agglomeration effect, thus bringing about the job expansion and wage increase. However, the competition among industries within the same cluster may crowd out industrial jobs by boosting the price of land, labor, and other inputs. In addition, the path dependence brought by the development of industrial clusters may result in industries being stuck in the low end of the industrial value chain, which is not conducive to the long-term development of the industry and the job expansion. Therefore, more empirical evidence are needed.

Chapter 7 constructs a conditional convergence model of urban industrial development, and empirically estimates the impact of urban industrial cluster development in terms of quantity and quality. Section 7.1 reviews literature on industrial clusters. Section 7.2 estimates the impact of cluster development from the perspective of industrial employment growth and tests its robustness. The empirical results show that cluster development significantly promotes the industrial employment growth. A one-standard-deviation increase in the strength of clusters from its mean level leads to an increase of 2.153 percentage points in the average annual growth rate of industrial employment in the future. The employment expansion effect of cluster development mainly comes from the emerging of new firms and the job expansion of existing firms. Considering that cluster development may be detrimental to the improvement of industrial quality due to path dependence, Section 7.3 studies the effect of industrial clusters in terms of quality. It is found that, in terms of quality, the impact of clusters on the growth of industrial quality indicators is not significant or even significantly negative. At the end of this chapter, the industrial job growth model is expanded and the differences in the cluster effect of industries at different positions of the industrial value chain are analyzed. The empirical results show that although the employment promotion effect exists at different positions in the industrial chain, due to the weaker forward and backward linkage and stronger competition effect, cluster effects on industries at similar industrial chain position as other industries within the same cluster are relatively weaker.

Chapter 8 analyzes the multiplier effect of urban manufacturing employment on service employment from the perspective of macroeconomic structural transformation, and further examines the impact of agglomeration effect. By summing up the literature on place-based policies, we find that the increase of manufacturing employment does not necessarily lead to the jump of local economy and employment from low-level equilibrium to high-level equilibrium, and agglomeration effect plays a significant role. When the agglomeration effect is not strong enough, the increase of manufacturing employment cannot promote the service industry employment, but crowd out service industry employment, which is not conducive to the development of service industry. In Section 8.1, mechanisms of the multiplier effect of manufacturing employment on service employment are described, and in Section 8.2, the data and models used in this chapter are introduced. Section 8.3 provides empirical results of the multiplier effect of manufacturing employment on service employment. Considering issues of reverse causality and omitted variable biases, an index measuring export shocks is constructed in this chapter as the instrumental variable of urban manufacturing employment, and the instrumental variable correlates positively with regional manufacturing employment and China's total exports in the year of investigation, and negatively correlates with the distance from the city to the coastal port cities. Estimates show that the increase of manufacturing employment will have a significant positive effect on the employment of local service industry, which has the greatest impact on the manual jobs with the highest degree of labor intensity. In view of the fact that agglomeration effect, elasticity of labor supply, and other factors' impact on the effect of place-based policies, Section 8.4 expands the model and examines the heterogeneity of employment multiplier effects in manufacturing industries in cities of different urbanization levels and sizes. It is found that only in regions with the highest urbanization level, the largest urban population or migration scale can manufacturing employment significantly promote the increase of service employment, while in small cities or regions with low urbanization levels, manufacturing employment may crowd out service employment.

Chapter 9 is the conclusion of the book. In this chapter, the book's conclusions and contributions are summed up, and several unresolved issues are raised. It is believed that the book comprehensively analyzes the influence of economic agglomeration effect on individual's urban labor market performance and urban industrial development, enriches the existing literature, and provides a basis for the formulation of China's urbanization and urban development policies. However, the focus of this book is to analyze the impact of agglomeration effect on the labor market, without analyzing the impact on transportation, environment and public security, etc., which are essential for residents' welfare. Nor the determinants of economic agglomeration and industrial cluster development are considered, which needs to be studied further in the future.

1.4 Main Contributions

This book comprehensively examines the impact of economic agglomeration on individual's labor market performance and urban industrial development. The main contributions include the following four aspects.

First, combining the literature of new economic geography and labor economics, the book analyzes the theoretical mechanisms by which economic agglomeration may affect individual's labor market performance, and uses data from China to conduct empirical tests from the perspectives of both employment and income. The existing literature of new economic geography proves the positive effect of economic agglomeration effect on labor productivity from the perspective of average wage or average output of laborers. However, it is difficult to reveal the influence of economic agglomeration on workers' welfare only from the perspective of average wages or output. The total income of workers including non-wage income, and the real income adjusted by prices are relatively more direct measures of workers' welfare. In addition, the existing literature lacks the analysis on how the economic agglomeration effect will affect the use of factors (such as labor employment). This book uses individual level survey data to examine how changes in the city size will affect workers' employment and nominal income, thus making up for the existing literature and providing micro-evidence from China for the existence of economic agglomeration effects. In addition, based on the price index constructed with two different methods, the effect of economic agglomeration on the real income of workers is also examined. The study of real income provides a basis to analyze how economic agglomeration will affect the welfare of workers, and the relevant results also serve as a basis to judge whether the spatial general equilibrium has been reached among Chinese cities.

Second, not only the average effect of economic agglomeration on the labor market is examined but the heterogeneity of its effects on workers with different income and educational background is also distinguished. The existing researches lack of analysis on the heterogeneity of economic agglomeration effect, and the understanding of heterogeneity is crucial for thinking about the change of income gap, making urban development policies and improving the "inclusiveness" of economic growth. The theoretical mechanisms underlying this heterogeneity are analyzed in detail and empirically tests are conducted. The results show that there are differences in the mechanisms by which workers with different income and skills benefit from the economic agglomeration effect. In the process of urban expansion, low-skilled and low-income workers mainly benefit from a greater increase in employment probability, which is mainly related to the expansion of the manual jobs in big cities. However, due to the stronger knowledge spillover effect in big cities, the income of highly skilled workers has been greatly improved in the process of economic agglomeration.

Third, the book presents a definition of clusters of China's manufacturing industries that is comparable across regions. Due to the limitations of data and methods, current researches on industrial clusters mainly focus on case studies, and conclusions from these studies are specific to regions or industries. Chapter 6 of the book systematically divides four-digit level manufacturing industries in China into clusters based on clustering analysis and comprehensive statistical evaluation, thus providing a foundation for the research on the development of regional industrial clusters and their economic development effects. The cluster definition we use has the following three advantages. Firstly, the cluster definition obtained by this method covers various forms of inter-industry relations including input–output relations and industrial spatial distribution characteristics, comprehensively reflecting the relations between different industries, and overcomes the defects of previous studies that only focus on one specific form of inter-industry relations. Secondly, this method makes use of statistical analysis to comprehensively evaluate the classification results of various industrial cluster definitions, so that the optimal classification results can be selected based on objective criteria. Thirdly, this method allows researchers to subjectively adjust the abnormal results of industrial cluster classification caused partly by data or method limitations. All the adjustment processes are transparent, avoiding subjective arbitrariness.

Fourth, this book provides reference for the formulation of urban place-based policies, urban development and regional policy improvements. On the choice of China's urbanization path, that is, whether to give priority to the development of large cities or small and medium-sized towns, there is still a debate in the academic and policy circles. Due to insufficient understanding of economic agglomeration effect, the government and urban residents tend to support policies to limit population expansion in large cities. One consequence of this is that China's population concentration is not only lower than that of land and production but also much lower than that of other countries with similar levels of economic development. From the perspectives of labor market and industrial development, the book emphasizes the importance of increasing economic agglomeration, showing that measures that hinder economic agglomeration are not only detrimental to economic efficiency but also do harm to the welfare of workers due to the adverse impact on their income and jobs. In addition, although place-based policies are the common practice of local governments in various countries, their effects and determinants have not been confirmed in the existing literature, which requires us to provide more evidence. Besides, it is still debated whether the government should introduce and develop high-tech industries in a "one-size-fits-all" manner, or should encourage the development of industries with stronger spillover effects based on local comparative advantages and strengthen the complementary effect between industries. By examining industrial cluster effect and the multiplier effect of manufacturing employment expansion on service sector employment, this book not only illustrates the importance of the complementary effect between industries to the influence of place-based policies but also explains the prerequisite for the effectiveness of place-based policies.

Chapter 2

Why Do Big Cities Rise: A Literature Review

The forces of economic agglomeration drive the concentration of population and economic activity toward the big cities. In 1970, there were only two megacities, New York and Tokyo, with populations of more than 10 million. Since then, the trend of population concentration toward megacities has continued to advance. By 2014, there were 28 megacities in the world, six of them in China, and Tokyo, with the largest population, had 37,833,000 residents. By 2030, it is expected that there will be 41 megacities with a population of more than 10 million (United Nations, 2014). In addition to macro statistics, empirical studies have also confirmed the widespread existence of economic agglomeration. Ellison and Glaeser (1997) found that among all 459 four-digit level manufacturing industries in the United States, 446 had an excess agglomeration tendency. Manufacturing employment is concentrated in New England in the northeast, the Mid-Atlantic coast, and the Midwest. In 1920, the manufacturing employment of these three major regions in the United States accounted for 71.88% of the manufacturing employment of the whole country (Fan Jianyong and Yang Bingjian, 2002). Literature review studies by Combes (2004) and Holmes and Stevens (2004) also confirm the widespread presence of economic agglomeration in the EU, Asia, and the US.

In China, economic agglomeration has also been confirmed by many studies. Basing on the provincial data of China from 1987 to 2001, Jin Yu *et al.* (2006) found that since the reform and opening up, the trend of industrial agglomeration in China has been gradually strengthened, and the inter-provincial (regional and municipal) gap of the proportion of industrial GDP of each province (region and municipality) in the national industrial GDP has gradually widened, with the coefficient of variation rising from 0.026 in 1987 to 0.030 in 2001. China's industrial agglomeration mainly revolves around the Yangtze River Delta and the Pearl River Delta. Ma Guoxia *et al.* (2007) measured the degree of regional agglomeration among different manufacturing industries by using China's input–output data in 1995 and 2003. They found an increasing concentration of manufacturing in China and a trend of concentrating toward coastal areas. Vertical input–output linkages and external economies of scale are the key reasons for China's manufacturing agglomeration. In addition, geographical proximity and local market effects also promote agglomeration through a circular cumulative effect. Similarly, Zhao Wei and Zhang Cui (2007) calculated the industrial geographical concentration index, or the Ellison–Glaeser Index, of 20 sectors of China's manufacturing industry and proved that from 1999 to 2003, most sectors in China had shown stronger spatial agglomeration tendency. Although economic agglomeration is widespread in China, generally speaking, the extent of concentration of economic activities in China is still smaller than that in western developed countries. According to Lu Jiangyong and Tao Zhigang (2006), 79.97% of the industries in China are low-concentration industries, while the ratio is only 10% in the US. In China, by contrast, only 6.31% industries are highly concentrated, lower than 16% in the UK, 25% in the US, and 27% in France. Fujita *et al.* (2004) also found insufficient agglomeration of economic activities in China.

What causes the spatial concentration of economic activities? Why do big cities rise? Based on the existing literature, this chapter will describe the driving force of economic agglomeration and its micro-foundations, and discuss the influence of economic agglomeration, especially the development of large cities, from the perspective of labor market and industrial development, so as to lay a theoretical foundation for the research in later chapters of this book.

2.1 Economic Agglomeration Effect: A Review

Marshall noticed the phenomenon of economic agglomeration as early as the end of the 19th century. In his opinion, input sharing, labor market pooling, and knowledge spillover are the causes of agglomeration

(Marshall, 1890). However, due to the limitations of methodology, early literature mainly focused on the impact of first nature geography factors on locating economic activities such as geography and natural endowment. After Krugman (1991a), economists began to study the agglomeration of production and consumption being generated endogenously from geographic areas with exactly the same prior conditions, i.e., the so-called second nature geography factors in the new economic geography literature. The first nature geographic factors are crucial to firm's location decisions in periods when production is highly dependent on resources and transportation costs which account for a large proportion of total production costs. With the development of technology and the decrease of transportation costs, economic agglomeration begins to play decisive role in modern production activities. For example, Fan Jianyong and Yang Bingjian (2002) show that the manufacturing center of the United States moved from New England in the northeast to the Midwest in the second half of the 19th century. New England's share of manufacturing employment in the country decreased from 37.2% in 1860 to 20.4% in 1920. Accordingly, the proportion of manufacturing employment in the central and western regions rose from 13.3% in 1860 to 34.8% in 1920, and the concentration of population to the Midwest was an important factor in the transfer of the manufacturing centers.

According to the literature of new economic geography, the location choice of economic activities is the result of both agglomeration effect and dispersion effect. Due to increasing returns to scale, consumer preferences for consumption diversity and lower transportation costs, manufacturers choose to produce and operate in regions with relatively large market demand, thus resulting in larger production scale and higher factor prices in the agglomeration areas. Although relatively higher factor prices in agglomeration areas become the force that drives economic activities to disperse, the higher labor productivity there becomes the centripetal force that balances the high factor prices and attracts the concentration of economic activities. Otherwise, profit-maximizing manufacturers will choose to produce in other areas where factor prices are relatively low.

2.1.1 *Micro-foundations of economic agglomeration effect*

Agglomeration can improve labor productivity mainly through three micro-mechanisms, namely, more widely input sharing, better production factor matching, and more learning opportunities (Duranton and Puga, 2004; Gill and Kharas, 2007). Firstly, the aggregation of manufacturers in a certain region can promote the sharing of the construction cost of indivisible equipment, thus increasing equipment investment. Agglomeration also attracts a wider range of manufacturers of raw materials and intermediate goods into the market and promotes specialization. Firms can better share risks because of agglomeration. All these factors can bring production functions with increasing returns to scale, which is the benefit of "sharing" brought by economic agglomeration. Secondly, a larger number of firms and workers in the agglomeration area improve the matching efficiency of the labor market, and the improvement of matching efficiency will greatly promote labor productivity, which brings the benefit of "matching" by economic agglomeration. In addition, improved matching efficiency also encourages division of labor and specialization of production, which also contributes to productivity improvement. Finally, agglomeration will create more learning opportunities for local firms and workers, promote innovation and the application of more efficient production methods through mutual learning among firms, and improve productivity, which brings the benefit of "learning" by economic agglomeration. In theory, therefore, economic agglomeration does boost productivity, which is the main reason why economic activity is widely concentrated rather than dispersed.

(1) Sharing: In terms that "sharing" will lead to economic agglomeration and the generation of cities, the most direct mechanism is to assume that some indivisible goods or equipment is used in the process of production, and the construction of such equipment requires high fixed costs. This indivisible equipment is essentially club goods (Buchanan, 1965). Club goods can be used by many consumers at the same time, but the use is excludable and it excludes consumers who are not club members. The increase in the number of consumers, on the one hand, can share the fixed costs of club goods, but on the other hand, it will also bring crowding-out effects. Therefore, there are trade-offs in determining the optimal number of consumers for club goods. Similarly, the theory of club goods can also be used to explain the development of cities. With the increase of urban population, some club goods that require large fixed cost, such as infrastructure, can be shared by more urban residents. But at the same time, the expansion of cities will also be limited by the crowding-out effect. The trade-off between the increasing return to scale brought by fixed cost sharing and the crowding-out effect will jointly determine the optimal city size. Club goods are the simplest description of the "sharing" mechanism.

The monopolistic competition model of Dixit and Stiglitz (1977) describes how monopolistic competition between intermediate goods producers will lead to the overall production function showing increasing returns to scale in the case of perfect competition between final goods producers and a production function with constant returns to scale. Based on the models of Ethier (1982), Dixit and Stiglitz (1977), and Chamberlin (1933), Duranton and Puga constructed the mechanism of "inputs sharing" theoretically. Their model shows that the nature of increasing returns to scale of the total production function comes mainly from its "sharing" of the benefits of the diversification of intermediate inputs. In addition, economic agglomeration not only enables cities to gain benefits by sharing more kinds of intermediate inputs but also enables cities to "share" the benefits of individual production specialization. The story of specialization first came from Adam Smith's *The Wealth of Nations*. According to Adam Smith, specialization works mainly through three mechanisms. First, specialization enhances the proficiency of workers, thus bringing about "learning by doing" effect. Second, specialization can reduce the cost of transformation that may occur when workers change jobs. Third, since simpler tasks are more likely to be replaced by machines, division of labor and specialization can encourage labor-saving technological progress. Fourth, as for the "sharing" mechanism, Duranton and Puga (2004) also believe that in the case of uncertainty, the economic agglomeration of cities may benefit widely by clustering labor market and encouraging workers and firms to share risks. Therefore, workers in the agglomeration areas can get relatively higher expected wages, and firms also get higher expected profits.

(2) Matching: The second mechanism of the agglomeration effect comes from "matching". Economic agglomeration can enhance labor productivity by increasing the probability of matching between firms and workers, improving the quality of the matching and reducing holding up behaviors. In labor economics literature, "matching" mechanisms are often linked to a "thick labor market".

First, the increase in the number of workers and firms in a city will increase the probability of successful matching. The key is to build a matching function related to the number of job seekers and that of vacant positions in a city. In order to explain the matching effect of economic agglomeration, the researchers constructed a matching function of increasing returns to scale. With the increase in the number of job seekers and the number of vacant jobs by a certain proportion in a city, the number of successful matches in a city will increase by a larger proportion. If the matching function has increasing returns to scale, with the increase in urban population, the search friction in the urban labor market tends to decline, thus reducing the unemployment rate and the proportion of vacant jobs (Coles, 1994; Coles and Smith, 1998).

Second, the expansion of urban scale will also improve the quality of labor market matching, thus promoting labor productivity (Helsley and Strange, 2014; Duranton and Puga, 2004). Empirically, based on US census data, Bleakly and Lin (2012) found that in areas with relatively dense population, the probability of labor force changing jobs or industries is lower, which provides evidence that the matching quality of the labor market in economic agglomeration areas is relatively higher. In addition, younger workers are more likely than senior workers to change jobs or industries, mainly because young people tend to try out multiple careers to find the best match, and such search costs are the lowest early in their careers. In theory, Duranton and Puga (2004) comprehensively explains how economic agglomeration affects the matching quality of the labor market. According to their model, workers' income will increase for the following two reasons as the urban workforce expands. On the one hand, due to the competition among firms, the increase of the number of firms is slower than that of the workers with the increase of urban labor force, which leads to the increase of firm's average employment size. In the case of fixed production costs, the increase in the average number of workers employed by a firm will raise the output per worker. On the other hand, the increase in the number of urban workers and firms will close the average gap between the skills possessed by workers and those needed by firms. That is, on average, workers can find job positions more suited to their skills. Therefore, economic agglomeration improves the quality of labor market matching and reduces the output loss caused by mismatching.

Third, economic agglomeration may also encourage workers to invest in human capital by reducing the possibility of firms' *ex-post* "hold-up" behaviors, thus improving labor productivity. In theory, if the contract is incomplete, and one party to the contract needs to invest in skills or capital that are specific to the contract beforehand, then the investor may be "held-up" by the other party through renegotiation (Williamson, 1985; Hart, 1995). The possibility of *ex-post* renegotiation reduces the incentive for contractors to invest a certain capital. As far as the urban labor market is concerned, a common phenomenon is that workers need to invest in specialized human capital to meet the production requirements of firms. However, if such specialized human capital cannot be applied to other firms, after the completion of the investment, the firm has an incentive to renegotiate the salary contract, and the optimal choice of the enterprise is to pay the workers only reservation wages. Given the outcome of this post-contract renegotiation, workers will rationally choose not to invest in specialized human capital beforehand. However, this equilibrium is not socially optimal, it will enable firms to obtain only the lowest level of profits, and workers will only obtain retained income. In economic agglomeration regions with a large number of potential employers, the possibility of renegotiation is lower. Competition among firms will force firms to pay workers according to their marginal output. In order to raise marginal output, workers have stronger incentives to invest in human capital beforehand, benefiting both firms and workers.

(3) Learning: The importance of the "learning" effect in the era of knowledge economy is self-evident. Jovanovic (1997) believes that modern economies invest 20% of their resources in learning. Since learning requires face-to-face communication between people, the acquisition of learning opportunities requires physical proximity, which also becomes a reason why economic activities tend to be concentrated in cities. As some workers become better educated, the productivity of others will increase through a variety of mechanisms.

Existing literature models knowledge spillover effect in two different ways. The first one is technical externalities. Human capital externality is modeled by introducing increasing returns to scale to the production function. Lucas (1988) believed that knowledge spillovers brought by social interaction would increase total factor productivity, and such knowledge externalities were an important factor to explain the widening gap of economic growth between countries after World War II. However, Lucas's description of knowledge externalities is only realized by introducing increasing returns to scale into the production function, and his model does not explain the causes of such externalities endogenously. Similarly, Glaeser (1999), Jovanovic and Rob (1989) also believed that people could improve their labor productivity by interacting with their high-skilled neighbors. The second way to model human capital externalities is pecuniary externalities. Acemoglu (1996, 1998) improved Lucas's model by interacting human capital with physical capital, and the conclusion of the model did not depend on the hypothesis of increasing return to scale of the production function. Firms' invest depends on the city's level of human capital. When there are frictions in the labor market, with the rise of city's human capital level, labor productivity is enhanced. This is another mechanism of human capital externalities, which does not depend on the direct interaction between workers, but is completely realized through the market mechanism. However, if education only serves as a signal for individuals' high abilities (Spence, 1973), but fails to really improve individual labor productivity, the private return to education may be lower than the social return, thus making human capital externalities negative.

A large number of empirical studies have confirmed the existence of knowledge spillover. Glaeser *et al.* (1995) found that after World War II, per capita income grew faster in cities with higher initial human capital levels, thus providing indirect evidence for the existence of human capital externalities. Rauch's study (1993) is often regarded as the first empirical study to identify human capital externalities in cities. Using the US census data in 1980, he found that wages were relatively higher in cities with higher levels of average human capital. On average, a one-year increase in a city's average years of education leads to a 3–5% increase in urban wages. Similarly, Moretti (2004b) found that every percentage point increase in the proportion of urban college graduates increased the labor productivity of enterprises by 0.6–0.7%. Moretti (2004c) also confirmed the existence of knowledge spillover effect by investigating workers' wages. He found that for every percentage point increase in the proportion of urban college graduates, the average wages grew by 0.6–1.2%. In addition, Jaffe *et al.* (1993) "captured" knowledge spillovers directly in an empirical model by using data of patent citations. They found that new patent applications more likely to cite existing patents in the same state and region (SMSA level), providing more direct evidence of localized knowledge spillovers.

Empirical studies on China have also confirmed the existence of knowledge spillovers. Fu Shihe and Hong Junjie (2008) found that every 1% increase in the average education level of workers in a certain manufacturing industry in the city would bring an increase of 0.21% in the output of that industry by using the data of China's 2004 economic census. Liu (2007) provided more direct evidence for the existence of human capital externalities by estimating the wage equation of workers. He found that human capital externalities in China is as big as the private return to education. On average, a one-year increase in the average number of years of schooling for urban workers would bring an 11–13% increase in income. Taking the national departments adjustment in the 1950s as the instrumental variables of urban human capital, Glaeser and Lu (2018) found that a one-year increase in average years of education in cities would lead to wage rising by about 22% per hour based on the data of China's urban household income survey in 2002, 2007, and 2013. Similar human capital spillover effect exists on the workers' aggregate wage incomes, but the level of human capital in cities does not affect the non-wage income of workers.

2.1.2 *Economic agglomeration and labor productivity: Empirical evidence*

In the above, mechanisms of economic agglomeration effect have been confirmed in the existing literature. Economic agglomeration promotes urban labor productivity through sharing, matching, and learning. Abundant evidence on the positive effect of economic agglomeration on labor productivity have also been provided. Sveikauskas (1975) found that compared with small cities, the labor productivity in large cities measured by the average output and the wages of employees was relatively higher. On average, for every doubling of the size of a city (measured by its population), labor productivity increases by about 4.77–6.39%. Ciccone and Hall (1996) found that there were huge spatial differences in labor productivity in the United States. In 1988, the average output of the workers in the state with the highest productivity levels was two-thirds more than those in the state with the lowest productivity levels. Economic density at the county level is crucial in explaining between-state labor productivity differences. On average, a doubling of county employment density would lead to a 6% increase in average state labor productivity. Glaeser and Resseger (2009) took urban population as the measure of the city size, and such indicators as the average output of urban workers, the real median household income, and personal hourly income as the measurement of the city's labor productivity, and the regression results at both the individual level and the city level show that the expansion of cities can improve labor productivity, and the positive effect is comparatively greater in cities with more university graduates.

Similarly, the effect of economic agglomeration on labor productivity also exists in China. Fan Jianyong (2006) used the data of prefectural cities and sub-provincial cities in 2004 and took urban land area as the instrumental variable of non-agricultural employment density to do the regression analysis, and the results showed that, in China, non-agricultural employment density had a significant positive effect on the labor productivity of non-agricultural industries. The two-stage least squares estimates show that every 1% increase in employment density would bring about an 8.8% increase in labor productivity, which was higher than the elasticity coefficient of about 5% in developed countries in Europe and America. Au and Henderson (2006) found that in China, there was a significant inverted U-shaped relationship between real income per capita and urban employment scale, that is, in the early stage of urban development, real income per capita would increase with the expansion of employment. After the urban expansion reached a certain extent, due to the crowding-out effect of transportation costs, the per capita real income tended to decline, but the decline of per capita real income caused by a city being oversized was far lower than the efficiency loss caused by the city being undersized. This inverted U-shaped relationship between per capita real income and city size indicated that in the early stages of urban development, the expansion of cities would lead to an increase in labor productivity.

It can be seen from the above literature that existing literature mainly focuses on discussing the influence of agglomeration on labor productivity, while there are few researches on the influence of economic agglomeration effect on the use of factors such as the amount of worker employment, labor remuneration or industry development. The literature on economic agglomeration in China also focuses on the causes of agglomeration while the results of economic agglomeration are largely ignored. However, modern and sustainable economic growth must benefit all social groups broadly, and the impact of economic growth on factors such as employment and income of workers is an important measure of whether workers benefit broadly from economic growth. In addition, the development of urban industries and the enhancement of urban competitiveness are important guarantees for the continuous improvement of urban labor market performance. In 2005, the World Bank put forward the concept of inclusive economic growth, which required that economic growth should put emphasis not only on speed but also on the mode of economic growth, so as to benefit different sectors broadly and integrate the majority of a country's labor force in the process of growth. Creating more job opportunities, promoting income growth and industrial development are essential.

2.2 Urban Labor Market Effect of Economic Agglomeration

Examining the determinants of labor employment and income is an important branch of the literature of labor economics. Economists often emphasize the role of personal human capital factors such as education and work experience in the study of employment and wage decisions. For example, the Mincer equation regards the determination of labor income as a function of individual worker's education level, work experience, and work experience squared, as shown in Equation (2.1) (Mincer, 1974), where y is income, and the explanatory variables are the natural logarithm of income. In different studies, researchers tend to measure total annual, monthly, or hourly wages. And the most important explanatory variables of income include level of education S, potential working experience X, and potential working experience squared.

$$\log y = \log y_0 + rS + \beta_1 X + \beta_2 X^2 \tag{2.1}$$

Since then, the empirical studies of the wages and income of individual workers are various extensions of the Mincer equation, and the related studies may refer to Lemieux (2006). In addition to the human capital, a large number of sociological and economic literature also believes that social network, social capital, and other factors, as informal institutions, will also have an impact on individual income and employment. Since social capital can reduce the information asymmetry between firms and individuals and reduce the searching cost in the process of job hunting, it can promote the employment of individual workers (e.g., Granovetter, 1973; Montgomery, 1991). In addition, the factor of social capital may represent the individual ability of workers and other unobservable factors, thus affecting the worker's jobs and incomes.

In general, human capital, social capital, and political capital are all characteristics at the individual level. In the labor market, however, it is not only the individual characteristics of workers that affect their jobs and incomes but also the characteristics of cities. However, the factors of cities have been neglected in existing studies. Our analysis in Section 2.1 has shown that economic agglomeration is the most important aspect of urban characteristics and a fundamental reason for the existence and development of cities. As is confirmed in the existing theories and empirical literature that the effect of economic agglomeration can promote labor productivity, it is believed that theoretically there is a mechanism in which economic agglomeration may affect the employment and income of workers. Examining how urban economic agglomeration affects labor market performance is critical to achieving inclusive and sustainable economic growth in China.

Based on the important role of agglomeration in modern economic growth and production activities and the policy debates on urbanization patterns, this book attempts to examine the impact of economic agglomeration on urban labor market from the perspectives of employment and income in Chapters 4 and 5. Our research will not only provide evidence from China for the existence of an economic agglomeration effect but will also provide a supplement to the existing literature on new economic geography and labor economics by investigating the impact of economic agglomeration on employment creation and income enhancement. First, we will directly examine the effect of economic agglomeration on urban labor market by using individual level data. According to existing literature, we will construct the employment and income determination model of individual workers, and use the number of urban permanent residents as the proxy variable of economic agglomeration to directly investigate the impact of economic agglomeration on the local labor market. Empirically, when investigating the impact of economic agglomeration on the wages of workers, researchers generally use urban population as the proxy of economic agglomeration. For example, Sveikauskas (1975) and Glaeser and Resseger (2009) all investigated the impact of the increase of urban population on the average output and income of workers. By investigating the influence of urban economic agglomeration on individual workers' employment probability and income, urban characteristics are introduced into individual employment and income determination model, which enriches existing new economic geography literature and researches on local labor market. Second, the heterogeneity of the impacts of economic agglomeration effect on workers with different levels of human capital will be examined, based on the differences of individual workers' education or income. By introducing economic agglomeration variables into the employment and income determination model of individual workers, we can only examine the average effect of economic agglomeration. However, human capital of individuals can affect their benefits from economic agglomeration, and this heterogeneity has been ignored in the existing literature. In Sections 4.4 and 5.3, mechanisms of heterogeneous agglomeration effects will be analyzed and the empirical results on the heterogeneous agglomeration effects across individuals with different levels of human capital will be provided.

2.2.1 *Economic agglomeration and employment of workers*

From the overview of the economic agglomeration effect in Section 2.1, it is found that economic agglomeration will promote the improvement of labor productivity through three mechanisms: more extensive input sharing, better matching of production factors, and more learning opportunities. The existing empirical literature has also confirmed the widespread existence of economic agglomeration effect.

In theory, employment and unemployment of individual workers are largely determined by the supply and demand of labors. Because economic agglomeration can improve labor productivity, with the urban expansion, at the same time when the urban labor supply increases, the demand for labors will also expand due to agglomeration effect. In equilibrium, as long as the labor supply curve slopes upward, given labor supply curve unchanged, the higher labor productivity brought by agglomeration will eventually reflect the outward movement of the labor demand curve, thus bringing about the simultaneous rise of the equilibrium wages and the number of employment. Therefore, higher wages and labor productivity in big cities may imply more employment opportunities. Keeping other factors unchanged, if the growth of job opportunities is faster than urban expansion, the employment probability of individual workers may rise.

In addition, as an important part of the modern economy, the non-tradable goods sector is an important source of urban job creation. Taking the non-tradable sector into consideration, the effect of economic agglomeration on employment is likely to be magnified. Moretti (2010) discusses the impact of exogenous shocks of the demand of an industry in the tradable goods sector on aggregate urban employment. If an industry producing tradable goods increases the demand for labors for some reason (such as the introduction of new inventions that increase the labor productivity), the shock will increase employment and wages in that industry. Since, in the absence of friction in the labor market, workers should be paid the same across sectors, wages and employment will rise across the city, thus increasing the total urban income. According to Clark's Law, an increase in total income will inevitably lead to an expansion of consumption demand in non-tradable goods sectors, and hence an increase in wages and employment in equilibrium in non-tradable goods sectors. Moretti (2010) tested this "employment multiplier effect" on the basis of the US census data in 1980, 1990, and 2000. The empirical results show that each additional employment opportunity in the manufacturing sectors will bring 1.59 jobs to non-tradable goods sectors, and the multiplier effect in high-skilled manufacturing industry employment increase more significantly. Moretti's analysis on the employment multiplier effect provides a new basis for considering the impact of city size on employment. Considering non-tradable goods sectors, economic agglomeration may bring more employment opportunities for workers, thus increasing the employment probability of individuals.

In Chapter 4, the Probit model of employment decision at the individual level will be constructed and empirically estimated, using data of the Chinese Household Income Project in 2002 and 2007 (CHIP, 2002; CHIP, 2007) and the data of the fifth National Census of China in 2000.

2.2.2 *Spatial general equilibrium and the income effect of economic agglomeration*

In addition to affecting the employment of workers, in existing literature, the effect of economic agglomeration on the improvement of labor productivity is also manifested through nominal indexes such as output per capita and wage. But nominal wages and output cannot fully reflect workers' welfare.

On the one hand, non-wage income, such as business income and property income, has become an increasingly important part of one's total income. Economic agglomeration will promote the rise of workers' non-wage income by lowering the entry barrier of firms, encouraging entrepreneurship and improving the efficiency of information transmission. Entrepreneurship is critical to increasing non-wage income. Because workers' starting a business often involves finding opportunities, access to resources, creating and coordinating resources (Garnsey, 1998), such effects as enhanced efficiency of information transmission, or increased upstream input supply and downstream demand brought about by agglomeration will reduce the costs of starting businesses, encourage starting businesses, and promote the improvement of business income. For example, Hoover and Vernon (1962) believe that, due to the concentration of capital, input factors and services in the city center, the costs of starting businesses there are relatively lower than those in periphery areas. Glaeser and Kerr (2007) believe that the emergence of entrepreneurs is often related to the existing industrial structure of cities. For example, workers tend to start businesses in areas where consumers or intermediate suppliers are concentrated. New ideas of innovation often come from nearby firms, and whether the firms can employ qualified employees at the early stage of businesses depends on the local labor market. Empirically, Glaeser and Kerr (2009) investigated determinants of the number of new manufacturing firms established and the number of workers employed by new firms in a region. They found that urban population and the increase of urban employment in the same industry will significantly increase the number of workers employed by new firms in this industry. On average, an increase of one standard deviation in urban population will lead to an increase of 0.5 standard deviation in the number of workers employed by new firms. Agglomeration at the urban industrial level explains 80% of the change in the number of newly hired workers. Similarly, Glaeser (2007a) found that the self-employment of workers in cities, as an aspect of entrepreneurship, would be affected by the number of urban elderly population and the number of intermediate product suppliers. The increase in the size of local small businesses and the number of employed workers in cities is related to the concentration of local intermediate goods suppliers and labors. Using enterprise data from the Netherlands ICT industry, Oort and Stam (2006) also found that agglomeration and diversification significantly promoted the creation of new firms, thus providing evidence for economic agglomeration encouraging entrepreneurship.

On the other hand, what is more important is, due to the impact of regional price disparities, the difference in nominal income is not equivalent to the difference in real income. The real income adjusted by regional price levels is a more comprehensive reflection of workers' welfare. The research results of Kravis and Lipsey (1988) based on cross-country data show that the prices and incomes of high-income countries are positively correlated because of higher labor costs and non-tradable goods prices. Similarly, within a country, regional price levels are related to local labor productivity and income, and the differences in prices are mainly caused by differences in the prices of non-tradable goods. Because labor flow among regions will affect non-tradable goods market demands and commodity prices, to present a more complete picture of economic agglomeration effects on workers' welfare, we need not only to examine directly the economic agglomeration effect on workers' income but also consider the interaction of the labor market and non-tradable goods market based on the spatial general equilibrium model.

Roback (1982) analyzed the interaction between the land market and the labor market, and provided the spatial general equilibrium model for the first time. Under the assumption of free labor mobility and inelastic land supply, Roback's (1982) model shows that changes in labor supply or demand in local labor market will eventually be capitalized into land prices. So in equilibrium, the utility of labor does not change. In a broad sense, as a special case of non-tradable goods sectors, the influence of urban labor supply changes on land prices can be regarded as its influence on the prices of non-tradable goods sectors. Based on Roback (1982), Moretti (2011) considered more general spatial equilibrium models such as limited labor mobility, heterogeneity in labor skills, or increasing returns to scale in regional economy. His research shows that local labor market demand and supply shocks will lead to the inflow or outflow of workers, which will lead to changes in the prices of non-tradable goods in the region, making the change of the real income of workers smaller than that of the nominal income. The change of prices of non-tradable goods is affected by both demand and supply in the process of economic agglomeration. In general, the more consumers prefer non-tradable goods, the greater the elasticity of labor supply is, or the higher the skills of the inflow workers are, and the greater the increase of local demand for non-tradable goods, the higher the prices of non-tradable goods are pushed up. Higher elasticity of supply of non-tradable goods will depress prices. With perfect free mobility of labors and inflexible supply of non-tradable goods sectors, the promotion of economic agglomeration on the nominal income of workers will be completely offset by the rise of the prices in non-tradable goods, so that the impact of urban expansion on real income is not significant.

Empirically, existing literature has proved that changes in local labor market conditions will bring about labor inflows or outflows. Blanchard and Katz (1992) investigated the impact of economic fluctuations on the labor market in 40 years after World War II. They found that while fluctuations in regional economic growth brought permanent changes in the number of employment in local economies, the unemployment rate remained unchanged. This is mainly because labors and businesses flow in and out of the region after booms and busts. The change in number of labors in regional economy will affect prices of local non-tradable goods through the change of demands, thus leading to the change of real income. Based on census data from 1980 to 2000 in the United States, Moretti (2013) found that if we took into account the differences in prices and workers' skills among regions, the real income gap between college graduates and high school graduates rose much less than the nominal income gap. Considering the movement of labors and the resulting differences in the prices of non-tradable goods between regions, we need to investigate the impact of economic agglomeration on the real income of labors based on the spatial general equilibrium model, so as to analyze the changes of laborers' welfare more comprehensively.

Chapter 5 will use the same database as Chapter 4 does to estimate the income determination model at the level of individual workers, and investigate the impact of economic agglomeration on the nominal income and real income of workers, respectively. The results in Chapter 5 will not only provide evidence for the existence of economic agglomeration effect in China but also further reveal the welfare effect of economic agglomeration by examining the impact of economic agglomeration on the real income of workers.

2.3 Economic Agglomeration and Place-based Policies

From the perspective of individual employment and income, we discussed how economic agglomeration affects an individual's labor market performance. In general, agglomeration effect will facilitate the increase of employment probability and income of workers due to the relatively higher labor productivity in the agglomeration area. Then, how is the effect of agglomeration effect on industrial development? The healthy operation of the local labor market is based on the sustainable development of industries. Chapters 6–8 focus on the development of manufacturing and service industries. Given the macro background of China's economic structural transformation, it is of great policy value to examine how economic agglomeration affects industrial development. Theoretically, the economic agglomeration effect may lead to multiple equilibria. From the perspective of regional economic development, an important question is: Can economic agglomeration effect benefit local economy as a whole, so as to boost the region's economic takeoff? The analysis of these problems will be based on place-based policies and structural changes of industries.

2.3.1 *Place-based policies*

In reality, no matter in developed or developing countries, local governments always attract firms by implementing various preferential policies (such as tax policies, land policies, etc.) to promote local economic growth and increase employment. Such place-based policies are particularly prevalent in the manufacturing industry.

Theoretically, the effectiveness of place-based policies mainly depends on economic agglomeration and the resulting increase in returns to scale. Kline (2010) introduced the agglomeration effect into the spatial general equilibrium model of place-based policies and found that only when agglomeration effects are present and strong enough will the place-based policies promote the local economy, making the local economy shift from a low-level equilibrium with low employment and wages to a high-level equilibrium with relatively higher employment and wages. However, some studies believe that local governments usually attract firms and investment through preferential policies, which often distorts the market mechanism and factor allocation, resulting in the inefficiency of local production and deadweight loss of residents' welfare. The loss is especially severe when local government officials formulate place-based policies in pursuit of personal benefits (Wilson, 1999; Glaeser, 2001). In addition, the increase of local wages brought by the increase of manufacturing employment will crowd out employment in other industries, thus weakening the positive impact of place-based policies on the local economy (Moretti, 2011). The crowding-out effect is particularly evident when labor supply is inelastic.

In practice, local governments often face different policy choices. There are still debates about whether local governments should give priority to high-tech and high-value-added industries in development, or should promote complementarities across related industries based on local industrial structure and comparative advantages. Compared with the "one-size-fits-all" introduction and development of high-tech industries, it needs to be empirically tested whether the policies to promote the development of industries with stronger complementarities are more effective.

Empirical studies on the effectiveness of place-based policies have reached different conclusions. Bondonio and Engberg (2000) found that the enterprise zone programs aimed at increasing employment within the region did not bring an increase in local employment, which might be because employment growth in the enterprise zone had a crowding-out effect on employment in other local industries and regions. Similarly, Hooker and Knetter (1999) analyzed the impact of defense employment on local labor market and also found that government-led employment increase would crowd out other local employment. The analysis by Charles *et al.* (2013) provided indirect evidence for the crowding-out effect of manufacturing employment increase on employment in other industries. It is found that while the decline in manufacturing employment had significantly increased the overall local unemployment rate, the negative impact on overall employment was much less than one-to-one effect. On average, a 1 percentage-point decline in manufacturing employment share of the local population leads to a 0.4 percentage point increase in the local unemployment rate. However, some other studies have found that place-based policies have positive spillover effects on other industries. Greenstone *et al.* (2010) used site selection decision data and county-level economic data from 1970 to 1999 in the United States to find that every time a firm of more than one million dollars was attracted to a place, aggregate wages of the firm's industry would increase by about 9%. At the same time, aggregate wages of other industries in the same region or of the same industry in neighboring regions will also rise, but by a relatively smaller amount. Moretti (2010) directly investigated the spillover effect of employment growth in tradable goods sectors on employment in non-tradable goods sectors. Using US data aggregated at the local labor market level, he found that each additional manufacturing job created 1.59 jobs in the non-tradable sectors of the local labor market, and that the multiplier effect of the increase in high-skill manufacturing jobs was more significant. Similarly, Moretti and Thulin (2013) found that the multiplier effect of manufacturing employment in the local labor market also existed in Sweden. Therefore, we need more empirical evidence on the effectiveness of place-based policies.

2.3.2 *Cluster effect and the development of manufacturing industry*

In terms of the development of manufacturing industry, we will focus on the impact of industrial clusters for the following three reasons. First, industrial clusters are not only a common feature of urban development and industrialization in various countries but also a major underpinning of China's manufacturing industry (Zhang Xiaobo and Ruan Jianqing, 2011).

However, due to the limitations of data and methods, there are few researches on industrial cluster effect, and the relevant researches mainly focus on case analysis. Secondly, the existing empirical literature on agglomeration effect mainly focuses on the localization effect of industries or the urbanization effect of the whole city. However, this dichotomy is oversimplified. In fact, the spillover effect in production can neither be confined within a single industry nor come from all industries in the city. It mainly comes from the various forms of links between related industries. Therefore, industrial cluster is a reasonable starting point. Third, as for place-based policy choices, especially in the process of development, there is still a debate about whether the local government should give priority to the development of high technology, high value-added industries, or should be based on the local industrial structure and comparative advantage to promote the development of related industries and encourage complementarities across industries, based on the industrial cluster, and thus more empirical evidence are needed.

Industrial cluster is a common feature of urban development and industrialization in various countries. The economic development and industrial upgrading of many countries and regions in the world are often accompanied by the development of industrial clusters (Bianchi, 1998; Sonobe and Otuska, 2006; Ali *et al.*, 2014). In definition, industrial cluster mainly refers to the geographical concentration of related industries and departments due to the connection of knowledge, technology, input–output, demand, and other aspects (Delgado *et al.*, 2016). Porter (1990), based on the "diamond model", analyzed the effect of inter-firm interactions on cluster innovation and growth, and believed that cluster-based industrial development is the main source of a country's industrial competitiveness, which is the key for a country to obtain competitive advantages. In China, not only the development of the manufacturing industry in the eastern coastal areas is mainly based on the industrial clusters, but even agricultural productions in the western areas are cluster-based. Cluster-based productions adapted to the resource endowment and institutional characteristics in the early stage of industrialization, which is conducive to lowering investment barriers and transaction costs and encouraging division of labor. Therefore, industrial cluster becomes a main underpinning for the development of manufacturing industry (Zhang Xiaobo and Ruan Jianqing, 2011). However, with the completion of industrialization and rising of labor costs, the initial development advantages of industrial clusters may be weakened. Not only the competition among industries within the same cluster may crowd out industrial employment by pushing up prices of land, labor, and other factors but also path dependence brought about by cluster development may lead to the city's industries being locked at the lower end of industrial value chain, which is not conducive to sustainable industrial development and employment expansion (Grabher, 1993; Chen Jiagui and Wang Qin, 2005). In addition, in practice, local governments often face the problem of how to promote the development of related industries and take advantages of the complementary effect between industries based on local comparative advantages. The research on industrial cluster and its industrial development effect can not only supplement the literature of new economic geography but also provide reference for the formulation of government's regional and industrial policies and business decisions of enterprises.

Although Porter put forward the concept of industrial cluster as early as in 1990, due to the lack of an effective method for classification of industrial clusters, there was little systematic research on industrial cluster, and there was no classification of China's manufacturing industrial clusters at present. The existing researches on industrial cluster and its economic development effect mainly focus on case analysis. Theoretically, the cluster development mainly promotes the labor productivity of the industry within the cluster through agglomeration effect. In Section 2.1, we have explained the micro-foundations and existing empirical findings of agglomeration effects. In general, agglomeration effects in the existing empirical studies are tested as localization effects or urbanization effects. Localization effect is mainly manifested as the externality caused by the concentration of a single industry in the region, and its positive effects on labor productivity mainly comes from the benefits of specialization. The urbanization effect refers to the advantages of industrial diversification brought by the expansion of the overall economic scale in a region. In terms of indicators, economists often use the employment number or the relative concentration of the industries to measure localization effect, while the urbanization effect is often measured by population or employment of cities (Rosenthal and Strange, 2004). Henderson (2007), for example, took industrial employment and regional overall employment as the measurement of the localization effect and the urbanization effect, respectively, and confirmed the positive effect of localization on enterprise labor productivity. Sveikauskas (1975), Glaeser and Resseger (2009) provided evidence for the existence of the urbanization effect by analyzing the impact of urban population on labor productivity and income. But in reality, there is no city with only one single industry, or a city with all the industries. The key for the agglomeration effect lies in the spillover effect between related industries, and the industrial cluster composed of related industries is a reasonable starting point. As for industrial clusters, the existing research mainly takes the form of case analysis to explain the role of industrial cluster from the following three aspects. First, the knowledge spillover effect brought by industrial clusters will reduce the technical or capacity barriers for enterprises to enter a certain industry. Therefore, in the early stage of industrialization, it is conducive to overcoming the adverse impact of entrepreneurs' low personal technical level or operational ability on industrial development (Zhang Xiaobo and Ruan Jianqing, 2011). Huang *et al.* (2008) illustrated the effect by summarizing the development of Wenzhou's shoe manufacturing industry cluster. In addition, industrial clusters are also conducive to the cultivation of the consumer market, so they will promote industrial development by increasing market opportunities (Sonobe *et al.*, 2002). Second, the division of labor and cooperation within clusters will help enterprises gain competitive advantages, thus promoting the growth of firms and industries. Many studies have found that the division of labor and cooperation along the industrial value chain have made important contributions to the development of export-oriented industries in developing countries, and development of the industrial clusters is the main reason for the development of labor-intensive industries in China (Humphrey and Schimitz, 1996; Long Xiaoning *et al.*, 2015). Third, the development of industrial clusters may promote the improvement of industrial productivity and industrial development in the region through overall innovation and quality improvement. Case studies on industrial clusters in developing countries show that the cluster-based production often leads to the problem of low product quality in the early stage of development (Sonobe and Otsuka, 2006). This is mainly because low-quality goods tend to have relatively higher market demand in the early stages of development when per capita income is lower. However, with the development of industrialization and the continuous increase of income per capita, the innovation ability and product quality of industrial clusters become the core determinants of cluster competitiveness. The three-stage model of industrial cluster transformation and upgrading of Ruan Jianqing *et al.* (2014) regards the period of cluster quality improvement as the key to industrial cluster development. According to them, the successful and sustainable development of industrial clusters needs to go through three stages: the period of quantity expansion, the period of quality improvement, and the period of growth based on R&D and brand innovation. The quality crisis and the change of regional comparative advantages are the main reasons for the three-stage development of industrial clusters. If path dependence leads to industrial cluster being locked in the low end of the industrial value chain, the development of cluster and related industries will be hindered. After the breakthrough of quality improvement, the development of industrial clusters will enter the third stage of growth based on R&D and brand innovation. If the clusters keep growing through quantity expansion without quality promotion, the fierce competition among enterprises may hinder the elevation of the position of industrial value chain, undermining sustainable growth of the cluster. Based on case studies of the woolen sweater cluster in Puyuan, China, and the lamp cluster in Wenzhou, China, Ruan Jianqing *et al.* (2014) confirms the important role of providing public goods with positive externalities in cluster evolution and upgrading.

In Chapter 6, based on the methods of Delgado *et al.* (2014), China's economic census data and input–output data will be used to classify all Chinese manufacturing industries into clusters, and on this basis, the current situation and regional distribution characteristics of China's manufacturing industry clusters will be further analyzed. One advantage of using Chinese data to classify industrial clusters is that China is a large economy. As a large economy, China has the advantage of complete industry categories and big differences among regions. In addition, with heterogeneity of the distribution of industrial clusters among regions, researches on the labor market effect of industrial clusters could provide enough variations for more detailed analyses. In Chapter 7, based on the classification of industrial clusters, we will comprehensively evaluate the effect of clusters on industry development from both aspects of quantity and quality, and emphasize the importance of complementarities of economic activities for regional economic development, thus providing a supplement to the literature of new economic geography.

2.3.3 *Agglomeration effect and employment multiplier effect of urban labor market*

In addition to the manufacturing industry, the book will also explore the economic agglomeration effect on the service industry. In particular, we mentioned in 2.2.1 that economic agglomeration effects may affect individual's labor market performance through the expansion of employment in non-tradable goods sectors. Therefore, examining how economic agglomeration affects employment in the tertiary industry is a natural extension of the study in Chapters 4 and 5.

Service economy is a typical characteristic of modern economy and its development plays an important role in modern economic growth. Since the beginning of the 21st century, almost all developed economies have transformed into a service economy, with the employment proportion of the service industry rising constantly, and almost all new job opportunities are created in the service industry (Schettkat and Yocarini, 2003). According to Clark's Law, with the growth of income, people will spend a larger share of income on the purchase of services, thus increasing the final demand for services and bringing about the continuous increase of employment in the service industry (Clark, 1957). Fuchs (1968) believed that the United States began to transition to a service economy as early as in the 1920s, and the initial feature of this transformation is the large-scale increase of employment in the service industry. He found that from 1947 to 1967 America created 17 million jobs, almost all of which were in the service sector. However, in China, the development of the service industry lags far behind in the face of continuous economic growth and rising industrialization level. An important manifestation of this is the long-term low proportion of employment in the service industry. Cheng Dazhong (2004) believes that, compared with other countries at similar levels of development, China has low percentage of added value, low employment proportion and low added value per worker in its service industry. Take employment as an example. In 2010, the employment of the tertiary industry accounted for 71.46% of the employment of all the OECD countries, while the employment of China's tertiary industry accounted for only 34.6% in the same period, far lower than that of OECD countries. However, as the future direction of economic development, service industry will be more and more important in absorbing employment. By using China's industrial employment data from 1979 to 2000, Yao Zhanqi and Xia Jiechang (2005) found that the employment growth in current China still needs to be driven by the development of the service industry. Especially for low-skilled workers, the development of the service sectors should be taken as the direction of absorbing them in the future (Yuan Fuhua and Li Yixue, 2008).

The tertiary industry as a whole has been playing an increasingly important role in the macro-economy in the post-industrialization period.

A new phenomenon in the US and European labor markets in recent years has been the growing share of high- and low-skilled service sector employment in the total employment. With the widespread use of computers, jobs are more and more concentrated to high-skilled and low-skilled service industries, which is called job polarization (Autor *et al.*, 2003). The changes in urban occupational structure, especially the expansion of employment in service industries, have been explained by existing researches in terms of technological progress and material capital (such as computers) replacing workers in production. Existing literature has found that skills-biased technological progress does not significantly worsen the employment prospects of low-skilled workers; on the contrary, more low-skilled workers find jobs in the low-skilled service sector. This is because in the process of technological progress, computers only replace some routine jobs that are generally taken by medium-skilled workers, such as typing. As for low-skilled manual jobs in service sectors such as babysitters or homemakers, and high-skilled abstract jobs such as lawyers and doctors, computers do not replace. In addition, technological progress has provided complementary services for high-skilled service industry, which has led to the increase of employment in high-skilled service industry. Goos and Manning (2007) confirmed the relationship between technology substitution and employment polarization through data from the UK. Similarly, Manning (2004) found that in the United States and the United Kingdom, the employment of low-skilled workers is increasingly concentrated in non-tradable goods sectors, and the increase of such employment is increasingly dependent on the geographical proximity of low-skilled workers and high-skilled workers. One possible explanation is that high-skilled workers have a higher consumption demand for low-skilled services.

Based on Ricardo's theory of comparative advantage, Acemoglu and Autor (2010) established a theoretical model for the impact of technological progress on the employment of labor force with different skills. According to them, the traditional model of career structures usually introduces technological progress into it as a factor augmenting element, and model the relationship between skills and careers as a one-to-one correspondence. Therefore, technological progress is bound to be accompanied by rising factor demand, increasing employment opportunities and higher wages. But traditional models cannot explain recent trends of polarization of employment and income in the labor markets of the United States and Europe. Acemoglu and Autor (2010) used Ricardo's theory of comparative advantage and improved the traditional models by choosing different occupations for workers with different skills according to their comparative advantages. Advances in technology in broader terms — replacement of routine jobs by computers, development of outsourcing services, and so on — forced medium-skilled workers to turn to the services hard to be codifiable for jobs by partly replacing their jobs, thus affecting the urban job structure. The comparative static results from this model better explain many previously unexplained phenomena of employment and wage structure in the labor market. Similarly, Autor and Dorn's (2013) model also started from the production function of computer development to replace routine jobs and complement high-skill service industry, and theoretically explained employment polarization. The empirical results of using data from 1980 to 2005 in the United States suggest that as the price of computers falls dramatically, local labor markets with more routine jobs at the very beginning will adopt more computer technology to replace routine jobs, leading to an expansion of low-skill service employment in these regions. However, the above researches mainly explain the changes of the employment structure of urban labor market from the perspective of production function, while the factors of the changes of market consumption demand are largely ignored.

Moretti's (2010) analysis on the employment multiplier effect investigated the factors affecting the employment in the service industry from the perspective of demand. The employment multiplier model discusses the spillover effect of employment changes between different urban sectors. To be specific, Moretti examines the effect of an expansion of jobs caused by an exogenous demand shock in an industry in the tradable goods sector of the city on employment in other industries of the city. An important concern is the impact of the expansion of jobs in the tradable goods sector on jobs in the non-tradable goods sector. The increase of jobs in the tradable goods sector will increase the jobs and wages of the city, thus bringing the increase of total income of the city. According to Clark's Law, the increase of total income will inevitably lead to the expansion of the demand of non-tradable goods sectors, and then increase the wages and jobs of non-tradable goods sectors in equilibrium. The employment multiplier is mainly related to the labor intensity of the non-tradable goods sectors, the technical level of the manufacturing industry, and the supply elasticity of the local labor market and housing market. Generally speaking, the higher the labor intensity of the non-tradable goods sectors and the higher the technical level of the employment in the expanded tradable goods sectors, the greater the employment multiplier effect. However, a smaller elasticity of labor and housing supply may restrain the employment multiplier effect, mainly because the low elasticity of labor and housing supply will lead to a more substantial increase in labor and housing prices, while the increase in factor prices will restrain the labor demand of firms. Moretti's (2010) empirical results verified the existence of the employment multiplier effect. His regression results showed that manufacturing employment did significantly promote non-tradable goods sector employment, with 1.59 jobs in non-tradable goods sector for each additional manufacturing sector employment on average. The multiplier effect of increased employment in highly skilled manufacturing industries was even more significant. Moretti's analysis of the employment multiplier effect provides a new basis for us to investigate how economic agglomeration affects the employment of the tertiary industry in cities from the perspective of demand.

There are few studies on how economic agglomeration affects service sector employment in China. Existing studies focus on high-skilled producer services such as finance and real estate, and focus on the analysis of the impact of producer services on the development of manufacturing industry, rather than the opposite. Chen Jianjun *et al.* (2009) studied the agglomeration of producer services in China. Using data of Chinese prefecture-level cities after calculating the spatial Gini coefficient of 14 Chinese service industries, they found that there is also a high degree of agglomeration in producer services in China, and the degree of manufacturing agglomeration, human capital, city size, government size, and foreign direct investment will affect the degree of agglomeration of producer services. Jiang Jing *et al.* (2007) theoretically modeled the effect of producer services development on that of the manufacturing industry under the framework of Dixit–Stiglitz monopolistic competition model, and tested the model by using province level panel data from China. They found that in China, the development of producer services boosted productivity growth in manufacturing. The regression results of the fixed effects model show that every 1% increase in labor input in producer services brings 0.927% increase in labor productivity in manufacturing industry. Gu Naihua *et al.* (2006) also showed that in China, the development of producer services can promote the competitiveness of the manufacturing industry, and regional marketization would further promote the interaction between producer services and manufacturing industry.

The development of the tertiary industry is crucial to the structural transformation and future sustainable growth of the Chinese economy. In developing countries, the ongoing process of urbanization requires cities to create more jobs to accommodate the continuous inflow of rural workers. Therefore, in Chapter 8, we will focus on how economic agglomeration affects the development of urban tertiary industry from the perspective of demand. How urban manufacturing employment changes affect services employment and the factors influencing local differences of the multiplier effect will be empirically investigated based on Moretti's (2011) model in Chapter 8. The research in Chapter 8 can provide not only evidence from China for the literature on place-based policies but also policy suggestions on how to realize the transformation and upgrading of local economy through the development of manufacturing industries.

Chapter 3

Spatial Distribution of the Manufacturing Industry in China since the Reform and Opening Up: Roles of Globalization, Economic Agglomeration, and Economic Policy

Not only are economic activities unevenly distributed among countries, but there is also a trend of these activities concentrating in large cities or city clusters within the same country. According to the theory of new economic geography, the agglomeration effect and the crowding-out effect jointly determine the spatial distribution of economic activities. Agglomeration effect includes any increase in firm or worker income caused by the increase of local economic scale, input–output relationship between firms, labor market pooling, and knowledge spillover, which are the three major driving forces of economic agglomeration. The crowding-out effect mainly comes from higher prices of production factors such as lands and labors, as well as the fiercer market competition, environmental pollution, and competition for local public goods in the concentrated areas.

Since the reform and opening up, economic activities in China show the trend of concentrating in the eastern coastal areas, especially the Yangtze River Delta, the Pearl River Delta, and the Beijing–Tianjin–Hebei metropolitan area. With the development of globalization and the growth of international trades, China's coastal areas have realized the initial concentration of economic activities due to their geographical advantages closer to the international market. The resulting economic agglomeration effect has constantly strengthened the advantages of the early development of coastal areas due to the accumulation cycle effect of agglomeration, which constitutes the new economic geographical advantages of the development of coastal areas. Jin Yu *et al.* (2006) uses the provincial data of China from 1987 to 2001 to find that since the reform and opening up, the trend of industrial agglomeration in China has gradually strengthened, and the gap between provinces (autonomous regions and municipalities) in the proportion of industrial GDP in national industrial GDP has gradually widened, with the coefficient of variation rising from 0.026 in 1987 to 0.030 in 2001. Similarly, by calculating the industrial geographic agglomeration index of 20 sectors in China's manufacturing industry, Zhao Wei and Zhang Cui (2007) confirmed that the trend of spatial agglomeration of most industries in China has continuously grown from 1999 to 2003.

This chapter mainly focuses on the characteristics and changes of the spatial distribution of the manufacturing industry. On the one hand, as the production sector of tradable goods, the spatial distribution of the manufacturing industry is prone to being influenced by economic geographical and new economic geographical factors to concentrate. In contrast, the agglomeration trend of the non-tradable sector is relatively weak. On the other hand, manufacturing industries not only play essential roles in absorbing and creating jobs in urban areas in most countries but also are the core forces driving economic development and technological innovation. Especially in China, manufacturing is the most important sector that absorbs employment and creates international trade surpluses. The competitiveness of the manufacturing industry is the core of China's global competitiveness. Even from the perspective of service sector development, employment growth in service sectors is largely dependent on the development of manufacturing industries. For policy considerations, apart from promoting employment and lowering the unemployment rate, the Chinese government also pays great attention to the spatial distribution of employment. Ignoring the structural changes behind the overall employment changes may lead one to overlook the dynamic changes of China's industrial development and labor market, and make one-sided conclusions and policy suggestions. The formulation of industrial and regional development policies must be based on an understanding of the development trends and spatial distribution patterns of different industries.

3.1 Spatial Distribution of Economic Activities: Agglomeration Effect vs. Dispersing Effect

Theoretically, the spatial distribution of economic activities is mainly determined jointly by the agglomeration effect and the dispersing effect. On the one hand, influenced by the input–output relationship between enterprises, labor market pooling, and knowledge spillover, economic activities tend to be concentrated spatially. The concentration of economic activities and the growth of the regional economic scale will promote the improvement of enterprise labor productivity and the increase of labor income (Combes and Gobillon, 2015). In the agglomeration area, more extensive input sharing, more efficient production factor matching, and more learning opportunities are the micro-mechanisms (Duranton and Puga, 2004). On the other hand, the concentration of production activities in some areas will also push up the prices of production factors such as land and labor, thus increasing the production cost of firms. In addition, fiercer market competition, environmental pollution, competition for local public goods, and other factors also constitute the dispersing force of economic activities. The final location choice of firms is the result of the tradeoff between agglomeration effect and dispersing effect. Higher production costs in the agglomeration area indicate the relatively higher labor productivity. Only increases in profits brought about by higher labor productivities can offset the negative impact of higher production costs. Otherwise, profit-maximizing firms will choose to turn to other areas with relatively low factor prices to produce and operate.

Despite the coexistence of the agglomeration effect and crowding-out effect, in cases when agglomeration effects dominate, even if we assume in advance that there is no difference among cities in terms of "first nature", the urban system will eventually turn into the core–periphery pattern. The agglomeration effect constitutes the "centripetal force" for factors to concentrate toward the central area, while the crowding-out effect becomes the "centrifugal force" for the urban system to expand outward. According to the simulation results of Fujita and Mori (1996, 1997), due to the interaction between centripetal and centrifugal forces, the market access of cities and the distance to the central cities show a ∽-shaped function relation. In the early stage of economic development, port cities attracted a large number of manufacturing firms due to their proximity to international markets and lower transportation costs. Even if transport costs become less important with technological progress, the early agglomeration advantages of port cities will be continuously enhanced (Fujita and Mori, 1996, 1997). Thus, port cities or traffic arteries develop into central cities in the core–periphery model. Better trade accessibility and increased concentration of production and consumption activities in central cities have brought about relatively higher local market potential. As the distance to the central city increases, transportation costs rise, and the market potential of the city tends to decline, firms' incentives to leave the central region and enter the peripheral regions for production are lowered. Areas where the market potential decreases with increasing distance are called urban shadows, where centripetal forces dominate. With the further increase in the distance to the central areas, the centrifugal force began to play a major role, promoting the development of domestic and regional trade market potential. As long as the market capacity is large enough, a new sub-center will be formed beyond a certain distance from the central area. However, when the distance becomes even longer, the market potential tends to decline again, thus forming a ∽-shaped relationship between market potential and the distance. Economic activities in a region are directly related to its market potential. In Fujita and Mori's models, market potential directly determines the size of the local economy.

Empirically, Hanson (2005) used the county-level data in the US and found that with the increase of distance from areas with high market potentials, the employment density of the area tended to decline. In addition, he also empirically tested the impact of market potential on workers' wages and found that market potential significantly improved workers' wages, and the effect is getting stronger over time. Xu Zheng *et al.* (2010) tested the ∽-shaped relationship between distance and market potential using the data of China's prefecture-level cities. By introducing the quadratic and cubic terms of cities' distance to Shanghai and Hong Kong into regressions, which are two major ports of China, they provided empirical evidence consistent with the simulation results of Fujita and Mori (1996, 1997). Regression results of Xu Zheng *et al.* (2010) showed the ∽-shaped relationship between the city's economic growth rate and its distance to the central big city, namely, with the increase in the distance to the central big city, big city's impact on the economic growth of the city changes dynamically, first restraining city growth and then promoting city growth. Similarly, Meng Keqiang and Lu Ming (2011) applied the core–periphery theory to the analysis of economic efficiency of the three metropolitan areas (city clusters) in China, the Yangtze River Delta, the Pearl River

Delta, and the Beijing–Tianjin–Hebei metropolitan area, and also confirmed the ∽-shaped relationship in Fujita and Mori (1996, 1997). In addition, they found that compared with the Pearl River Delta metropolitan area, core cities in the Yangtze River Delta had a relatively stronger agglomeration effect and a wider radiation scope.

The above analysis shows that the development of central cities and the interaction between cities will affect the overall spatial distribution of employment and wages. The spatial distribution of market potential will determine economic activities in cities with different geographical locations, thus affecting local employment. In Section 2, the spatial distribution characteristics of production activities in China's manufacturing industry will be described based on the core–periphery theory. Consistent with the theory of new economic geography, China's manufacturing activities tend to be highly concentrated in the eastern regions. This is mainly because of the following: On the one hand, the eastern coastal area, due to its geographical advantage of being close to the international market, got priority in the early stage of the reform and opening up. On the other hand, the concentration of economic activities in the eastern regions has brought the advantage of early agglomeration, which has been continuously strengthened under the influences of new economic geographical factors. As the distance to the coastal areas increases, the intensity and density of economic activities in the central and western regions decrease.

In addition to the economic geographical and new economic geographical factors, the impact of economic policies on the spatial distribution of economic activities is also crucial. On the one hand, the early industrial development in coastal areas was closely related to the reform and opening up and other related preferential policies. But on the other hand, policies to reduce inter-regional income disparities will also strengthen the dispersing effect and lead to the trend of premature dispersion or inward migration of manufacturing industries, bringing efficiency loss. A common misunderstanding about urban and regional development is to equate "coordinated development between regions" with "synchronized development between regions" and to further contrast "economic agglomeration" with "coordinated development between regions". In terms of policies, it tries to narrow the development gap between different regions and cities of different sizes, so as to balance the welfare of residents in different regions and cities.

3.2 Features and Changes of the Spatial Distribution of China's Manufacturing Industry since the Reform and Opening Up

As is mentioned in the previous section, the agglomeration effect and the dispersing effect together shape the economic map of China's manufacturing industry. China's economic development since the reform and opening up mainly benefits from globalization, especially the tremendous development of international trade. The eastern coastal areas are given priority due to their proximity to the international markets. This is the "first nature" factor driving the concentration of economic activities toward China's eastern coastal area. The concentration of economic activities in the eastern regions has brought the advantage of early agglomeration. Under the influence of new economic geographical factors, the advantage of early agglomeration has been continuously strengthened. As the distance to the coastal areas increases, the intensity and density of economic activities in the central and western regions keep declining, which is the macro background of the spatial distribution characteristics of China's manufacturing activities.

Data show that China's manufacturing industry is mainly concentrated in the eastern regions, declining from the east to central and western regions. The trend of agglomeration has been continuously strengthened since the reform and opening up. In history, after the founding of the People's Republic of China, China implemented the strategy of catching up and the fundamental mode of macroeconomic operation is planned economy. In order to realize industrialization as soon as possible and give priority to the development of capital-intensive industries, the government lowered the prices of agricultural products, labor, and capital through central planning, so that state-owned enterprises (SOEs) would be able to hand over as much surplus as possible to the state in the form of industrial enterprise profits and improve the overall accumulation rate of the country. Although this growth mode at the expense of agriculture and household consumption can realize industrialization quickly in the short term, it violated China's comparative advantage at that time, distorted investment and industrial structure, and is therefore inefficient and unsustainable. In addition, for the sake of national defense and security, China has implemented the strategy of balanced development among regions, the third-line construction was a typical example. Based on the distance from the fronts of land and coastal borders, a large number of labors, especially high-skilled ones, migrated from the relatively developed coastal areas to the inland areas for the third-line construction, forming a large-scale constructive migrant flow during the planning period. Therefore, in the early stage of the reform and opening up, the spatial agglomeration trend of China's industry was not obvious. In 1982, the proportion of the industrial employment population in the eastern regions in the whole country was 45.28% (Table 3.1).

The system of central planning was abandoned after 1978, price controls were lifted, agricultural and industrial output grew rapidly, and China's economy began to take off in the 1980s. The most important reforms in the 1980s were the reform of the price system for agricultural products and the land contract system. On this basis, the economic growth mode driven by rural industry and consumption was established. Among them, the development of township and village enterprises (TVEs) is the most remarkable, so much so that Deng Xiaoping called it "the biggest unanticipated harvest" in the process of reform and development. In the 1980s, the overall degree of competition in the product market was relatively low, and the importance of agglomeration effect in production had not yet appeared, which provided development opportunities for TVEs located in rural areas without economies of scale. TVEs have played an

Table 3.1. Regional Distribution of Manufacturing Production (%) (1982–2000)

	1982	1990	2000
East	45.28	49.76	62.90
Central	21.18	20.10	16.01
West	17.80	16.57	13.64
Northeast	15.74	13.57	7.44

Note: (1) The data of 1982, 1990, and 2000 are from the third, fourth, and fifth population census of the People's Republic of China. (2) The eastern regions include 10 provinces or municipalities: Beijing, Tianjin, Shanghai, Hebei, Jiangsu, Zhejiang, Fujian, Shandong, Guangdong, and Hainan. The central regions include six provinces: Shanxi, Anhui, Jiangxi, Henan, Hubei, and Hunan. The western regions include 12 provinces, regions or municipalities: Inner Mongolia, Guangxi, Chongqing, Sichuan, Guizhou, Yunnan, Tibet, Shaanxi, Gansu, Qinghai, Ningxia, and Xinjiang. Northeastern regions consist of three provinces: Liaoning, Jilin, and Heilongjiang. (3) The data of 1982 shows the proportion of regional industrial employment in the national industrial employment, and the industrial employment is calculated as follows: Industrial Employment = regional population × percentage of employed population in total population × percentage of industrial employment in employed population.

important role in absorbing surplus rural labor force, increasing farmers' income, reducing poverty, narrowing urban–rural income gap, and strengthening market competition. They are the "catalyst" for China's successful economic transformation. China had not yet entered the era of large-scale globalization in the 1980s, and the driving force of economic growth mainly came from market-oriented reforms in rural areas, especially the development of TVEs. Compared with TVE, investment from Hong Kong, Macao, and Taiwan and foreign countries played a small role in employment. In 1985, firms from Hong Kong, Macao, and Taiwan and foreign-invested firms employed a total of 60,000 people, while TVEs employed 28.27 million people in the same year. Even in 2016, Hong Kong, Macao, and Taiwan firms and foreign-invested firms created 26.66 million jobs, which was still lower than the number of employment in TVEs in 1978. The development of TVEs has reduced the number of rural poor and significantly narrowed the income gap between urban and rural areas. The ratio of urban per capita disposable income to rural per capita net income fell from 2.57 in 1978 to only 1.84 in 1984. Under the circumstance that large-scale labor flow between urban and rural areas is still restricted, the labor supply of TVEs mainly comes from the surplus labor force in local rural areas, so the distribution is relatively scattered. Although China's economy began to take off in the 1980s after the market-oriented reform, the spatial agglomeration trend of economic activities has not yet emerged. Take the proportion of manufacturing employment in different regions as an example, the proportion of manufacturing employment in eastern regions accounted for 49.76% of that in the whole country in 1990, only 4.48 percentage points higher compared with that in 1982, which is 45.28%. In comparison, the proportion of manufacturing industry in central, western and northeast China didn't decrease significantly, from 21.18%, 17.80%, and 15.74% in 1982 to 20.10%, 16.57%, and 13.57% in 1990, respectively (Table 3.1).

Since the 1990s, the focus of the economic reform has shifted from rural areas to cities, and the economic agglomeration effect is the source of urban development vitality. In particular, Deng Xiaoping's South Tour Talks in 1992 ushered in a new era of reform and opening up in China. Globalization and marketization accelerated, and FDI and private capital grew rapidly. Statistics show that FDI investment expanded rapidly in the middle of the 1990s (Figure 3.1), and the employment proportion of SOEs and collectively owned enterprises (COEs) decreased significantly (Figure 3.2). The reform of SOEs and urban labor market enhanced the

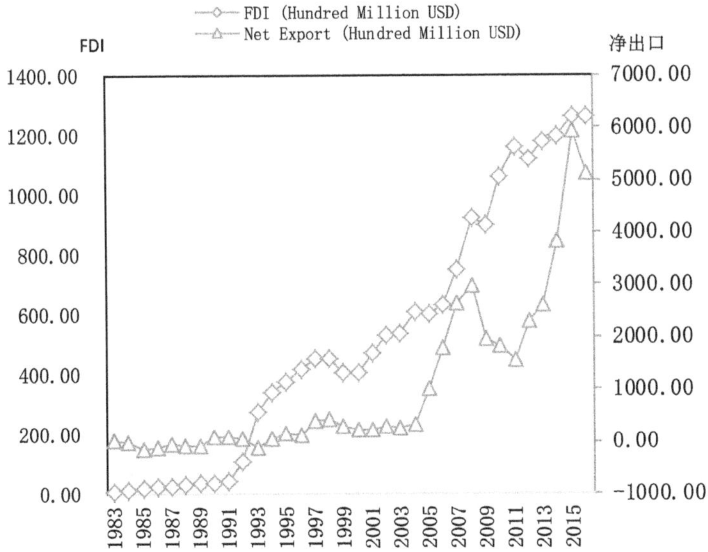

Figure 3.1. Urban Foreign Direct Investment and Net Export

Source: *China Statistical Yearbook.*

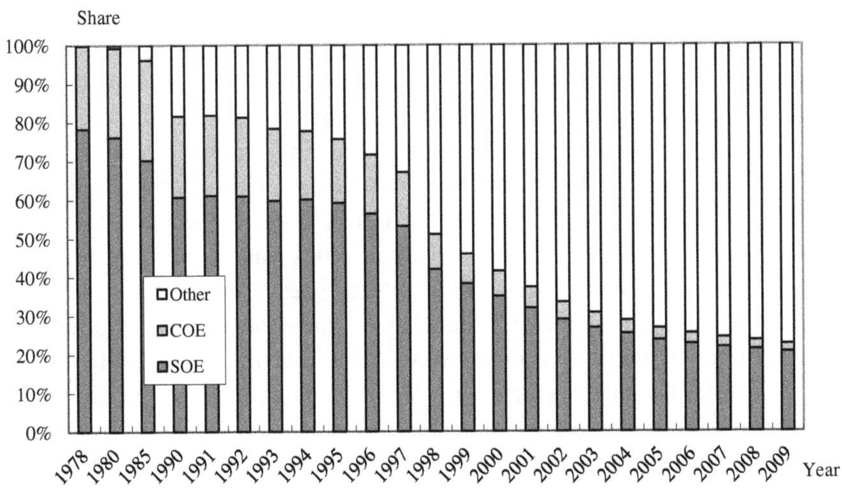

Figure 3.2. Employment Proportion of Different Types of Ownership in Urban Areas

Source: *Statistical Yearbook of China's Population and Employment.*

competitiveness of SOEs, the rapid development of foreign capital and private economy intensified product market competition, large-scale urban and rural migration continuously reduced surplus labor force in rural areas. As a result, the competitive advantage of TVEs gradually lost in the mid-1990s. The improvement of the economy's opening to the outside world highlights the importance of economic agglomeration. As TVEs are usually geographically remote and small in scale, their benefit from economic agglomeration is low, restricting the endogenous growth of productivity. Zhong Ninghua (2011) found that although the employment growth in TVEs significantly closed the urban–rural income gap, its effect continued to decline in the 1990s and its net effect even turned negative in some years. In the 1990s, expansion of TVEs had little effect on narrowing the urban–rural income gap. Since the mid-1990s, thanks to the trend of globalization and global value chain specialization, export-oriented manufacturing industries have gained great development in China. Although net exports are still relatively small compared with those after 2000, they have been consistently positive since the mid-1990s, when exports replaced consumption as the main driver of economic growth (Figure 3.1).

The miracle of "Made in China" owes much to a number of market-oriented reforms in the 1990s. First, the reform of state-owned firms in urban sectors has lowered entry barriers of the private sector, and private manufacturing firms have obtained great opportunities for development. According to the economic census data, the growth of manufacturing firms from 1994 to 2005 followed the "Double 70 Law", that is, 70% of the total industrial added value of manufacturing enterprises came from private firms, and 70% of the total added value of private firms came from newly established firms (Wei *et al.*, 2017). Second, the establishment of special economic zones and coastal open cities has pushed the market-oriented reform of the urban sectors further. Special economic zones and open cities have become experimenting grounds for a series of development policies. Successful policies were quickly replicated elsewhere and rolled out across the country. In addition, given the limited financial resources of the state, special economic zones and open cities were granted priorities in financial resource allocations so that infrastructure constructions there can be constructed, creating good conditions for the development of the private sectors and FDI. Third, the fiscal reform in 1994 provided incentives for local governments to attract FDI and encourage the development of private firms. Local governments' share of budget revenue decreased after the reform, while their budget expenditures have not changed much. The widening gap between revenue and expenditure weakened local governments' ability to subsidize local SOEs and TVEs. To increase fiscal incomes and broaden the tax base, local governments have instead raced to attract private and overseas investment by offering industrial land at low prices and lowering labor and environmental standards. Local governments competing for growth becomes a significant characteristic of China's growth.

Under the influence of globalization, agglomeration effect, and economic policy, manufacturing activities in China begin to gather at an accelerating pace. According to analysis based on the 2000 National Population Census data, the employment proportion of the manufacturing sectors in the eastern regions reached 62.9% in 2000, while the employment proportion of the central, western, and northeastern regions decreased from 20.10%, 15.57%, and 13.57% in 1990 to 16.01%, 13.64%, and 7.44% in 2000, respectively. The decline of manufacturing employment in northeast China was the most obvious, with a drop of 6.13 percentage points (Table 3.1). Analysis using micro-level firm data also shows a trend of economic concentration in the east. Table 3.2 uses the above-scale industrial firm data in 2004 to calculate the proportion of manufacturing employment, total output, and operating profit in different regions of China in 2004. The statistical results show that no matter what index is used, under the joint influence of economic geographical and new economic geographical factors, China's manufacturing industry is mainly concentrated in the eastern regions. In 2004, 66.93% of all manufacturing employment in China was concentrated in the eastern regions, while 14.69% in the central regions, 11.84% in the western regions, and 6.54%

Table 3.2. Regional Distribution of Manufacturing Production in 2004 (%)

Regions	Employment	Total Output	Business Profit
East	66.93	71.84	73.66
Central	14.69	11.65	11.12
West	11.84	9.34	9.97
Northeast	6.54	7.17	5.25

Note: The definition of the eastern, central, western, and northeastern regions is the same as Table 3.1.

in the northeastern regions. The regional distribution calculated with the total industrial output and operating profit as indicators shows a similar tendency. Generally speaking, the trend of the concentration of firm operating profit in the eastern regions is more obvious and shows the relatively stronger profitability of firms in the eastern regions.

However, after 2000, the trend of further concentration of manufacturing activities in the east slowed down. Even in some industries, the trend of dispersing began to emerge, and the proportion of manufacturing employment in the east remained stable on the whole. Theoretically, higher factor prices in the concentrated areas begin to crowd out the production activities of some industries, leading to the spatial relocation of industries, thus narrowing the income gap between regions. The inverted U-shaped pattern, in which the income gap between regions rises first and then declines with economic development, is a common phenomenon in the development of all countries, which is known as the "spatial Kuznets curve". Theoretically, the shape of the spatial Kuznets curve is driven by the structural transformation of urban development, that is, the relocation of industries between cities. The spatial distribution patterns of production and employment differ across various industries or stages of development. Desmet and Henderson (2014) found that in recent years, the dispersion of manufacturing employment in the US has been increasing, and regions with higher levels of manufacturing development at the initial stage have a slower growth of manufacturing employment. However, compared to the manufacturing industry, the growth of service employment in regions with different initial developments of service industry takes the form of an S-shaped curve, that is, in regions where the development of the service industry is at a medium level at the initial stage, the growth of service employment is relatively the fastest. A similar situation exists in Europe. In regions with high levels of initial density or economic development, expansions of the service sector tend to crowd out manufacturing industries due to the crowding-out effect. Economic agglomeration raises prices of non-tradable goods, especially land prices, pushing up production costs of manufacturing. The crowding-out effect is relatively weaker for land-intensive industries such as service industries.

In addition to economic geographical and new economic geographical factors, the spatial distribution of China's economic activities is significantly affected by economic policies. On the one hand, the early industrial development in coastal areas was closely related to the reform and opening up and other related preferential policies. Economic policies not only directly promoted the early agglomeration of manufacturing activities in the eastern regions but also magnified influences of both economic geographical and new economic geographical factors. On the other hand, policies to balance inter-regional development will also strengthen the dispersing effect, thus making the dispersing of manufacturing industries and bringing efficiency loss. A common misunderstanding about urban and regional development is to equate "coordinated development between regions" with "synchronized development between regions" and to further contrast "economic agglomeration" with "coordinated development between regions". Policies tried to narrow the gap between different regions and cities of different sizes, so as to achieve the goal of balancing the welfare of residents in different regions and cities. The implementation of the strategy of western development, the plan for the rise of the central regions, and the revitalization strategy of the old industrial bases in northeast China all show the government's resolutions on the balanced development among regions. Our research in Chapters 4 and 5 will show that economic agglomeration promotes labor productivity through a variety of mechanisms, which in turn leads to job expansion and higher income levels. However, due to policy restrictions, most cities in China suffer from insufficient agglomeration, resulting in huge efficiency losses (Au and Henderson, 2006).

Table 3.3 shows eastern region's national share of manufacturing industries from 2004 to 2012, and shares of employment, total industrial output, and operating profit are calculated, respectively. The results show that the proportion of manufacturing employment in the eastern regions increased year by year from 2004 to 2010, rising from 66.93% in 2004 to 68.87% in 2010, but the overall rising tendency slowed down. After 2010, the employment share of the eastern regions began to decline, from 68.87% in 2010 to 66.30% in 2012. The proportion of output and profit decreased more prominently, the proportion of total output and profit decreased from 71.84% and 73.66% in 2004 to 62.37% and 61.47% in 2012.

There may be several reasons for the growing dispersing effect in the spatial distribution of the manufacturing industry, leading to the trend of dispersion after 2010. First, China's manufacturing industry is mainly export-oriented. Affected by the impact of the financial crisis in 2008, declining external demand has restrained the expansion of manufacturing production, while areas closer to the coastal areas, especially the Yangtze River Delta and the Pearl River Delta, have been hit harder. In Chapter 8,

Table 3.3. Proportion of Manufacturing Production in Eastern Regions 2004–2012 (%)

Year	Employment	Total Output	Business Profit
2004	66.93	71.84	73.66
2005	67.68	71.47	76.08
2006	68.40	70.91	72.07
2007	68.52	69.17	66.14
2008	68.57	67.48	65.67
2009	68.68	67.51	65.23
2010	68.87	74.16	68.65
2011	66.68	61.71	59.23
2012	66.30	62.37	61.47

Note: (1) The definition of the eastern regions is the same as in Table 3.1. (2) In 2011, the National Bureau of Statistics changed the definition of "above-scale" firms by increasing the annual sales revenue of enterprises from at least 5 million yuan to 20 million yuan. As this standard is applicable to all regions, and the table only involves the calculation of the proportion of manufacturing activities in each prefecture-level city, we did not change the sample accordingly. In order to ensure the robustness of the analysis results, we tried to limit the sample before 2011 to firms with sales revenue higher than 20 million yuan and calculated the proportion of the manufacturing industry in the eastern regions, and the overall results got little change.

according to the instrumental variables regressions at the first stage, the export shocks have a significant impact on the change of manufacturing employment in prefecture-level cities, exports increase will lead to the expansion of manufacturing employment and vice versa. Export impact significantly depends on the distance of the city to port cities in the Yangtze River Delta and the Pearl River Delta. Second, in order to cope with the adverse impact of the financial crisis on the overall macroeconomy and maintain economic growth, the government implemented a series of economic stimulus policies, and the effects of the economic stimulus plan were more prominent in the central and western regions with low levels of marketization and high proportions of SOEs (Wen and Wu, 2014; Qian *et al.*, 2015). The government's economic development policies mainly favor the central and western regions and northeastern regions (Shen Kaiyan and Chen Jianhua, 2014). Moreover, the constant expansion of China's assets and liabilities crowds out the real economy greatly after 2008. The essence of the four trillion stimulus plan is partial financial liberalization. To meet funding requirements for investment in infrastructure projects, local governments have either obtained loans from banks by injecting capital into financing vehicles or obtained financing from shadow banks through trust products or other means. Financial liberalization may increase the distortion of the financial market and worsen the efficiency of capital allocation when local governments intervene in the allocation of financial resources. Housing prices in the eastern regions were further pushed up under the impact of the four trillion plans, and the production costs of firms increased, thus the crowding-out effect began to appear. Corresponding to declines in the proportion of manufacturing in the eastern regions, the proportion of manufacturing employment in the central regions increased from 14.75% in 2004 to 16.11% in 2012 and that in the western regions increased from 6.54% in 2004 to 6.83% in 2012, and the changing trends of output and profit were more obvious.

Results of the distribution of manufacturing activities in prefecture-level cities also show a trend of dispersion. The Gini coefficient of manufacturing activities across prefecture-level cities is used to represent the distribution of manufacturing over the whole country, and a higher Gini coefficient represents a higher regional concentration. We calculated the Gini coefficient with the number of manufacturing employment, the number of firms, and the total output of prefectural-level cities, respectively. Results show that the Gini coefficient of employment declined from 2004 to 2012, and declines in the Gini coefficient calculated by the number of firms or the total output were even more significant. The Gini coefficient of urban manufacturing employment in China dropped from 0.67 in 2004 to 0.65 in 2012, while the Gini coefficient of enterprise number and total output dropped from 0.71 and 0.73 in 2004 to 0.63 and 0.64 in 2012, respectively. That is to say, the manufacturing production activities tend to be dispersed among prefectural cities in China, and the crowding-out effect and policies restraining agglomeration are the main reasons.

3.3 Knowledge Spillovers and Changes in Spatial Distribution of Manufacturing Industries

Within the manufacturing sector, patterns of the spatial distribution of different industries are prominently different, among which the industry skill is the most important determinant. The impact of skills is especially evident in the era of the knowledge economy. Physical proximity between people and increases in learning opportunities enhance labor productivity. As is summarized in Chapter 2, a large number of studies have confirmed the existence of the knowledge spillover effect. Geographical proximity in agglomeration areas will enhance knowledge spillovers between enterprises and industries, while highly skilled industries, which are more dependent on knowledge and innovation, will be more significantly affected and thus are likely to grow faster. On the contrary, low-skilled industries are relatively less dependent on innovation and more sensitive to the rising costs of inputs such as land and labor force. Therefore, the geographic relocation of industries with different skill levels may be different, which is manifested in further concentration of high-skilled industries to the agglomeration areas and the departure of low-skilled industries from these areas under the influence of the crowding-out effect.

Taking the proportion of workers with a bachelor's degree or above in the total labor force as the proxy variable of the industrial skill level, we calculated the industrial skill level in 2004 and tried to figure out its correlation with the region's future changes in employment shares. Figure 3.3 depicts the relationship between the skill level of the manufacturing industry at the four-digit code level in 2004 and the industry's changes in employment shares in various regions of China from 2004 to 2012. The horizontal axis of the four figures shows the proportion of graduates with a bachelor's degree or above in the industry, while the vertical axis shows the industry's employment share changes in the eastern, central, western, and northeastern regions from 2004 to 2012, respectively, from the top left to the bottom right. The linear fitting lines show that there is a positive correlation between industry skill level and growth employment share in the eastern regions of China, with a correlation coefficient of 0.238. However, this relationship is insignificant in the central regions, with a correlation coefficient of 0.007. In contrast to the eastern and central regions, the change of the employment share and the industry skill level in the western and northeastern regions are significantly negatively correlated, with the correlation coefficient being –0.261 and –0.219, respectively.

So, what are the overall trends of different manufacturing industries? Using the industrial firm data from China, we found that in the era of the knowledge economy, industries with higher technology levels grow

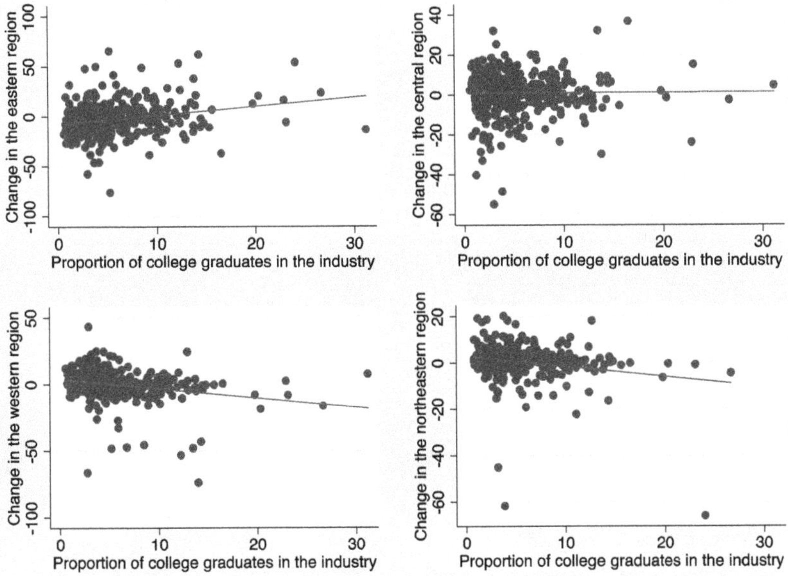

Figure 3.3. Changes in Industry Skill Level and Industry Employment Share in Different Regions

faster. Industries were classified into five categories, depending on whether the percentage of college graduates employed in 2004 is higher than the 80th, 60th, 40th, and 20th percentile of all manufacturing industries. We label an industry's skill level with the values of 1, 2, 3, 4, or 5, of which 1 represents the lowest skill level and 5 represents the highest skill level. On average, industries with the lowest skill level grow noticeably more slowly than other industries or even show negative growth. Total employment growth in manufacturing industries with the lowest skill level is only 80.42% from 2004 to 2012, which is significantly lower than the growth rate of higher than 100% in those with higher skill levels (Table 3.4).

In terms of regional distribution, from 2004 to 2012, the high-tech industry generally concentrated in the eastern region, while the western region suffered from the greatest loss of employment in high-tech industries (Table 3.5). In Table 3.6, industries are divided into five skill levels according to the employment share of college graduates in 2004, and the

Table 3.4. Manufacturing Employment Growth by Skill Levels

Skill level	5	4	3	2	1
Growth (%)	133.58	102.26	157.29	122.96	80.42

Table 3.5. Changes in Regional Employment Proportion of Industries with Different Skill Levels from 2004 to 2012 (percentage points)

Skill Levels	East	Central	West	Northeast
5	3.34	1.74	−2.32	−2.31
4	0.64	−4.35	−3.93	−3.91
3	2.92	2.77	4.07	2.30
2	0.09	0.33	3.25	2.11
1	−6.99	−0.49	−1.06	1.81

Table 3.6. Employment Growth Rate (%) of Industries with Different Skill Levels from 2004 to 2012

Skill Levels	East	Central	West	Northeast
5	143.82	156.31	76.04	102.81
4	121.03	82.22	57.61	87.89
3	155.75	171.09	149.35	150.82
2	113.39	138.64	129.25	151.54
1	69.22	129.91	85.64	150.43

changes of the industries' employment shares in aggregate regional manufacturing employment from 2004 to 2012 are calculated. The results show that the employment proportion of the eastern region with the highest skill level with the skill value of 5 increased by 3.34 percentage points from 2004 to 2012, and correspondingly, the employment proportion of industries with the highest skill levels in the western and northeastern regions decreased by 2.32 percentage points and 2.31 percentage points, respectively. The employment shares in industries with the second highest skill level with the skill value of 4 in the central and western regions and the northeast region also declined significantly. The employment share in the lowest-skilled industries declined significantly in the eastern region, with the proportion dropping by 6.99 percentage points. By contrast, employment share in the lowest-skilled industries rose by 2.11 percentage points in the northeast.

The regional heterogeneity of the employment growth rate of industries with different skill levels also indicates the trend of high-skilled industries concentrating in the eastern regions. From 2004 to 2012, the employment growth rate of the industries with the highest skill level with the skill value of 5 in the eastern region was 143.82%, far higher than the growth rates of 76.04% and 102.81% in the western region and the northeast region, respectively. The employment growth of industries with the second highest skill levels shows similar trends among regions, and the employment of the high-skilled industries does not show a trend of convergence among regions. Unlike high-skill industries, employment growth in low- or medium-skilled industries is the fastest in the central region. Employment growth in industries with the lowest skill level valued 1 in the central region is 129.91% during the period, far higher than the 69.22% growth in the eastern region. Manufacturing employment growth is the slowest at all skill levels in the western region, with employment growth concentrates in medium- or low-skilled sectors. It is worth noting that since the size of employment in the eastern region is much higher than that of the central and western regions, the higher growth rate of the high-skilled industries there will lead to a larger increase in the number of high-skilled jobs and a further concentration of high-skilled industries in the eastern region.

The analysis above is consistent with our theoretical predictions. We believe that the knowledge spillover effect of economic agglomeration is more important for industries with higher skill levels, while knowledge spillover is more sensitive to the proximity of geographical distance. Therefore, the agglomeration trend of industries with high skill levels is particularly obvious in the era of the knowledge economy. Generally, low-skilled industries are more sensitive to the rising costs of input factors such as land and labor, so they will be more significantly affected by the crowding-out effect in the agglomeration area, showing a tendency of dispersion. The change of industries with different skill levels in the agglomeration area will influence the labor market performance of the labor force with different skill levels, which is the focus of our analysis in Chapters 4 and 5.

3.4 Summary

This chapter mainly reviews the spatial distribution characteristics and evolution of China's manufacturing industry since the reform and opening up. Based on theory and literature, we believe that economic geographical, new economic geographical, and economic policy factors jointly shape the economic map of China's manufacturing industry. In the early stage of reform and opening up, market-oriented reforms became the main driving force for China's economic take-off, and the emergence and development of TVEs were especially remarkable. Although the eastern region has obvious advantages in economic development, the trend of spatial concentration of economic activities was not prominent in the 1980s. Since the 1990s, under the joint impacts of globalization, agglomeration effect, and policy effect, the largest migration flow in human history emerged. Large-scale cross-regional labor migration provides capital in coastal areas with abundant labor supply, the competitive advantages of China's manufacturing industries were thus established. However, after 2008, due to the impact of declining exports, the government's policies of reducing regional development gap, as well as rising land and labor costs in agglomeration areas, manufacturing activities did not show a further trend of agglomeration, and even the trend of dispersion began to appear in some industries.

In addition, we find that the roles of agglomeration effect in industries with different skill levels are different. Analysis at the national level of industry growth shows that employment in higher-skilled industries has grown faster, while employment in low-skilled industries has fallen sharply. At the regional level, with the stronger crowding-out effect and the implementation of the policies aiming at balancing inter-regional development, China's manufacturing production showed a trend of dispersion, which was especially obvious after the 2008 financial crisis. However, data show that industries with trends of relocation to inland areas are mostly low-skilled, while high-skilled industries which are not sensitive to input prices and have a higher dependence on the agglomeration effect tend to remain concentrated in the eastern region. There is no tendency of convergence in the employment of high-skilled industries among regions. High-skilled industries tend to be concentrated in the eastern region, and the faster employment growth in the central and western regions relative to the eastern region mainly comes from low-skilled manufacturing industries.

This chapter descriptively provides evidence for the spatial distribution characteristics and changes of economic activities. However, the spatial agglomeration of economic activities observed at the macro level does not necessarily imply the welfare of workers and industrial development at the micro level. More empirical evidences will be provided in the following chapters of the book.

Chapter 4

Economic Agglomeration and the Employment of Urban Workers

Urban development should help to improve individual welfare. Whether an individual can be employed and how much the income can be improved in the process of urban development are important indicators. The World Bank put forward the concept of "inclusive growth" in 2005, stressing that a country should not only pay special attention to the speed of economic growth but also attach great importance to its economic growth pattern. Countries should include the majority of their labor forces into the process of economic growth so that achievements of economic prosperity could be widely enjoyed by the public. Jobs and incomes are not only related to the effective allocation of workers but also important indicators of an economy's inclusiveness. Other things equal, the employed will directly share the benefits of economic growth, especially the boost to labor productivity by agglomeration, while the unemployed will not. Income, especially real income, is directly related to one's personal well-being. In addition, in terms of macroeconomic growth and structural transformation, increases in aggregate incomes and employment will in turn promote economic growth through consumption expansion, which is crucial for China's current growth strategy of expanding domestic demand.

As for policies, formulating regional development policies and improving the urban system largely depend on how economic agglomeration affects labor employment and income at the present stage. A relevant and widely discussed policy issue related to patterns of urbanization is whether the development of large cities or small and medium-sized towns should be given priority. Japan, South Korea, and other countries have taken measures to limit population growth in large cities during their development. The advantages of big cities are mainly reflected in the relatively stronger economic agglomeration effect. The development of small and medium-sized cities and towns may reduce the psychological cost of migration for rural labors, better integrate urban and rural markets, and reduce the cost of city construction. Moreover, there is a widespread fear that cities may not be able to create enough jobs as their population expands. Fiercer competition in the urban labor market may reduce worker incomes and increase unemployment, especially for low-skilled workers.

So, is that the case? Theoretically, the optimal city size reflects trade-offs between the agglomeration effect and crowding-out effect brought by urban expansion. Under the interaction of the two forces, the relationship between urban labor productivity (and per capita income) and city size is inverted U-shaped. In the early stage of cities' development, the expansion of the city size brought the rise of real income per capita. However, if the urban population is too large, due to the crowding-out effect, the further expansion of the city size will reduce the per capita real income, so there is an optimal city size. In current China, neglects of economic agglomeration benefits and excessive concerns about crowding costs have imposed restrictions on the development of large cities. Under restrictions of the urban household registration system, urbanization in China is localized, and the scale economy advantages of cities cannot be brought into play, impeding the improvement of urban labor productivity and economic growth. It is estimated that 51–62% Chinese cities are too small in size, and the resulting output loss accounts for about 17% of the average employee output (Au and Henderson, 2006). In fact, the development of large cities or small and medium-sized towns are not mutually exclusive. The development of small and medium-sized towns can be based on the development of large cities and benefit from the spillover effects there (Xu *et al.*, 2010). Therefore, when the agglomeration effect brought by urban development is stronger than the crowding-out effect, blindly restricting the size of large cities too early may bring about huge efficiency loss.

How to coordinate the development of cities of different sizes and improve the inclusiveness of economic growth is a major strategic problem that needs to be solved in China. In this chapter and the next one, we will study the effect of economic agglomeration on individual's labor market performance in China, from the perspectives of employment and income. Heterogeneous influences of agglomeration on workers with different skill levels will also be investigated.

4.1 City Size and Employment: Theory

The effect of city size on the employment of workers is mainly determined both by the agglomeration effect and the crowding-out effect. Interactions between the two effects result in an inverted U-shaped relationship between urban labor productivity (and per capita income) and city size, so there is an optimal city scale. On the one hand, city expansion brings about increases in labor supply, intensifying labor market competition. But on the other hand, as city expands, agglomeration effect will raise labor productivity, thus increasing labor demand. As is stated in Chapter 2, due to the increasing returns to scale, consumers' preference for consumption diversity, and transportation costs, firms will choose to locate in places with larger market, resulting in larger scales of production and higher overall prices there. In equilibrium, higher factor prices in the agglomeration area must be compensated with higher labor productivities; otherwise, profit maximizing firms will choose to locate in other places where factor prices are relatively lower. More extensive input sharing, better matching of production factors, and more learning opportunities are the micro foundations of economic agglomeration to promote the labor productivity.

The employment rate of workers is mainly determined by both labor supply and demand. In equilibrium, as long as the labor supply curve slopes upward and other factors remain unchanged, the positive effect of agglomeration on labor productivity will push the labor demand curve move outward, thus leading to the simultaneous rise of equilibrium wages and employment. Therefore, higher wages and labor productivity in big cities imply more employment opportunities. If the increase of employment opportunities is faster than the expansion of urban populations, individual employment probability will rise.

In addition, as an important part of the modern economy, the non-tradable goods sector constitutes a major source of urban jobs. Considering this sector, the effect of city size on employment will be magnified. Moretti (2010) discusses how changes in labor demand of an industry in the tradable sector would influence aggregate urban employment.

Empirical results based on the US census data in 1980, 1990, and 2000 show that each additional manufacturing job creates 1.59 job opportunities in the non-tradable sector, known as the "employment multiplier effect". In addition, he found that the multiplier effect in high-skilled manufacturing industries was more significant. Moretti's analysis of the employment multiplier effect provides a new basis for considering the impact of city size on employment. Agglomeration increases labor productivity in the tradable goods sector, which in turn leads to a simultaneous increase in equilibrium wages and employment. The increase of employment and wages in the tradable goods sector will enhance the city's aggregate income, thus increasing the demand for non-tradable goods and creating more jobs for the non-tradable sector. Therefore, considering the non-tradable goods sector, economic agglomeration may bring more employment opportunities for workers and further improve the employment probability of individuals.

While all workers may enjoy agglomeration benefits as city expands, benefits to workers with different skills may vary. Theoretically, there are two reasons why the benefits to workers with different skills may be heterogeneous. On the one hand, since job opportunities of low-skilled workers are more concentrated in low-skilled service industries, which are an important part of the non-tradable goods sector, low-skilled workers may enjoy more benefits from agglomeration than medium- and high-skilled workers. Highly skilled workers have higher consumption demand for low-skilled service. Mazzolari and Ragusa (2013) found that due to the higher opportunity cost of time for highly skilled workers, there is a higher consumption demand for low-skilled services such as nannies and homemaking. As cities grow in size, concentration of highly skilled workers may create more jobs for the low-skilled workers. On the other hand, different occupations depend on learning and innovation to different extent. As a result, different occupations may benefit from knowledge spillover effects in big cities to different degrees. A large number of studies have proved the existence of knowledge spillover effect. These studies suggest that the expansion of cities, especially the agglomeration of highly skilled workers, will provide workers with more opportunities for learning and innovation, thus improving labor productivity. For example, Rauch (1993) found that wages and land rent were higher in cities with a higher average human capital. Moretti (2004a) found that for every one percentage point increase in the proportion of urban college graduates, the labor productivity of firms would increase by 0.6–0.7%. As for knowledge spillover in China, Glaeser and Lu (2018) found that as the education per capita of cities increased by one year, the hourly wage of workers increased by about 22%. Due to the strong learning ability of workers in high-skilled industries and their greater dependence on knowledge and innovation, labor productivity could be more significantly enhanced.

To summarize, increases in city population size will not only increase labor productivity but also bring benefits to workers by increasing employment opportunities. Workers with different skill levels will benefit from city expansion differently. However, estimates of city size's impact on employment may suffer from the two-way causality problem because the unemployment rate of a city will in turn affect city size through people's immigration choices. In addition, employment and city size may be influenced by other unobservable factors simultaneously, leading to missing variables bias. In this chapter, we will use the natural logarithm of urban population growth from 1953 to 1982 as the instrumental variable of city size, and estimate the model using instrumental variable estimation.

4.2 Economic Agglomeration and the Employment of Workers: Baseline Regression Results

To investigate how the change of city size will affect the employment of labors, we use the data of the Chinese Household Income Project (CHIP) in 2002 and 2007, combining with the *China Urban Statistical Yearbook* and the data of census. The CHIP data were jointly collected by the Chinese Academy of Social Sciences and the National Bureau of Statistics of China, and the two-stage stratified systematic random sampling scheme was used. Cities and counties/towns for survey were selected randomly in the first stage, and then in the second stage, households were selected using a multi-phase sampling scheme. The 2002 sample covers 70 cities from 10 provinces and 2 municipalities, including Beijing, Shanxi, Liaoning, Jiangsu, Anhui, Henan, Hubei, Guangdong, Chongqing, Sichuan, Yunnan, and Gansu, with a sample size of 6,835 households and 20,632 individuals. The 2007 sample covers 19 cities from 7 provinces and 2 municipalities, including Shanghai, Jiangsu, Zhejiang, Guangdong, Anhui, Henan, Hubei, Chongqing, and Sichuan. A total of 5,000 households and 14,699 individuals are included in the

2007 survey. All the individuals in the CHIPS urban survey have urban *hukou* identity, which means rural residents and migrant workers are not included in this study. The data include detailed demographic and economic and social information of individual workers, enabling us to identify the impact of city size on workers' employment probabilities, with individual characteristics controlled.

The basic identification strategy in our study relies on the comparison of employment probabilities for otherwise similar individuals who live in cities with different scales. In different regressions, the natural logarithm of the number of permanent urban residents and the natural logarithm of the number of college graduates are used as measures of city size. Economic agglomeration may promote employment through a variety of channels. On the one hand, agglomeration can enhance the labor productivity of firms and thus increase their labor demand. On the other hand, economic agglomeration will bring increases in the aggregate income of the city. According to Clark's Law, increases in total income will raise worker' demand for non-tradable goods, thus bringing more employment opportunities in the non-tradable goods sector. The positive effect of economic agglomeration on employment in the non-tradable sector may be more obvious in cities with a higher concentration of high-skilled workers. This is mainly because high-skilled workers have a relatively higher demand for low-skilled services, resulting in "consumption spillovers" of high-skilled workers to low-skilled workers. As a result, we expect workers to find jobs more easily in large cities with larger populations or more college graduates, which is one of the central assumptions tested in this chapter. City-level data on the number of permanent residents and university graduates are from the Fifth Population Census of the People's Republic of China in 2000. In addition, a number of other urban features that may affect employment are controlled in the regression, such as physical capital investment, industrial structure, government expenditure and transportation infrastructure, etc. The data for city-level characteristics are from *China City Statistical Yearbooks* for years 1997–2001.

The econometric model used is the Probit model of employment decision at the individual level, as shown in Equation (4.1):

$$Prob(Employed_{ij} = 1) = \Phi(\beta'\mathbf{X}_{ij} + \theta_1 Size_j + \alpha'\mathbf{City}_j) \qquad (4.1)$$

where subscripts i and j represent the individual i living in city j. The regression sample used is limited to population at working ages, that is, males between the ages of 16 and 60 and females between the ages of 16 and 55. In addition, our regression excludes those who are not in the labor force, individuals with the urban status of officially off-duty (*Lixiu*), retired, unable to work, full-time homemaker, full-time student, or waiting for job assignment or entering a higher school.[1] The dependent variable *Employed* is a dummy variable regarding the employment status of individuals. An individual who is employed will be valued 1, and who is unemployed, valued 0.

On the right-hand side of the regression equation, $\mathbf{X}_{ij}$ is a vector of personal characteristics that may affect employment, including gender, marital status, years of education, potential work experience and its squared term, CPC member or not, ethnic minority or not. Age is not included in regressions, because the variable of potential work experience, which equals to one's age minus the sum of years of education and 6, has already been included in the regression. If both age and work experiences are included in the regression, perfect collinearity will be brought about. Labors' years of education are used as a proxy for their skill levels. In literature, as it is hard to measure the skill levels of workers directly, education is usually used as a measurement for workers' skill level. In addition, abnormal samples with potential experience less than 0 years and more than 44 years, or with years of education are more than 22 years, are excluded from regressions.

The core explanatory variable $Size_j$ is a measurement related to the size of a city. We take the natural logarithm of the number of permanent urban residents or the natural logarithm of the number of college graduates as the proxy for the size variable. It should be noted that municipal level population is divided into the total urban population and the total rural population in the fifth national census. Here, the total urban population is chosen as the measure. Total urban population includes the population who are living in the city without urban *hukou* identity, which is essentially a measure of the permanent urban population. Most existing studies used urban population as the measurement of urbanization effect,

[1] The proportion of individuals who are waiting for job assignment or entering a higher school accounts for 0.685% of all the working-age population in our sample. According to the definition in labor economics, they should be regarded as those who are not in the labor force. However, as they may partly reflect disguised unemployment, we also run regressions which include them as the unemployed population. The main results of our study do not change with this adjustment.

such as Sveikauskas (1975), Glaeser and Resseger (2009), among others. Besides, the number of urban college graduates is used as another measure of city size. Theoretically, externalities generated by the agglomeration of highly skilled labor force is an important source of agglomeration effect, and the levels and scales of human capital in cities are often highly positively correlated. For example, Glaeser (2007b) found that cities with a higher proportion of college graduates in the initial years had a faster future population growth. Statistics show that there is a strong positive correlation between urban population and the number of college graduates. In our regression sample, the correlation coefficient between the two is as high as 0.905. The magnitude and significance of θ_1 are our focus. If large cities do generate more employment opportunities for workers, θ_1 is expected to be significantly positive, meaning that the expansion of cities will increase the employment probability of workers.

Other urban characteristics that may affect employment are included in the $\mathbf{City}_j$ vector, including the average FDI over average GDP in 1996–2000, average fixed asset investment over average GDP in 1996–2000, road size per capita in 2000, the city's number of buses for every 10,000 persons in 2000, and a dummy variable indicating whether a city is a province capital or not. By controlling these variables, the omitted variable bias that may be caused by labor demand factors or supply factors could be alleviated. A city's physical capital stock is generally correlated with city size and employment. Larger cities attract more capital inflows because of the benefits from economic agglomeration, and capital accumulation itself increases job opportunities for urban residents. Therefore, ignoring capital accumulation in regressions will lead to a biased estimate of θ_1. Another reason why capital accumulation needs to be considered in the individual employment decision model involves human capital externalities. When there are frictions in the labor market and there is complementarity between physical capital and human capital, the improvement of the education of some urban residents will encourage firms' physical capital investment. Increases in physical capital investment will enhance labor productivity, thus raising the labor demand of firms (Acemoglu, 1996, 1998). Controlling FDI and fixed asset investment in cities can reduce the potential missing variable bias due to demand shocks from the urban labor market. We control per capita road area and the number of buses per 10,000 people in the city in regressions, mainly because transportation and other infrastructure will affect the matching efficiency of the labor market and promote information transmission, thus increasing employment probability. In addition, the improvement of urban infrastructure will facilitate the inflow of labors, thus increasing city sizes. Unlike regression models in Chapter 5 in which agglomeration effect on labor income is estimated, we do not control variables related to urban amenity in regressions. This is mainly because there is no channel through which urban amenity may affect employment rate directly. In models of spatial general equilibrium, workers are willing to give up part of their income for better urban amenity. So, in equilibrium, urban amenity may have a negative impact on income. In regressions of this chapter, we only control the variables related to urban investment and transportation infrastructure. Table 4.1 is a description of the variables contained in the regression. Descriptive statistics of the relevant variables entering the regression sample are shown in Table 4.2.

In Table 4.3, estimates of the Probit model are reported. In Regressions 1 and 2, city scale is measured as the natural logarithm of urban total population or urban number of college graduates, respectively. Marginal effects are displayed. To save space, we divide the table into two parts, with coefficients of city scale and individual characteristics being displayed in Columns (1) and (2). The coefficients of other city characteristics are listed in Columns (3) and (4). We find the impact of city size on individual employment probability to be insignificant.

However, Probit results might be biased. Effects of city size on individual employment probability might suffer from two-way causality problem. Cities with higher employment rates encourage an influx of workers by increasing the expected benefits of the labor force, resulting in a relatively large urban population. In addition, although we have controlled city-level variables as many as possible in regressions to mitigate omitted variables biases, other unobservable labor demand or supply shocks in the urban labor market may still affect city size and employment at the same time. Therefore, in Section 4.3, we will estimate the individual-level model of employment probability using instrumental variables estimation, so that the possible endogenous biases could be mitigated.

4.3 Looking for the Instrumental Variable of City Size

Considering potential biases from problems of two-way causality and missing variables, in all the regressions following, instrumental variable regressions are adopted. We use the natural logarithm of the population

Table 4.1. List of Explanatory Variable

Variable	Definitions
Individual Characteristics	
Employment	1 for employed and 0 otherwise
Gender	1 for male and 0 otherwise
Married	1 for married and 0 otherwise
Eduyr	Years of education
Exp	Potential experience = Age − Years of education − 6
Expsq	Experience squared
CP	1 for Communist Party members and 0 otherwise
Minority	1 for minority and 0 otherwise
City Characteristics	
Population	Ln (Urban population (million))
College	Ln (Number of college graduates (million))
PopGrw	Ln (Population in 1982 (million)) – Ln (Population in 1953 (million))
FDI	Average FDI in 1996-2000 (10,000 RMB)/Average GDP in 1996–2000 (10,000 RMB)
Investment	Average fixed asset investment in 1996–2000 (10,000 RMB)/Average GDP in 1996–2000 (10,000 RMB)
Road	Road size per capita in 2000 (m^2)
Transportation	Number of buses for every 10,000 persons in 2000
Year07	1 for year 2007 sample and 0 otherwise

Note: (1) Since CHIPS 2007 does not have information on one's Communist Party membership, we construct the party membership variable for the 2007 sample using CHIPS 2002 data. An individual's Communist Party membership is proxied by the city's share of Communist Party members in the 2002 sample. If a city is included in the 2007 sample, however is not included in the 2002 sample, the Communist Party membership of individuals in that city is proxied by the national share of Communist Party members in 2002.
(2) In order to ensure the geographical unity of the cities involved in the 1953, 1982, and 2000 censuses, the county or city codes in the national censuses in 1953, 1982, and 2000 have been changed into the codes of administrative divisions in 2010. Therefore, the indicators of city size we use in regression are not affected by the adjustment of administrative areas in history.

growth of a city from 1953 to 1982 as the instrumental variable of city size, in which the population data in 1953 are from the First National Census of the People's Republic of China, and the data of 1982 are obtained from the Third National Census of the People's Republic of China.

Table 4.2. Summary Statistics of Variables

Variable	Mean	Standard Deviation	Min	Max
Individual Characteristics				
Employment	0.886	0.318	0	1
Gender	0.549	0.498	0	1
Married	0.856	0.351	0	1
Eduyr	11.606	2.941	0	22
Exp	22.131	10.509	0	44
CP	0.240	0.326	0	1
Minority	0.020	0.141	0	1
City Characteristics				
Population	0.792	0.727	−0.943	2.673
College	−1.576	0.951	−3.371	0.826
PopGrw	0.393	0.595	−1.821	1.865
FDI	0.062	0.062	0.003	0.248
Investment	0.332	0.203	0.184	1.596
Road	5.788	3.031	1.100	17.500
Transportation	9.056	13.787	0.600	95.700
Year07	0.427	0.494	0	1

An important feature of the Chinese economy from 1953 to 1982 is the dominance of central planning. In order to implement the big-push industrialization strategy and accelerate the development of capital-intensive industries, the market's role in resource allocations was curtailed. Consistent with the planned economic system, one of the main characteristics of cross-region allocation of labors from 1953 to 1982 was highly administration dominant. According to Ge and An (2010), there were three main forms of migration in China between 1953 and 1982. The first is national defense immigration in the border area. Construction corps were established in the border areas of Heilongjiang, Inner Mongolia, and Xinjiang from 1953 to 1959, and immigration was organized by the state through plans to migrate young or middle-aged people from the mainland to the border areas. The second type is construction migration from relatively more advanced coastal areas to inland areas, especially those with high skill levels, to promote the development of

Table 4.3. City Size and Employment: Probit Results

Variables	(1) Regression 1	(2) Regression 2	Variables	(3) Regression 1	(4) Regression 2
Population	0.00840		FDI	0.250***	0.268***
	(0.00605)			(0.0743)	(0.0767)
College		0.00621	Investment	−0.0194	−0.0190
		(0.00480)		(0.0204)	(0.0197)
Gender	0.0560***	0.0560***	Road	−0.00157	−0.00150
	(0.00626)	(0.00626)		(0.00243)	(0.00245)
Married	0.0562***	0.0565***	Transportation	8.33e-05	8.74e-05
	(0.0126)	(0.0127)		(0.000404)	(0.000401)
Eduyr	0.0120***	0.0120***	Year07	0.0328***	0.0331***
	(0.00137)	(0.00138)		(0.00910)	(0.00891)
Exp	0.00546***	0.00543***	Pseudo R^2	0.076	0.076
	(0.00119)	(0.00119)	Observations	14,960	14,960
Expsq	−0.000150***	−0.000150***			
	(2.51e-05)	(2.52e-05)			
CP	0.0855***	0.0854***			
	(0.00980)	(0.00982)			
Minority	−0.0314	−0.0323			
	(0.0200)	(0.0202)			

Note: *, **, and ***, respectively, denote significance at 10%, 5%, and 1%. Robust standard errors clustered at district level are in parenthesis. The marginal effect of a dummy variable is calculated as the change of employment probability relative to the reference group; as for continuous variables, the marginal effect is calculated at the mean.

inland areas. The most typical example of constructive migration is the Third Front Construction program, which began in 1964. For the sake of national defense and security, the division of the first, second, and third line is mainly related to the distance of a region away from the frontier of borders. Western China was regarded as the third line of defense and thus would be least damaged if by any chance war broke out. As a result of the low skill level of the inhabitants of those places during that time, workers from the coastal area, especially those with high skill levels, were dispatched to these provinces. The third type of migration was the Down to the Countryside Movement in the late 1960s and early 1970s. A great many young people were sent to the countryside and employed in the farming sector. However, the migration from cities to rural areas in the movement did not have a clear direction between regions or cities with different population sizes. According to Ge and An (2010), the migration scale due to the Down to the Countryside Movement was quite limited, and all cities, regardless of size, became sources of migrants. Except for the above migration administered by the central or local government, spontaneous migration was rare during the planned economy period (Zhao, 2004). Migrants without government permission, in addition to being unable to obtain food stamps, cloth vouchers, and the like for the purchase of daily necessities, would also be immediately deported to their homelands. So, in general, migration from 1953 to 1982 was mainly led by the government, and the migration direction was mainly determined by exogenous factors such as geography.

Moreover, the natural rate of population growth during this period has little relevance to future economic prospects of the region. Figure 4.1 shows the relationship between the natural growth rate of urban population and urban economic development. The natural rate of population growth is obtained by subtracting the death rate from the birth rate. In the absence of earlier data, we use the data of urban GDP per capita in 1990 as a measure of urban economic development. We find that there is almost no correlation between the natural growth rate of urban population in 1982 and GDP per capita in 1990, with a correlation coefficient of −0.048. In general, when urban characteristics such as city size, investment, and amenity are controlled, migration administered by the government and natural population growth from 1953 to 1982 are not related to the error terms of the regression model, while the scale of spontaneous migration in the same period is almost negligible. Therefore, we believe urban population growth from 1953 to 1982 to be exogenous and constitute a reasonable instrumental variable for the current city size.

As a further test, we examine in Figures 4.2 and 4.3 the relationship between urban population growth (rate) from 1953 to 1982 and GDP per capita in 1990, and find urban economic development to be uncorrelated with changes in population in history. The correlation coefficient between urban population growth from 1953 to 1982 and GDP per capita in 1990 is only −0.017, while the correlation coefficient between population growth rate and GDP per capita is 0.099.

However, increases in urban population in history have positive effects on future population, and is therefore correlated with the urban

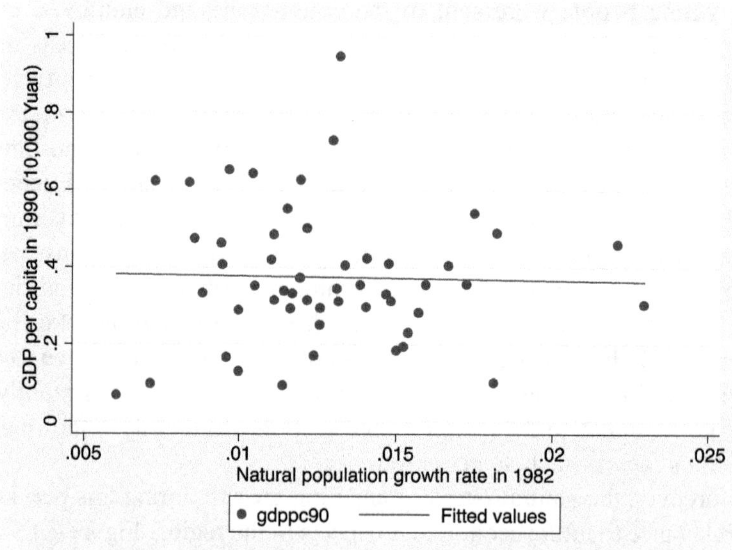

Figure 4.1. Natural Growth Rate of Urban Population and GDP Per Capital

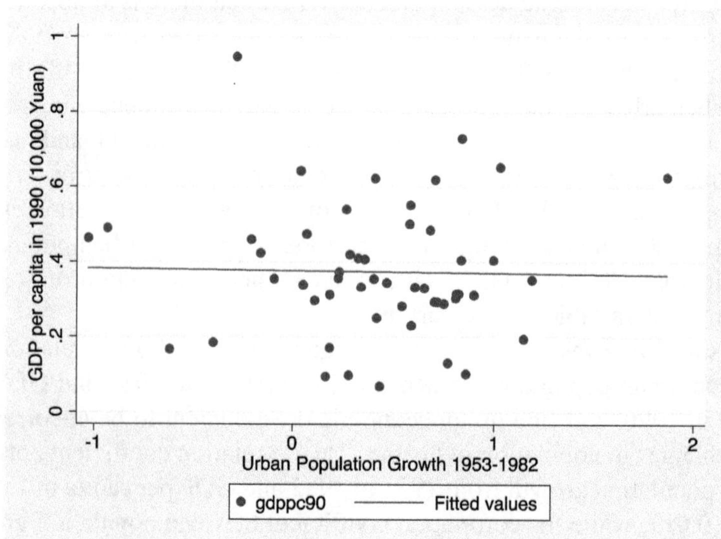

Figure 4.2. Urban Population Growth from 1953 to 1982 and GDP Per Capita in 1990

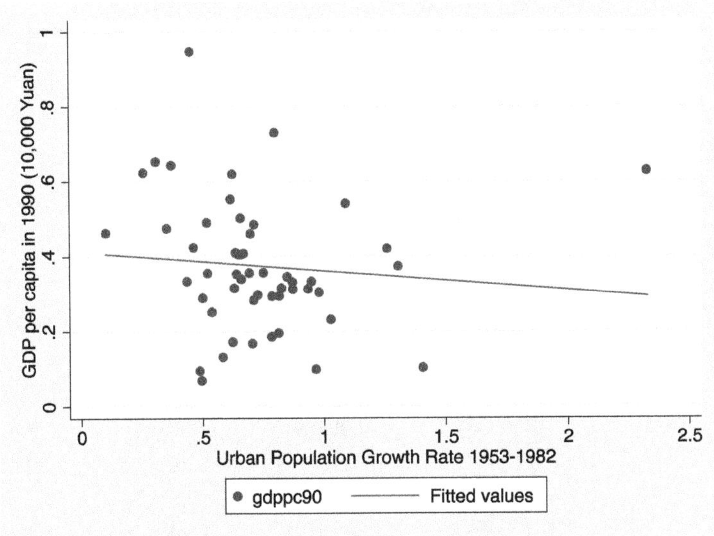

Figure 4.3. Urban Population Growth Rate from 1953 to 1982 and GDP Per Capita in 1990

population in 2000. In subsequent regressions, we will use the natural logarithm of the population increase of the city from 1953 to 1982 as the instrumental variable of the city size, and estimate the model by using instrumental variable method.

Instrumental variables estimates are presented in Table 4.4. Columns (1) and (3) report IV probit estimates of regression coefficients, and a city's urban population and a city's number of college graduates are used as scale measures in Regressions 3 and 4, respectively. We calculate the marginal effects of city scale on employment using Newey's two-step estimator, and marginal effects are presented in Table 4.5.

We first check the relevance of the instrumental variable, and first stage regression results are reported in Columns (2) and (4) of Table 4.4. We find that the expansion of urban population from 1953 to 1982 has significantly positive impacts on urban population and the number of college graduates in 2000. With other city-level characteristics controlled, every 1% increase in population from 1953 to 1982 would increase the current urban population by 0.98% and the number of college graduates by 1.34%, respectively. F statistics of the instrumental variable are

Table 4.4. City Size and Employment: IV Probit

	(1)	(2)	(3)	(4)
	Regression 3		Regression 4	
	IV Probit	First Stage	IV Probit	First Stage
Variables	Employed	Population	Employed	College
Population	0.133**			
	(0.0518)			
College			0.0972***	
			(0.0368)	
Population Growth 1953–1982		0.979***		1.337***
		(0.143)		(0.176)
Gender	0.322***	−0.00603	0.322***	−0.0130
	(0.0328)	(0.00669)	(0.0329)	(0.00865)
Married	0.305***	−0.0928***	0.307***	−0.155***
	(0.0588)	(0.0229)	(0.0587)	(0.0328)
Eduyr	0.0675***	0.0118***	0.0667***	0.0240***
	(0.00846)	(0.00349)	(0.00849)	(0.00571)
Exp	0.0325***	−0.00428	0.0321***	−0.00186
	(0.00682)	(0.00300)	(0.00682)	(0.00388)
Expsq	−0.000910***	0.000198**	−0.000905***	0.000217**
	(0.000141)	(7.75e-05)	(0.000142)	(0.000100)
CP	0.505***	−0.0486**	0.504***	−0.0564**
	(0.0561)	(0.0207)	(0.0562)	(0.0283)
Minority	−0.176*	0.00450	−0.187*	0.117
	(0.0980)	(0.0585)	(0.0984)	(0.0764)
FDI	1.052*	3.280**	1.352***	1.445
	(0.542)	(1.411)	(0.520)	(1.686)
Investment	−0.173	−0.165	−0.162	−0.332
	(0.190)	(0.618)	(0.168)	(0.641)
Road	−0.00191	−0.00974	−0.00136	−0.0200
	(0.0159)	(0.0303)	(0.0157)	(0.0395)
Transportation	−0.00120	0.0356***	−0.00102	0.0470***
	(0.00259)	(0.00366)	(0.00254)	(0.00461)
Year07	0.164***	0.189**	0.170***	0.197*
	(0.0564)	(0.0957)	(0.0543)	(0.119)
Observations	14,960	14,960	14,960	14,960

Note: *, **, and ***, respectively, denote significance at 10%, 5%, and 1%. Robust standard errors clustered at district level are in parenthesis.

Table 4.5. City Size and Employment: IV Probit (Marginal Effects)

	(1)	(2)		(3)	(4)
Variables	Regression 3	Regression 4	Variables	Regression 3	Regression 4
Population	0.0227**		FDI	0.180**	0.231***
	(0.00977)			(0.0789)	(0.0730)
College		0.0166**	Investment	−0.0296	−0.0276
		(0.00724)		(0.0185)	(0.0187)
Gender	0.0564***	0.0565***	Road	−0.000327	−0.000232
	(0.00632)	(0.00633)		(0.00232)	(0.00234)
Married	0.0598***	0.0604***	Transportation	−0.000205	−0.000175
	(0.0127)	(0.0128)		(0.000453)	(0.000450)
Eduyr	0.0115***	0.0114***	Year07	0.0276***	0.0286***
	(0.00137)	(0.00138)		(0.00869)	(0.00856)
Exp	0.00556***	0.00549***			
	(0.00121)	(0.00120)	Pseudo R^2	0.077	0.077
Expsq	−0.000156***	−0.000155***	Observations	14,960	14,960
	(2.61e-05)	(2.60e-05)			
CP	0.0863***	0.0862***			
	(0.00982)	(0.00985)			
Minority	−0.0336*	−0.0359*			
	(0.0203)	(0.0206)			

Note: (1) *, **, and ***, respectively, denote significance at 10%, 5%, and 1%. Robust standard errors clustered at district level are in parenthesis. In Probit estimation, the marginal effect of a dummy variable is calculated as the change of employment probability relative to the reference group; as for continuous variables, the marginal effect is calculated at the mean.
(2) The table is divided into two parts. Columns (1) and (2) report impacts of city scale and individual characteristics on employment probability. The effects of other city characteristics are displayed in Columns (3) and (4).

47.13 and 57.45. Therefore, weak IV is not a great concern here. In addition, we find that after controlling related city-level variables such as city size, investment, and public infrastructure, the city size in history has little direct impact on current employment. As shown in Columns (1) and (3), when instrumental variable estimates are used, no matter which measure of city size is used, increases in city size significantly promote the employment probability of workers.

However, the results in Table 4.4 only report the estimated coefficients of the Probit model, and marginal effects are not displayed. To provide an intuitive explanation of the effect of each explanatory variable, in Table 4.5, the Newey's two-step method is used to calculate the marginal effects of each explanatory variable on the dependent variable. Results show that when city size is measured by the total urban population, every 1% increase in city size will bring an increase in individual employment probability by 0.023 percentage points. Every 1% increase in the number of urban college graduates will raise the individual employment probability by 0.016 percentage points.

In addition, influences of other individual level socioeconomic characteristics and urban features on employment are presented. Regression results show that most of the individual level characteristics have significant impacts on employment, and the directions are consistent with theoretical expectations. Men and the married are more likely to be employed. On average, the employment probability of men is 5.64–5.65 percentage points higher than that of women, while the employment probability of married workers is 5.98–6.04 percentage points higher than that of unmarried ones. Education has significantly increased the employment probability of workers. On average, every one-year increase in education raises one's employment probability by 1.14–1.15 percentage points. The influence of work experience on employment shows an inverted U-shape: with the increase of experience, the employment probability of the individuals increases, but when experience becomes higher than the turning point, experience is not conducive to employment any longer. This may be because people with more work experience tend to be older, while older workers are at a disadvantage in terms of both health and knowledge. According to the regression results, the turning point of experience's impact on employment probability is about 17.85 and 17.74 years, that is, when the experience is less than 17 years, the increase of working experience enhances one's employment. However, after more than 17 years of experience, age disadvantage begins to play a major role, and the increase of experience is detrimental to employment. In our regression sample, about 66.44% of workers are to the left of the turning point. CPC membership also significantly improves the employment probability of workers, which indicates the relatively higher ability or richer social capital of the CPC members. In addition, the identity of ethnic minority significantly reduces one's employment probability, which may indicate some disadvantages of ethnic minorities in the labor market, such as language barriers or discriminations during job hunting.

We control city-level characteristics in regression to capture the impact of labor demand factors and labor supply factors on employment.

It is found that FDI has a significantly positive impact on employment, while the impact of fixed asset investment is not significant. This suggests that cities that rely more on domestic investment for growth are not creating more job opportunities than those that rely more on other components of GDP, such as consumption or net exports. Existing empirical studies have found that in China, local governments tend to give priorities to the development of capital-intensive industries for tax reasons, so high local investment-GDP ratios are often accompanied by low capacities in creating job opportunities (Lu and Ou, 2011). Moreover, increases in urban road areas and a more convenient public transportation system will enhance urban labor demand by improving the information transmission efficiency and matching efficiency, and thus increase the demand for labors. However, these variables are found to be insignificant in our study.

4.4 Does Economic Agglomeration Harm Equity: Heterogeneous Influences of City Size on Employment

In the previous section, we obtained an average effect of city size on the employment of all workers, and differences in agglomeration effect on individuals with different levels of education were not distinguished. In theory, labors with different skill levels may benefit differently from city size. On the one hand, employment of low-skilled workers is highly concentrated in low-skilled service industries. Therefore, compared with the medium-skilled or high-skilled workers, low-skilled workers may enjoy benefits from agglomeration more. On the other hand, different vocations depend on learning and innovation to different extents, so they will benefit from city expansions to different degrees when there are knowledge spillovers. Therefore, in this section, we divide individuals into three groups based on their years of education, including individuals with years of education fewer than or equal to 9 years, from 9 to 12 years, and more than 12 years, respectively. Regressions will be conducted respectively to investigate the heterogeneous impacts of city size across individuals with different skill levels.

Table 4.6 reports Probit results on heterogeneity in city size effects. In all regressions, personal and city characteristics are controlled. To save space, we report only the impact of the logarithm of the total urban population and the logarithm of the number of urban college graduates on

Table 4.6. Heterogeneous Effect of City Size on Employment: Probit Results

	Probit		
Years of Education	≤9	9–12	>12
Population	0.0196*	0.0108	0.000447
	(0.0116)	(0.00785)	(0.00503)
Individual characteristics	Controlled	Controlled	Controlled
City characteristics	Controlled	Controlled	Controlled
Observations	4,339	5,850	4,771
Number of college graduates	0.0140	0.00854	0.000733
	(0.00912)	(0.00620)	(0.00367)
Individual characteristics	Controlled	Controlled	Controlled
City characteristics	Controlled	Controlled	Controlled
Observations	4,339	5,850	4,771

Note: *, **, and ***, respectively, denote significance at 10%, 5%, and 1%. Robust standard errors clustered at district level are in parenthesis.

employment. According to the Probit results, generally speaking, the least-educated workers have benefited the most from the expansion of cities. Increases in the number of permanent urban residents significantly promote the employment probability of workers with years of education fewer than or equal to 9, while increases in the number of college graduates also enhance employment probability marginally. However, similar to the full sample regressions, results based on Probit regressions may also be biased due to two-way causality problems and missing variables.

Similarly, urban population growth from 1953 to 1982 is used as an instrumental variable for city size in 2000, and IV Probit estimates for the heterogeneous agglomeration effects are reported in Tables 4.7 and 4.8. Tables 4.7 and 4.8 report the marginal effects of city size computed using the two-stage method, and significance levels are obtained based on robust standard errors clustered at district level.

Regression results show that workers at all skill levels benefit from the expansion of cities, and low-skilled workers benefit the most compared with higher-skilled ones. On average, every 1% increase in city size will increase the employment probability of workers with years of education fewer than or equal to 9 by 0.028–0.038 percentage points. For workers with 9–12 years of education and those with more than 12 years of

Table 4.7. Heterogeneous Effects of City Size on Employment (City Size Measured by Urban Population): IV Probit Results

Variables	(1) Regression 11 ≤9	(2) Regression 12 9–12	(3) Regression 13 >12
Population	0.0384**	0.0225*	0.0149**
	(0.0728)	(0.0597)	(0.0758)
Gender	0.110***	0.0647***	0.0164***
	(0.0529)	(0.0473)	(0.0693)
Married	0.0823***	0.0418**	0.0234**
	(0.0897)	(0.0877)	(0.116)
Eduyr	−0.00544	0.00834	0.00550**
	(0.0211)	(0.0298)	(0.0283)
Exp	0.0237***	0.00975***	0.00579***
	(0.0130)	(0.0116)	(0.0156)
Expsq	−0.000491***	−0.000248***	−0.000173***
	(0.000243)	(0.000254)	(0.000382)
CP	0.126***	0.104***	0.0389***
	(0.115)	(0.0814)	(0.0970)
Minority	−0.0266	−0.0491	−0.0180
	(0.182)	(0.143)	(0.176)
FDI	0.276*	0.320**	−0.0212
	(0.658)	(0.667)	(1.243)
Investment	−0.164*	0.00265	0.00793
	(0.371)	(0.0912)	(0.200)
Road	−0.00184	−0.000517	0.000673
	(0.0192)	(0.0154)	(0.0295)
Transportation	0.000549	−0.000101	−0.000416
	(0.00413)	(0.00248)	(0.00496)
Year07	0.0565***	0.0132	0.0115*
	(0.0821)	(0.0636)	(0.0932)
Observations	4,339	5,850	4,771

Note: *, **, and ***, respectively, denote significance at 10%, 5%, and 1%. Robust standard errors clustered at district level are in parenthesis. In Probit estimation, the marginal effect of a dummy variable is calculated as the change of employment probability relative to the reference group; as for continuous variables, the marginal effect is calculated at the mean.

Table 4.8. Heterogeneous Effects of City Size on Employment (City Size Measured by the Number of College Graduates): IV Probit Results

Variables	(1) Regression 14 ≤9	(2) Regression 15 9–12	(3) Regression 16 >12
College	0.0283**	0.0164**	0.0111**
	(0.0529)	(0.0423)	(0.0531)
Gender	0.110***	0.0648***	0.0166***
	(0.0530)	(0.0474)	(0.0694)
Married	0.0840***	0.0420**	0.0239**
	(0.0895)	(0.0879)	(0.117)
Eduyr	−0.00586	0.00760	0.00529**
	(0.0213)	(0.0304)	(0.0283)
Exp	0.0233***	0.00975***	0.00572***
	(0.0130)	(0.0117)	(0.0156)
Expsq	−0.000485***	−0.000249***	−0.000173***
	(0.000242)	(0.000255)	(0.000383)
CP	0.125***	0.103***	0.0391***
	(0.115)	(0.0814)	(0.0974)
Minority	−0.0316	−0.0520*	−0.0186
	(0.182)	(0.143)	(0.177)
FDI	0.355**	0.376***	0.00611
	(0.630)	(0.654)	(1.079)
Investment	−0.160*	0.00433	0.00818
	(0.346)	(0.0863)	(0.183)
Road	−0.00145	−0.000439	0.000725
	(0.0196)	(0.0151)	(0.0291)
Transportation	0.000553	−7.60e-05	−0.000388
	(0.00414)	(0.00240)	(0.00491)
Year07	0.0579***	0.0142	0.0119
	(0.0797)	(0.0619)	(0.0896)
Observations	4,339	5,850	4,771

Note: *, **, and ***, respectively, denote significance at 10%, 5%, and 1%. Robust standard errors clustered at district level are in parenthesis. In Probit estimation, the marginal effect of a dummy variable is calculated as the change of employment probability relative to the reference group; as for continuous variables, the marginal effect is calculated at the mean.

education, the effects are 0.016–0.023 and 0.011–0.015 percentage points, respectively. The effect of city size on the employment rate of workers decreases with the increase of years of education.

In addition, some interesting results can be obtained from regression results by different education groups. Results show that the lower the skill level, the greater the difference in employment probability between men and women. For individuals with fewer than 9 years of education, males have an average 11.0 percentage points higher chance of employment than females, while for one educated for 12 or more years, the gender difference is only about 1.6–1.7 percentage points. Moreover, the return to education is relatively the highest for the most-educated workers. On average, the employment probability of highly skilled workers increases from 0.53 to 0.55 percentage points for each additional year of schooling. However, for workers with 12 or fewer years of education, the impact of education is not significant. Li *et al.* (2012) found that in China, high school education mainly plays the role of selecting potential college students, rather than improving labor productivity as a human capital investment. In terms of city characteristics, we find that FDI mainly promotes employment probabilities of the workers with 12 or fewer years of education, while increases in fixed asset investment significantly reduce the employment probability of workers with the lowest skill levels. This shows that the cost from inefficiencies in job creation by domestic investment is mainly borne by workers with low education levels.

The difference to which workers with different skill levels benefit from the expansion of cities is mainly related to the occupational and industrial structure of the city. Employment of workers with the lowest skill levels is mainly concentrated in low-skilled service industries such as catering and nannies. As cities grow in size, especially with the concentration of highly skilled workers, the demand for low-skilled services in cities will increase, so that employment prospects for low-skilled workers are improved. In Table 4.9, we divide all the employed workers into three groups according to the industries they belong to, including manufacturing, low-skilled manual jobs, and high-skilled abstract jobs, and the average years of education of the three groups are calculated respectively. We find that workers in low-skilled manual jobs have the lowest average years of education of 10.82 years, compared with 11.00 years in manufacturing and 13.07 years in high-skilled abstract jobs. As a result, low-skilled services absorb the highest proportion of low-skilled workers.

Table 4.9. Occupation and Education

	Manual	Manufacturing	Abstract
Years of Education	10.82	11.00	13.07

Note: Average years of education are calculated for each occupation using data from individuals who are in the labor force in CHIPS 2002 and 2007. Manual jobs include: transportation, storage, post office and communication; wholesale, retail and food services; social services. Abstract jobs include: information technology and software; finance and insurance; real estate; health, sports and social welfare; education, culture and arts, mass media and entertainment; scientific research and professional services; government agents, party organizations and social groups. Individuals working in the farming, mineral, construction, electricity, gas, and water supply facilities sectors are excluded in the calculation here.

The expansion of cities benefits low-skilled workers by creating higher demand for low-skilled services. We divide all cities in our sample into three groups according to their permanent resident population or the number of their college graduates, namely large, medium-sized, and small cities. Employment proportions of low-skilled services are calculated for each group. As is shown in Table 4.10, the proportion of low-skilled service jobs in urban employment rises with city sizes. In small cities, low-skilled service workers account for about 22.2–22.5% of all employment. In big cities, the proportion rises to 31.5–31.9%. Similar conclusions are reflected in Figures 4.4 and 4.5. The vertical axis is the city's share of manual job workers in all labors, while the horizontal axis is the size of cities, measured by urban population or the number of college graduates. A significantly positive relationship between the proportion of low-skilled service workers in urban labor force and city sizes is revealed. Therefore, with growth in city sizes, more jobs in low-skilled services are created, thus increasing the employment probability of the lowest-skilled workers.

The results in Table 4.9 show that employment of medium-skilled workers is concentrated in manufacturing. With the expansion of cities, the proportion of manufacturing employment displays an inverted-U shape. In the early stage of urban development, manufacturing enterprises choose to enter larger cities for the benefits of increased labor productivity and reduced production and transportation costs. Local governments also encourage the development of manufacturing industries for revenue and

Table 4.10. City Size and Employment Share of Manual Jobs

	Small Cities	Medium-Sized Cities	Big Cities
Groups based on urban population	0.225	0.245	0.319
Groups based on number of college graduates	0.222	0.254	0.315

Note: Cities with sizes smaller than the 33.3% percentile of all city sizes are grouped as small cities. Cities with sizes larger than the 66.7% percentile of all city sizes are grouped as big cities. The remaining are medium-sized cities.

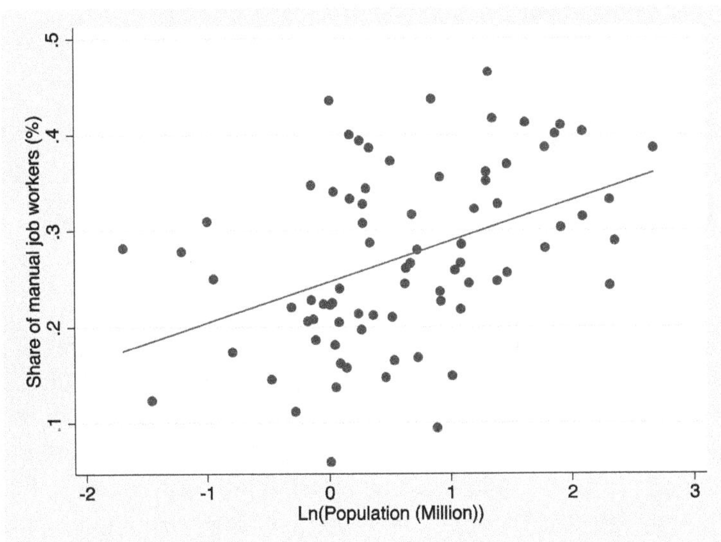

Figure 4.4. City Size and the Share of Manual Job Workers (City Size Measured by Population)

employment considerations. Therefore, as cities grow in size, a large number of manufacturing jobs are created. However, as cities grow further, due to issues such as environmental protection, industrial structure upgrading, etc., the proportion of service industry will increase, especially the high-skilled service industry such as finance, international trade, and real estate. In addition, due to the intensification of crowding-out effect such as rising wages and rising land prices, higher factor prices in

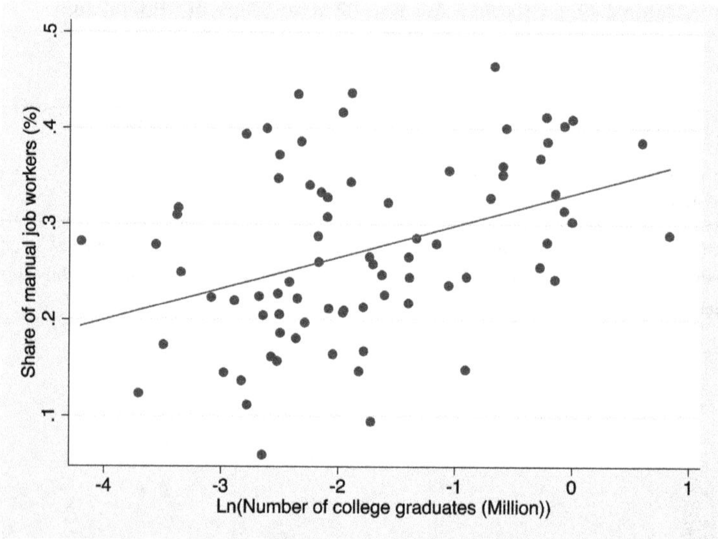

Figure 4.5. City Size and the Share of Manual Job Workers (City Size Measured by the Number of College Graduates)

agglomeration areas begin to crowd out the production activities of some industries, thus bringing about the spatial reallocation of industries. Manufacturing enterprises generally have stronger incentives to relocate to small and medium-sized cities with relatively lower production costs. Land-intensive service industry suffers less from crowding-out effect, so the city experiences structural transformation. For example, Desmet and Henderson (2014) found that in recent years, manufacturing employment in the United States has shown an increasing dispersion trend, and the higher the degree of manufacturing development in the initial period, the slower the growth of manufacturing employment in the future. Different from the manufacturing industry, the employment growth of the service industry takes the form of an ∽-shaped curve, for regions with a medium-level development of the service industry at the initial stage, service industry employment growth in the future is relatively the fastest. In Table 4.11, we calculate the proportion of manufacturing employment in cities of different sizes. Results show that with the expansion of cities, the change of the employment proportion of manufacturing industry presents an inverted U-shaped pattern. Similar results are shown in Figures 4.6 and 4.7. In Figures 4.6 and 4.7, the fitting line shows a clear inverted U-shaped

Table 4.11. City Size and Employment Share of Manufacturing Jobs

	Small Cities	Medium-Sized Cities	Big Cities
Groups based on urban population	0.183	0.208	0.195
Groups based on number of college graduates	0.179	0.207	0.196

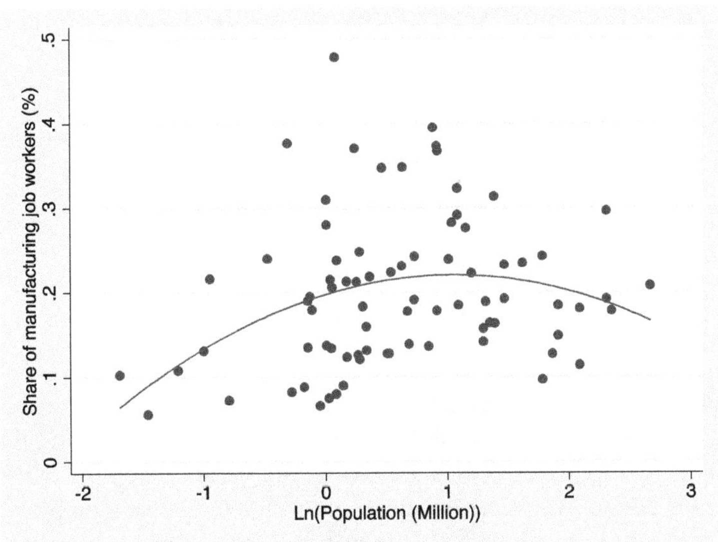

Figure 4.6. City Size and the share of Manufacturing Job Workers (City Size Measured by Population)

relationship between city size and the employment proportion of urban manufacturing industries.

Since the employment of the medium-skilled labor force is mainly concentrated in manufacturing enterprises, the impact of city expansion on their employment probabilities presents an inverted-U shape. Whether medium-skilled workers can benefit from urban expansion depends largely on whether most cities are to the left or the right of the turning point. Moreover, if workers with different skill levels complement each other in production, medium-skilled workers may still benefit directly from the concentration of highly skilled workers. Our empirical results

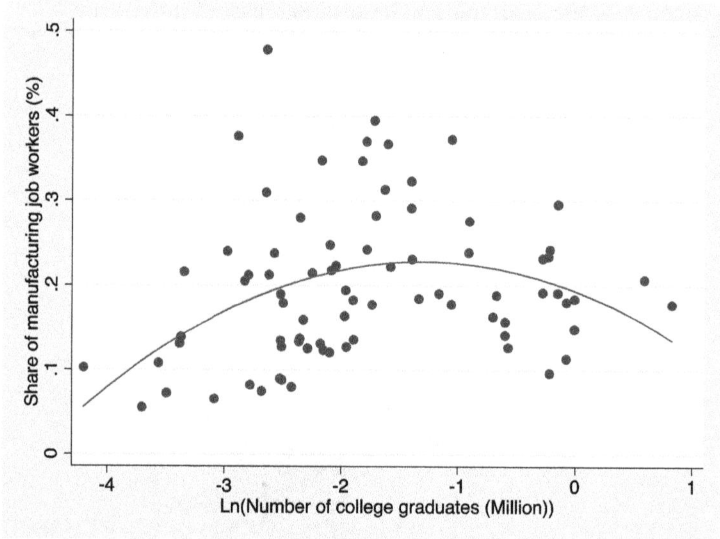

Figure 4.7. City Size and the Share of Manufacturing Job Workers (City Size Measured by the Number of College Graduates)

show that the expansion of city size significantly improves the employment probability of medium-skilled workers in general, implying that the vast majority of Chinese cities are still in the period when the expansion of cities is conducive to the development of manufacturing employment.

Finally, for workers with the highest skill levels, there are two reasons why the effect of city expansion on their employment is significantly positive. On the one hand, the expansion of city size brings more learning opportunities and stronger knowledge spillover effect. Due to its knowledge-intensive characteristics, high-skilled services can benefit more from the city expansion. High-skilled workers are mainly concentrated in high-skilled services. Therefore, city expansion increases the employment probability of high-skilled labors through the increase of employment opportunities. On the other hand, as cities expand, the manufacturing industry also upgrades, and the quality of low-skilled manual jobs also improves. Industrial upgrading and the improvement of service quality make it possible for the manufacturing and manual jobs which were low-skilled in the past to absorb more high-skilled workers. Table 4.12 divides cities into three groups, namely small cities, medium-sized cities, and big cities, based on their sizes of population or college

Table 4.12. City Size and the Proportion of High-Skilled Workers in Manufacturing Industry

	Small Cities	Medium-Sized Cities	Big Cities
Groups based on urban population	0.198	0.215	0.257
Groups based on number of college graduates	0.167	0.221	0.260

Note: Cities with sizes smaller than the 33.3% percentile of all city sizes are grouped as small cities. Cities with sizes larger than the 66.7% percentile of all city sizes are grouped as big cities. The remaining are medium-sized cities.

Table 4.13. City Size and the Proportion of High-Skilled Workers in Manual Jobs

	Small Cities	Medium-Sized Cities	Big Cities
Groups based on urban population	0.127	0.147	0.231
Groups based on number of college graduates	0.122	0.150	0.230

Note: Cities with sizes smaller than the 33.3% percentile of all city sizes are grouped as small cities. Cities with sizes larger than the 66.7% percentile of all city sizes are grouped as big cities. The remaining are medium-sized cities.

graduates. For each group, we calculate the proportion of high-skilled workers, those with more than 12 years of education, in manufacturing jobs. Results show that the proportion of high-skilled workers in manufacturing industry in small cities is the lowest at 16.7–19.8%. The proportion in medium-sized cities is relatively higher of about 21.5–22.1%, and the highest in the largest cities. Similar results hold for low-skilled manual jobs. In small cities, 12.2–12.7% of low-skilled service jobs are occupied by high-skilled workers, while in medium-sized cities and large cities the proportion is 14.7–15% and 23.0–23.1%, respectively (Table 4.13).

The upgrading of industrial skills experienced by the manufacturing industry and manual sector with the expansion of cities are also shown in Figures 4.8–4.11. Among them, the vertical axes of Figures 4.8 and 4.9 are the proportion of high-skilled workers in the manufacturing industry, and the horizontal axes are the natural logarithm of city population or the number of urban college graduates respectively. A significant positive correlation between city size and the skill level of the manufacturing

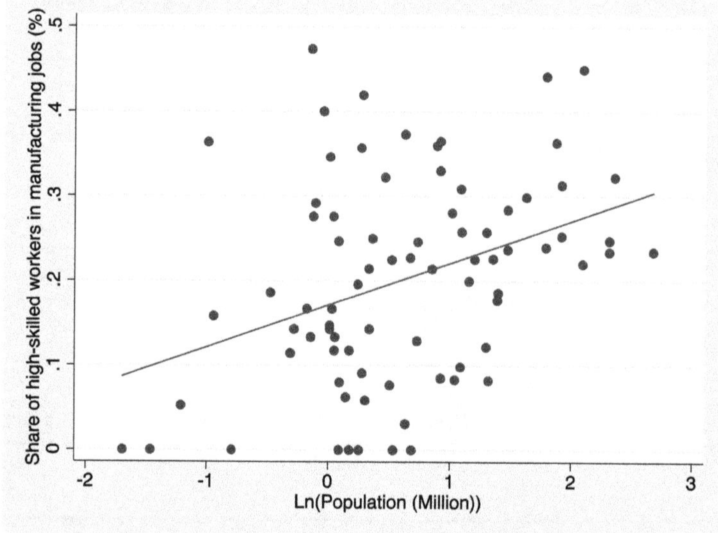

Figure 4.8. City Size and the Proportion of High-Skilled Workers in Manufacturing Jobs (City Size Measured by Population)

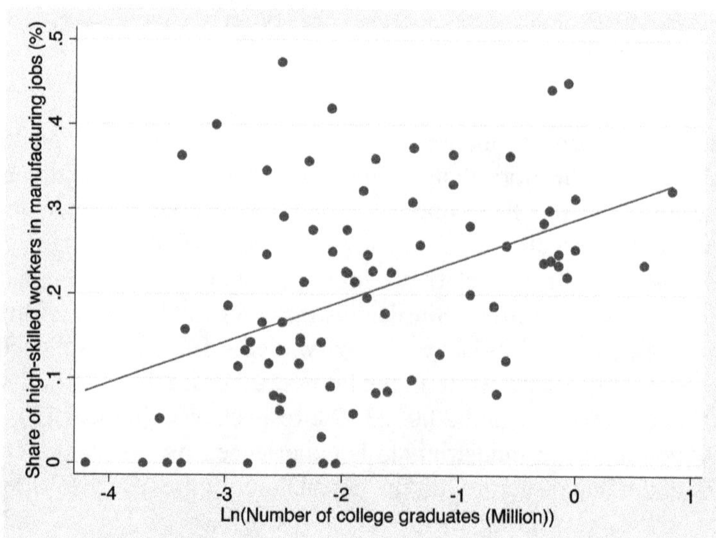

Figure 4.9. City Size and the Proportion of High-Skilled Workers in Manufacturing Jobs (City Size Measured by the Number of College Graduates)

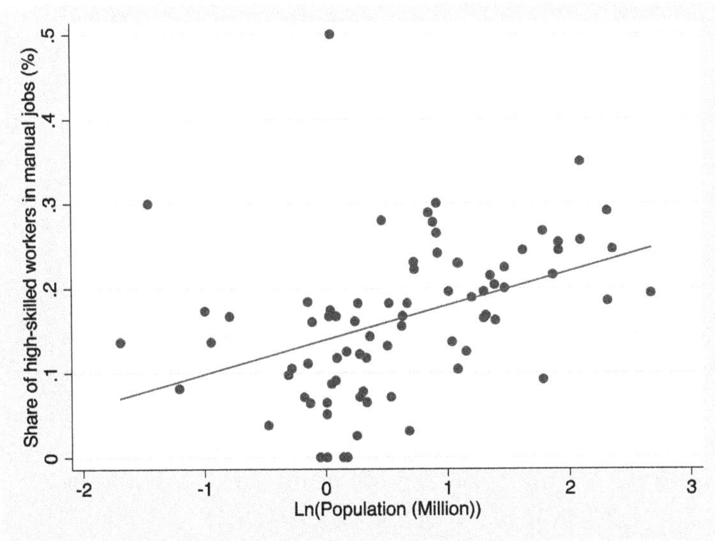

Figure 4.10. City Size and the Proportion of High-Skilled Workers in Manual Jobs (City Size Measured by Population)

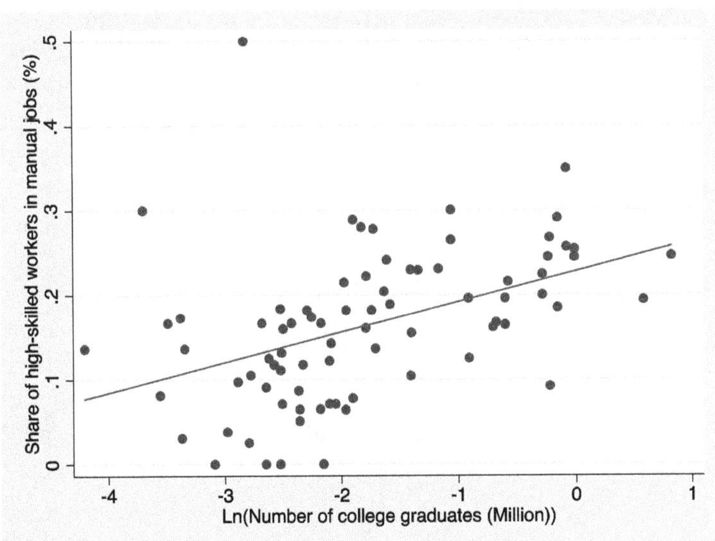

Figure 4.11. City Size and the Proportion of High-Skilled Workers in Manual Jobs (City Size Measured by the Number of College Graduates)

industry is revealed. The vertical axes of Figures 4.10 and 4.11 show the proportion of high-skilled workers in the manual sector. The linear fitting line also show that with the expansion of cities, the manual sector attracts more high-skilled labor force, thus bringing improvement of service quality.

4.5 Summary

This chapter examines the impact of city size on individual employment, using individual level data from the 2002 and 2007 Chinese Household Income Project Surveys for urban households, the *China Urban Statistical Yearbook* (1997–2001), and the National Population Census of the People's Republic of China in 1953, 1982, and 2000. Using urban population growth from 1953 to 1982 as the instrumental variable for city size, we identify the effect of economic agglomeration on the employment probability of individual workers. On average, for every 1% increase in urban population, the probability of individual employment will increase by 0.023 percentage points. A 1% increase in the number of urban college graduates will also increase one's employment probability by 0.017 percentage points. Individuals with different skill levels benefit from urban population growth differently. Although workers of all skill levels have benefited significantly from city expansions, the least-skilled workers have benefited the most compared with higher-skilled workers, mainly because employment in the labor-intensive manual sector increases the most significantly with the expansion of cities.

From the perspective of labor employment, this chapter shows that market-oriented urban expansion can increase the employment rate of urban residents, and that low-skilled workers benefit more from urban expansion. Therefore, policies restricting urban population especially those with low skills are neither efficient nor equitable. This provides a micro empirical foundation for deregulating the size of large cities and promoting further agglomeration of population.

Chapter 5

Economic Agglomeration and the Income of Urban Residents

Analysis in Chapter 4 shows that the expansion of cities is accompanied by the creation of more jobs, which is conducive to improving the employment probability of urban residents, and agglomeration benefits are the greatest for the least-skilled workers. Will the expansion of employment come at the expense of depressing the income of urban residents? In order to fully present the effect of economic agglomeration on individuals' labor market performance, this chapter further investigates the impact of city size on individual income.

The literature of new economic geography confirms the positive effect of economic agglomeration on wages or output per capita. But wages are not a comprehensive reflection of workers' welfare. On the one hand, non-wage income, such as business income and property income, is becoming increasingly more important in total income. On the other hand, what is more important is that differences in nominal income are not always the same thing as differences in real income, and roles of regional price disparities cannot be neglected. The real income adjusted by regional prices should be a more comprehensive measure of workers' welfare. As people concentrate in large cities, prices of local non-tradable goods will be pushed up, thus offsetting the positive effect of agglomeration on nominal income. Therefore, examining how economic agglomeration affects workers' income, especially their real income, is essential for us to understand the impact of economic agglomeration on workers' welfare.

Using individual-level data from the 2002 and 2007 Chinese Household Income Project Surveys (CHIPS, 2002, 2007) for urban households, this chapter estimates the impact of city size on workers' nominal income and real income, and examines the heterogeneity between workers with different incomes. Similar as Chapter 4, urban population growth from 1953 to 1982 is used as the instrumental variable for city size, and the instrumental variable method is used to estimate the individual level income model. Empirical results show that the expansion of cities has a positive effect on the income of workers. On average, a 1% increase in city size leads to an increase of about 0.190% in nominal annual income and 0.189% in nominal hourly income for workers. The positive effect of city size on workers' income is not completely offset by the relatively higher prices in large cities, and city size still plays a significant role in promoting the real income of workers after adjusting regional prices. On average, every 1% increase in city size brings an increase of 0.084–0.143% in real annual income and 0.083–0.142% in real hourly income of workers. Moreover, we find that the effect of city size on the income of workers is not linear. While workers at all income levels have benefited from the expansion of cities, those with the lowest income levels have benefited relatively less than those with higher incomes.

5.1 City Size and the Income of Workers: A Theoretical Analysis

Theoretically, the impact of city size on income mainly works through the positive effect of economic agglomeration on productivity. Based on the Mincer equation of wage determination, we construct a simple theoretical model to analyze how city population affects the wage of local firms. The production function of firm i is assumed to be as follows, in which firm output is jointly determined by its total factor productivity and the quantity of capital and labor.

$$Y_i = A_i K_i^{\alpha} L_i^{1-\alpha} \tag{5.1}$$

Here Y is the total output of the firm, A is the total factor productivity, and K and L are capital and labor inputs, respectively. All firms are assumed to face the same interest rate r, and operate in a complete competitive labor market. So to maximize profit, firms pay workers wages according to their marginal output. The first-order condition of firm profit maximization is shown in Equations (5.2) and (5.3):

$$A_i \alpha K_i^{\alpha-1} L_i^{1-\alpha} - r = 0 \quad (5.2)$$

$$A_i (1-\alpha) K_i^{\alpha} L_i^{-\alpha} - w_i = 0 \quad (5.3)$$

From these, the expression of wage w_i can be obtained:

$$w_i = A_i^{\frac{1}{1-\alpha}} (1-\alpha) \left(\frac{\alpha}{r}\right)^{\frac{\alpha}{1-\alpha}} \quad (5.4)$$

According to Glaeser and Gottlieb (2008), economic agglomeration is assumed to affect firm TFP through the functional expression in Equation (5.5):

$$A_i = \varphi N^{\rho} \quad (5.5)$$

Here, N is city population, and $\rho > 0$ means the magnitude of agglomeration effect. Existing literature has proved that the expansion of cities will enhance productivity through three mechanisms, including the wider sharing of input, higher matching quality of production factors, and more learning opportunities. Taking the natural logarithms of both sides of Equation (5.4), and substituting Equation (5.5) in it, the following expression of the relationship between wages and urban population can be reached:

$$lnw_i = \frac{\rho}{1-\alpha} lnN + \frac{1}{1-\alpha} ln\varphi + \ln\left[(1-\alpha)\left(\frac{\alpha}{r}\right)^{\frac{\alpha}{1-\alpha}}\right] \quad (5.6)$$

where $\frac{1}{1-\alpha} ln\varphi + \ln\left[(1-\alpha)\left(\frac{\alpha}{r}\right)^{\frac{\alpha}{1-\alpha}}\right]$ is a constant. Because $\rho > 0$ and $\alpha \in (0,1)$, the marginal effect of urban population on wages of workers is positive, and the elasticity of wages to the change of urban population is $\frac{\rho}{1-\alpha}$. The above model shows that due to the economic agglomeration effect, the expansion of cities will raise workers' wages through enhancing firm TFP.

As we mentioned in Section 2.2.2, the influence of economic agglomeration on labor productivity can be reflected through its influence on nominal output per capita, nominal wages, or other nominal indicators. For example, Sveikauskas (1975) found that labor productivity in large cities, which is measured by average output or wage of employees, is higher than that in small cities. Fan Jianyong (2006) analyzed the influence of China's non-farm employment density on non-farm outputs by using the data of prefecture-level cities and sub-provincial cities in 2004, and found that every 1% increase in employment density would increase the average output of non-farm labors by about 8.8%, which is higher than the elasticity coefficient of about 5% in European and American countries. However, nominal wages cannot fully reflect the welfare of workers. On the one hand, non-wage incomes such as business income and property income are becoming an increasingly more important part of individual total income. Economic agglomeration can promote the increase of non-wage income of workers by lowering the entry threshold of firms, encouraging entrepreneurship and improving information transmission efficiency.

On the other hand, regional differences in prices also affect workers' real income, which is a better measure of workers' welfare. The cross-regional movement of labors influences demands and prices of non-tradable goods. As a result, the influence of economic agglomeration on the real income of workers may vary across regions considering price changes, which has been largely ignored in the existing literature. Roback's (1982) modeled the interaction between land market and labor market, and showed that changes in labor supply or demand in the local labor market would eventually be capitalized into land prices. With free mobility of labors across regions, labors' utility would be equalized across different regions considering wages, price levels, and urban amenity. Based on the spatial general equilibrium model of Roback (1982), Moretti (2011) modeled such situations as incomplete labor mobility, differences of workers' skills and increasing returns to scale in regional economy, and found that local labor market demand or supply shocks would lead to inflows and outflows of labors, resulting in changes in prices of non-tradable goods. Considering price differences, changes in workers' real income being less than that of the nominal income, price of non-tradable goods will be affected by both demand and supply shocks in economic agglomeration. In general, the more consumers prefer non-tradable goods, the greater the elasticity of labor supply becomes, or the higher the skill levels of workers are, the more the demands for local non-tradable goods increase and the further non-tradable good prices are pushed up. Under assumptions of complete free mobility of labors and completely inelastic non-tradable goods supply, the positive effect of economic agglomeration on nominal income will be completely offset by rises in the prices of non-tradable goods, so that the impact of urban expansion on real income may not be significant. In this chapter, based on the spatial equilibrium model, we will empirically investigate the impact of city size on labor's real income.

5.2 Economic Agglomeration and the Income of Labors: Baseline Regression Results

As in Chapter 4, empirical analysis in this chapter will be based on individual level data from the Chinese Household Income Project in 2002 and 2007 (CHIP, 2002, 2007). Whether changes in city sizes will have impacts on individual incomes will be investigated. The total income includes wage income and non-wage income, which is mainly composed of business income, property income, and transfers. In different regressions, we use annual total income or hourly income as dependent variables, respectively, and study differences in the impact of city size on nominal value and real value of incomes. Economic agglomeration can promote the nominal income of workers by increasing labor productivity and encouraging entrepreneurship. However, the concentration of labor force in cities also leads to higher prices in the local non-tradable goods sector, which may offset the benefits of economic agglomeration. Kravis and Lipsey (1988) used cross-country data to find that there is a positive correlation between the levels of income and prices of a country, and relatively higher labor costs and prices of non-tradable goods in high-income countries is the main reason. According to Roback's (1982), under the assumption of free labor mobility, real incomes of labors in different cities tend to converge. This is mainly because changes in urban labor supply or demand will eventually be manifested as changes in land prices. In extreme cases with completely free labor mobility and inelastic supply of non-tradable goods, changes in city sizes will be completely capitalized into the price of non-tradable goods, completely offsetting their positive impact on nominal income. Therefore, the effect of city size on workers' real income is uncertain in theory. We use permanent urban population from the Fifth National Population Census of the People's Republic of China in 2000 to measure the city size in this chapter. A number of other urban characteristics that may influence local labor market conditions are controlled in regressions. Data on urban characteristics are obtained from the *China Urban Statistical Yearbook* from 1997 to 2001.

Based on the individual level income determination model shown in Equation (5.7), the impact of city size on incomes of urban residents will be investigated. Existing studies usually investigate the impact of personal characteristics on incomes. For example, the basic Mincer Equation examines the influences of education and experience on income, and follow-up studies examine the effects of socio-economic characteristics at the individual level. But city characteristics were largely neglected. Based on the theoretical model in Section 5.1, we expand the Mincer Equation by adding urban population and other city-level control variables into regressions. According to Equation (5.6), urban population is included in the regression in the form of natural logarithm rather than absolute value.

$$ln\text{Income}_{ij} = c + \beta'\mathbf{X}_{ij} + \theta_1 lnPop_j + \alpha'\mathbf{City}_j + \varepsilon_{ij} \tag{5.7}$$

In Equation (5.7), subscript i and j mean an individual i living in the city j. As in Chapter 4, our regression samples are limited to the working-age population, i.e., males between the ages of 16 and 60 and females between the ages of 16 and 55. Individuals who are not in the labor force are excluded from our regression samples. The dependent variable is the natural logarithm of income at the individual level. Real incomes are calculated based on two different methods. In the first method, real income is obtained by deflating nominal incomes of workers by the province-level price index from Brandt and Holz (2006). Brandt and Holz (2006) computed a cross-province comparable price index in China from 1984 to 2004 using household consumption data. The index takes into account household spending on food, clothing, daily necessities, culture and entertainment, housing and energy. This chapter uses the price index in 2002 to calculate the real income of workers. In addition, as a robustness check, we also construct a prefecture city level-data of housing prices in 2002 and 2007, and use it as a proxy variable for the price of urban non-tradable goods. City-level housing prices are calculated as total commercial housing sales divided by commercial housing sales area. Thus, a second measure of real income is obtained by dividing nominal income with city housing price levels.

On the right-hand side of the regression equation, c is the constant term, and X_{ij} is the vector of personal characteristics. In general, the personal characteristics that affect a worker's income are similar to those that affect labor employment, including gender, marital status, years of education, potential work experience and its square term, CPC membership, and ethnic minority status. Potential work experience is obtained by subtracting one's years of education from age and then subtracting 6 from the result. Abnormal samples with the potential experience of less than 0 year and more than 44 years and those educated for more than 22 years are excluded from our sample. $lnPop_j$ is the natural logarithm of urban permanent population. In this chapter, we focus on the magnitude and significance of θ_1. As the expansion of city size increases the nominal income of workers through the agglomeration effect, θ_1 is expected to be significantly positive. However, there are differences in prices among regions, and the rise of prices will partially offset the positive effect of economic agglomeration on workers' income. In the case of completely free flow of labors and inelastic supply of non-tradable goods, the economic agglomeration effect will be completely offset by rises in local price levels, making the impact of city size on the real income of workers insignificant. So θ_1's sign and significance on real income of workers is theoretically uncertain.

In addition, demand or supply shocks in the urban labor markets may influence both city sizes and incomes. Ignoring these factors will lead to estimation bias of θ_1. Therefore, we further control the vector of city characteristics $\mathbf{City}_j$ in regressions. City-level characteristics include average FDI over average GDP in 1996–2000, average fixed asset investment over average GDP in 1996–2000, road size per capita, the city's number of buses for every 10,000 persons, number of hospitals or hospital beds per 10,000 people, and green coverage rate in built-up areas. Estimates of θ_1 will be affected by both demand and supply shocks in the urban labor market. On the demand side, as physical capital investment will affect both city sizes and individuals' incomes, ignoring it in regressions will lead to biased estimates of θ_1. On the one hand, economic agglomeration in big cities raises returns to capital, and thus attract more enterprises and capital investment. On the other hand, as capital and labor inputs usually complement each other in production, increases in physical capital in production will enhance the marginal output of labors, and then raise workers' wages. In this chapter, we attempt to mitigate the impact of demand shocks in the urban labor market by controlling city-level FDI and physical capital investment in regressions. In addition, urban road size and transportations infrastructures are also controlled in regressions as a factor that may influence labor demand. This is mainly because constructions of road and transportation infrastructures of a city are not only related to city sizes but will also affect the matching efficiency of the labor market by facilitating information transmission between people. Among supply shocks in the labor market, we control the city's number of hospital beds and green coverage as measures of amenity. On the one hand, hospital beds and green areas will improve urban residents' quality of living. As a result, cities with better amenities are more attractive to workers, especially those with higher skill levels, leading to an expansion of city size. On the other hand, better amenities compensate for the utility of residents, so residents are more willing to accept a relatively lower income in areas with a higher amenity level (Moretti, 2011). Otherwise, areas where residents have better qualities of life will attract more workers, resulting in fiercer local labor market competition and restraining the rise of workers' income. In equilibrium, residents would be different across different cities. Besides, we control in regressions the dummy variable indicating whether the sample belongs to the survey in 2007, so as to capture the systematic difference between the 2007 survey sample and the 2002 survey sample. Tables 5.1 and 5.2 are the definitions and the descriptive statistics of relevant variables.

This section first investigates the effect of city size on workers' nominal incomes. Due to the two-way causality relationship between city size and workers' income, as well as the possible biases from omitted variables, instrumental variables estimation is used. Due to space limitations, we do not report OLS regression results in this chapter. As in Chapter 4, the natural logarithm of the population growth from 1953 to 1982 of the cities in which individual workers live are used as the instrumental variable for the city size in 2000. As is described in Section 4.4, China's migration in the period of planned economy are mainly national defense migration, constructive migration to promote the development of inland areas, and migration in the Down to the Countryside Movement, which were greatly government administered and exogenous. There is little correlation between the natural growth rate of urban population and future economic conditions over the same period. However, the change of

Table 5.1. List of Explanatory Variables

Variable	Definitions
Individual Characteristics	
Income	Ln (annual total income (yuan))
RealInc1	Ln (annual total income (yuan)/price index of the provincial administrative region)
RealInc2	Ln (annual total income (yuan)/housing price index of local prefecture-level city)
IncomeHr	Ln (hourly income (yuan))
RealIncHr1	Ln (hourly income (yuan)/price index of local provincial administrative region)
RealIncHr2	Ln (hourly income (yuan)/housing price index of local prefecture-level city)
Gender	1 for male and 0 otherwise
Married	1 for married and 0 otherwise
Eduyr	Years of education
Exp	Potential experience = Age − Years of education − 6
Expsq	Experience squared
Health	1 for "very good" or "good" health statuses and 0 otherwise
CP	1 for Communist Party members and 0 otherwise
Minority	1 for minority and 0 otherwise
City Characteristics	
Population	Ln (Urban population (million))
PopGrw	Ln (Population in 1982 (million) − Population in 1953 (million))
FDI	Average FDI in 1996–2000 (10,000 RMB) / Average GDP in 1996–2000 (10,000 RMB)
Investment	Average fixed asset investment in 1996–2000 (10,000 RMB) / Average GDP in 1996–2000 (10,000 RMB)
Road	Road size per capita in 2000 (m^2)
Transportation	Number of buses for every 10,000 persons in 2000
HospitalBed	Number of hospital beds for every 10,000 persons in 2000

(*Continued*)

Table 5.1. (*Continued*)

Variable	Definitions
Green	Green coverage rate in built-up areas (%)
Year07	1 for year 2007 sample and 0 otherwise

Note: (1) Due to the lack of the indicator of CPC membership in the 2007 sample, one's Communist Party membership in 2007 is proxied by the city's share of Communist Party members in the 2002 sample. If a city appears in the 2007 sample, however is not included in the 2002 sample, the Communist Party membership of individuals in that city is proxied by the national share of Communist Party members in 2002.
(2) In order to ensure the geographical unity of the cities involved in the 1953, 1982, and 2000 censuses, the county or city codes in the national censuses in 1953, 1982, and 2000 have been changed into the codes of administrative divisions in 2010. Therefore, the indicators of city size we use in regression are not affected by the adjustment of administrative areas in history.

population in the history of cities will significantly promote the current urban population growth, so the urban population growth from 1953 to 1982 is an appropriate instrumental variable.

Table 5.3 examines the impact of changes in city size on nominal income of workers. We divide the regression results into two parts: in Columns (1) and (2), the coefficients of city size and personal characteristics that may affect labor income are reported, while in Columns (3) and (4) other coefficients of city-level characteristics are reported. We find that increases in urban population growth from 1953 to 1982 significantly enhance urban population in 2000. On average, with population growth increased by 1% from 1953 to 1982, the population would increase by about 0.78% in 2000. F-values of the instrumental variables are 34.76 and 34.65, respectively, indicating that there is no problem of weak instrumental variable. Instrumental variable estimates show that city expansions will significantly enhance incomes of labors. On average, every 1% increase in urban permanent population brings a rise of 0.190% in nominal annual income and 0.189% in nominal hourly income, respectively.

Other individual and city-level characteristics that may affect labor income are controlled in the regressions. Consistent with existing studies, males and the married have significantly higher incomes. On average, men earn 16.9% more in annual income and 13% more in hourly earnings than women. The gap of annual income and hourly earnings between the incomes of married and unmarried people is 21.4% and 17.8%, respectively. Education raises the income of workers. In our regression results, the return on education was about 4.5–5.01% per year. The effect of experience on the

Table 5.2. Summary Statistics of Variables

Variable	Mean	Standard Deviation	Min	Max
Individual Characteristics				
Income	9.44	0.78	3.18	13.49
RealInc1	9.36	0.76	3.05	13.22
RealInc2	7.38	0.75	1.04	11.28
IncomeHr	1.78	0.85	−4.38	5.74
RealIncHr1	1.70	0.82	−4.51	5.47
RealIncHr2	−0.28	0.81	−6.52	3.54
Gender	0.56	0.50	0	1
Married	0.87	0.34	0	1
Eduyr	11.71	2.96	0	22
Exp	22.23	10.24	0	44
Health	0.71	0.45	0	1
Minority	0.02	0.15	0	1
CP	0.26	0.37	0	1
Year07	0.32	0.47	0	1
City Characteristics				
Population	0.71	0.68	−0.94	2.35
PopGrw	0.41	0.52	−1.03	1.87
Investment	0.33	0.21	0.18	1.60
FDI	0.06	0.06	0.00	0.25
Road	5.58	2.58	1.10	12.00
Transportation	6.90	5.25	0.60	31.20
HospitalBed	58.44	18.65	18.83	100.85
Green	31.59	7.57	11.80	45.50

personal income of workers shows an inverted U-shape. Based on the estimation coefficient, we find that the turning points of the effect on the total annual income and hourly income of the labor force are about 30.92 and 34.16 years, respectively. In our regression samples, approximately 76.20% and 88.24% of the labors are located to the left of the turning point. Comparing with the results in Chapter 4, we find that the turning point of experience's influence on workers' income is higher than that of

Table 5.3. City Size and Nominal Income of Workers

Variables	(1) Regression 1 Income	(2) Regression 2 IncomeHr	Variables	(3) Regression 1 Income	(4) Regression 2 IncomeHr
First Stage#					
PopGrw	0.7771***	0.7763***			
	(0.1318)	(0.1319)			
Second Stage					
Population	0.1904***	0.1894***	Investment	−0.3261*	−0.3365*
	(0.0613)	(0.0614)		(0.1852)	(0.1928)
Gender	0.1692***	0.1303***	FDI	2.0317***	2.1575***
	(0.0119)	(0.0135)		(0.6248)	(0.6481)
Married	0.2142***	0.1777***	Road	0.0222	0.0161
	(0.0225)	(0.0229)		(0.0152)	(0.0148)
Eduyr	0.0453***	0.0501***	Transportation	0.0136	0.0136
	(0.0032)	(0.0039)		(0.0104)	(0.0107)
Exp	0.0205***	0.0196***	HospitalBed	−0.0003	−0.0011
	(0.0043)	(0.0047)		(0.0015)	(0.0015)
Expsq	−0.0003***	−0.0003***	Green	−0.0024	−0.0007
	(0.0001)	(0.0001)		(0.0039)	(0.0041)
Health	0.0325**	0.0165	Year07	0.6173***	0.6849***
	(0.0153)	(0.0159)		(0.0405)	(0.0380)
Minority	−0.0133	-0.0426			
	(0.0393)	(0.0428)			
CP	0.1271***	0.1155***	Observations	10,741	10,655
	(0.0235)	(0.0228)	R^2	0.4446	0.4465

Note: (1) # is first stage regression results, and are from regressions of the endogenous variables (city size) on the instrumental variable and other control variables.
(2) *, **, and *** respectively denote significance at 10%, 5%, and 1%. Robust standard errors clustered at city level are in parenthesis.

experience's influence on employment. The empirical results in Chapter 4 show that after working for about 17 years, the employment probability of workers tends to decline with the increase of ages and working experience. But for the vast majority of the workforce, the income return from experience has been positive, and annual income and hourly income keep rising as experience increases. In addition, consistent with the existing literature, CPC membership has significantly increased labor income. However, we find that influences of ethnic minority do not have to be insignificant, which may indicate that due to policies aiming at promoting ethnic equality and encouraging the development of ethnic minority regions that China has adhered to for many years, the disadvantages of the employed ethnic minority workers in the labor market are not significant any longer.

Impacts of city characteristics on workers' income are reported in Columns (3) and (4). It is found that after controlling city sizes, most city characteristics do not have significant impacts on labor income. Of all the variables, only those related to investment have significant influences on labor income. Contrary to our expectations, rather than enhancing labor income, fixed asset investment has reduced it, implying that cities that rely more on fixed asset investment have lower levels of labor productivity and income than those that rely more on other components of GDP such as consumption or exports. Contrary to domestic fixed asset investment, the proportion of FDI in GDP has significantly promoted labor income, which may be because market-oriented FDI is more efficient than fixed asset investment. Moreover, workers' income of the 2007 sample is higher than the 2002 sample, reflecting the five-year increases in urban workers' incomes.

Results above have displayed the effect of city size on nominal labor income. However, as what was mentioned before, the positive effects of city size on nominal income can only confirm the existence of agglomeration effect, but changes in workers' welfare are not fully reflected. As cities expand, local prices, especially prices of non-tradable goods, rise due to higher consumer demand. Higher prices will partially offset the positive effect of economic agglomeration on nominal income. We therefore need to use regional comparable real income measure adjusted by price indexes as a more comprehensive index of workers' welfare. Roback (1982) found that in the case of complete free labor mobility and inelastic land supply, changes in labor supply or demand in the local labor market would eventually be capitalized into land prices. Therefore, other things equal, changes in city sizes will not have a significant effect on the real income of workers if labor mobility is completely free. Otherwise, workers will choose to leave cities with low real incomes and move to cities with high real income levels. Fiercer competition of the labor market in regions with labor inflows will reduce incomes of the local labor force, and city sizes will keep changing until real incomes among regions reach an equilibrium. On the contrary, when there are barriers to free labor mobility, benefits from urban expansions will not be fully captured by marginal migrants due to migration cost. As a result, city expansion may still have positive influences on real income of labors. How city sizes affect real incomes of labors is the second core issue to be studied in this chapter.

Table 5.4 displays instrumental variable regression results when the provincial price index is used to deflate nominal income of workers. Estimates show that the expansion of city size significantly increases the real income of labors. On average, for every 1% increase in the size of a city, the real annual income and real hourly income of workers rise by 0.084% and 0.082%, respectively. Although city size growth promotes the increase of real labor income, its marginal effect is smaller than the impact of city size on nominal income. This suggests that as cities grow in size, local prices of non-tradable goods rise accordingly, narrowing the income gaps among cities of different sizes. However, the effect of city size on real labor income is still significantly positive. This suggests that there are still barriers to labor mobility between cities of different sizes in China, especially when workers migrate to big cities. It is more expensive for workers to move to big cities where *hukou* policies are more stringent. What is more, higher migration costs prevent workers from moving into big cities and enjoying benefits from agglomeration effect. The effects of other personal and city characteristics on real income are similar to that in Table 5.3.

The real income in Table 5.4 is deflated by the price index at the provincial level and does not distinguish differences among different prefectural cities within the same province. As robustness checks, we further construct prefecture level commercial housing prices, and use it as another deflator of nominal incomes. Instrumental variable estimates are shown in Table 5.5. Similar to the results in Table 5.4, the marginal effect of urban population on real income of workers is smaller than that on nominal income. City expansions still contribute significantly to the rise in the real income of workers. On average, every 1% increase in the size of a city raises the real annual and hourly income of labors by 0.143% and 0.142%, respectively.

5.3 The Heterogeneous Influence of City Size on the Income of Workers

The empirical results in Section 5.2 confirm the positive effects of city expansion on labor incomes, and these influences are not completely offset by the relatively higher prices in large cities. So in larger cities, workers

Table 5.4. City Size and Real Income (Province Level Price Index)

	(1)	(2)		(3)	(4)
	Regression 3	Regression 4		Regression 3	Regression 4
Variables	RealIncl	RealIncHrl	Variables	RealIncl	RealIncHrl
Population	0.0836**	0.0824*	Investment	−0.5191***	−0.5309***
	(0.0410)	(0.0421)		(0.1344)	(0.1423)
Gender	0.1689***	0.1301***	FDI	1.4197***	1.5436***
	(0.0117)	(0.0134)		(0.5101)	(0.5314)
Married	0.2165***	0.1801***	Road	0.0093	0.0032
	(0.0221)	(0.0219)		(0.0113)	(0.0110)
Eduyr	0.0458***	0.0507***	Transportation	0.0237***	0.0238***
	(0.0031)	(0.0038)		(0.0074)	(0.0078)
Exp	0.0202***	0.0195***	HospitalBed	0.0018	0.0010
	(0.0043)	(0.0047)		(0.0011)	(0.0011)
Expsq	−0.0003***	−0.0003***	Green	−0.0045	−0.0027
	(0.0001)	(0.0001)		(0.0028)	(0.0029)
Health	0.0414***	0.0254	Year07	0.6158***	0.6834***
	(0.0152)	(0.0159)		(0.0347)	(0.0330)
Minority	−0.0162	−0.0451			
	(0.0397)	(0.0421)			
CP	0.1316***	0.1197***	Observations	10,741	10,655
	(0.0230)	(0.0222)	R^2	0.4162	0.4189

Note: (1) The result of first stage is from regressions of the endogenous variables (city size) on the instrumental variable and other control variables.
(2) *, **, and *** respectively denote significance at 10%, 5%, and 1%. Robust standard errors clustered at city level are in parenthesis.

do benefit from the agglomeration effect in terms of income. The previous analysis only examines the average effect of city size on incomes. In theory, the extent to which workers of different income levels benefit from city expansions may not be linear.

First, workers with different human capital levels are complementary to each other in production. Therefore, when cities expand for different reasons, workers with different human capital may benefit differently. Theoretically, the production function with constant elasticity of substitution

Table 5.5. City Size and Real Income of Workers (Prefecture City-Level Price Index)

	(1)	(2)		(3)	(4)
	Regression 5	Regression 6		Regression 5	Regression 6
Variables	RealInc2	RealIncHr2	Variables	RealInc2	RealIncHr2
Population	0.1432**	0.1418**	Investment	−0.2150	−0.2255
	(0.0572)	(0.0575)		(0.1700)	(0.1772)
Gender	0.1699***	0.1310***	FDI	1.7897***	1.9164***
	(0.0119)	(0.0135)		(0.5673)	(0.5918)
Married	0.2181***	0.1814***	Road	0.0270*	0.0208
	(0.0222)	(0.0226)		(0.0140)	(0.0136)
Eduyr	0.0444***	0.0493***	Transportation	0.0075	0.0076
	(0.0031)	(0.0038)		(0.0097)	(0.0100)
Exp	0.0203***	0.0195***	HospitalBed	−0.0010	−0.0018
	(0.0043)	(0.0047)		(0.0014)	(0.0014)
Expsq	−0.0003***	−0.0003***	Green	−0.0028	−0.0010
	(0.0001)	(0.0001)		(0.0036)	(0.0037)
Health	0.0316**	0.0156	Year07	0.5333***	0.6010***
	(0.0151)	(0.0157)		(0.0414)	(0.0390)
Minority	−0.0196	−0.0490			
	(0.0399)	(0.0431)			
CP	0.1288***	0.1172***	Observations	10,741	10,655
	(0.0231)	(0.0223)	R^2	0.4015	0.4066

Note: (1) The result of first stage is from regressions of the endogenous variables (city size) on the instrumental variable and other control variables.
(2) *, **, and *** respectively denote significance at 10%, 5%, and 1%. Robust standard errors clustered at city level are in parenthesis.

can be used to describe the production behavior of workers with different skill levels. If the expansion of cities is mainly caused by the concentration of high-skilled workers, the marginal output of low-skilled workers will be increased even more due to the complementary effect, thus raising the wages of the low-skilled workers more. However, the high-skilled are competing with each other, which will reducing the positive effect from their geographical concentration. On the contrary, if the expansion of cities is mainly caused by the concentration of low-skilled labors, the marginal effect of the city expansion on high-skilled people will be greater due to complementarities between high- and low-skilled workers. As workers' incomes are highly correlated with their human capital, workers of different wages will benefit differently from the expansion of cities.

Second, workers with different income levels are generally employed in different industries, and the influence of economic agglomeration on labor productivity may differ across different industries. City expansions bring increases in the demand for non-tradable goods, especially those provided by low-skilled manual jobs such as nannies and homemakers. Meanwhile, labor productivity in the consumer service sector grows relatively slowly (Kravis and Lipsey, 1988). With abundant labor supply, urban residents' higher demand for the manual service will be manifested as employment expansions in that sector rather than rises in prices or wages. The results in the previous chapter show that, compared with high-skilled workers, urban expansion has enhanced the employment probability of low-skilled workers the most, and one important reason is that the employment of low-skilled workers is more concentrated in the low-skilled non-tradable goods sector. Therefore, if employment of low-income labors is more concentrated in low-skilled manual jobs, the positive effects of city size on incomes will be restrained.

Third, just as the importance of learning and innovations in various jobs is different, different jobs benefit from urban expansion differently. A large number of studies have confirmed the existence of knowledge spillover effect. These studies suggest that the expansion of cities, especially the concentration of high-skilled workers, will bring more learning and innovation opportunities to workers, thus increasing labor productivity (see the review articles of Audretsch and Feldman (2004) and Moretti (2004a)). Rauch (1993) found that wages and land rents were higher in cities with higher level of average human capital. Similarly, Moretti (2004b) found that an increase of 1 percentage point in the proportion of college graduates in cities would increase the labor productivity of enterprises by 0.6–0.7%. Moretti (2004c) also illustrated the existence of knowledge spillover effect. He found that for every 1 percentage point increase in the share of urban college graduates, wages would increase by about 0.6–1.2%. Since workers in high-skilled industries have relatively better learning ability, and high-skilled industries themselves are relatively more dependent on knowledge and innovation, the improvement of labor productivity may be more significant in knowledge-intensive industries.

Finally, analysis of real incomes needs to take into account price differences of non-tradable goods across different regions, and the spatial distribution patterns of workers at different income levels are found to be different. Moretti (2013) found that the spatial distribution of workers at different skill levels was not uniform. Based on the US census data from 1980 to 2000, he showed that college graduates were increasingly more concentrated in areas with higher housing prices. Rising living costs explains 25% widening of the nominal wage gap between college graduates and high school graduates from 1980 to 2000. After taking living costs into account, the real income gap could be narrowed significantly. In 2000, for example, the wage gap between college and high school graduates narrowed from 60% to 51% after taking into account the cost of living. Similarly, Diamond (2016) found that college graduates tended to concentrate in regions with high housing prices. Therefore, considering the cost of living, the effect of city size on the welfare of workers at different income and skill levels may be different.

In order to investigate whether there are differences in the impact of city size on workers with different income levels, quantile regressions are used in this part (see Koenker and Bassett, 1978). In Table 5.6, we first report the quantile regression results of the impact of city size on the income of workers with nominal incomes at the 10th, 25th, 50th, 75th, and 90th percentiles, respectively. Part A presents the quantile regression results of θ_1, and Part B shows the instrumental variable estimates of the quantile regression. We use a two-stage method to estimate the quantile instrumental variable model. In the first stage, city sizes are regressed on the instrumental variable and other exogenous variables, from which we obtain the residual which captures factors related to the error term in the endogenous variable. In the second stage, we further control in regressions the residual obtained in the first stage, thus obtaining the instrumental variable estimates of the quantile regression. To save space, only coefficients and standard errors of city size are reported. Other personal and city characteristics are similar to the results in Section 5.2 and are not reported here.

Quantile regression results show that the expansion of cities significantly promotes the nominal income of workers at all income percentiles, and therefore workers at different income levels generally benefit from city expansions. But workers with lower incomes benefit less from city expansion than those with higher incomes. Workers with incomes at the 25–90th percentile benefit similarly from city expansion. On average, every 1% increase in city size will bring an increase of 0.177–0.206% in the nominal annual income of these workers, and an increase of 0.180–0.200% in their nominal hourly income. For workers with the lowest income levels, every 1% increase in city size only brings the increase of their nominal annual income and nominal hourly income of 0.124% and 0.125%, respectively, which is significantly lower than those of other income levels.

Impacts of city size on real income of workers at different percentiles are reported in Table 5.7. Similar to Table 5.6, only the coefficient and significance level of the city size are reported. It is found that compared to nominal incomes, the positive effect of city expansion on the real income of workers at all percentiles are significantly reduced, no matter province level or city-level price indexes are used. This is mainly because prices are also relatively higher in areas with larger populations. In addition, similar to the results using nominal income as the explained variable, the workers at the 10th percentile benefit significantly less from city expansions than those at other income percentiles, but the gap between the two is narrowed. For example, when province level price index is used to

Table 5.6. Heterogeneous Influences of City Size on the Nominal Income of Workers: Quantile Regression Results

	(1)	(2)	(3)	(4)	(5)
Dependent Variable	10th	25th	50th	75th	90th
A. Quantile regressions					
Income	0.174***	0.207***	0.225***	0.253***	0.273***
	(0.0174)	(0.0119)	(0.00933)	(0.0126)	(0.0146)
IncomeHr	0.191***	0.219***	0.235***	0.260***	0.263***
	(0.0164)	(0.0139)	(0.0109)	(0.0127)	(0.0184)
B. Instrumental variable quantile regressions					
Income	0.124***	0.177***	0.191***	0.206***	0.206***
	(0.0251)	(0.0152)	(0.0160)	(0.0179)	(0.0212)
IncomeHr	0.125***	0.180***	0.200***	0.199***	0.195***
	(0.0222)	(0.0194)	(0.0173)	(0.0205)	(0.0242)

Note: *, **, and *** denote significance at 10%, 5%, and 1%, respectively. Each entry is a separate regression studying the impact of city size on the income of workers at the corresponding percentile with individual- and city-level characteristics controlled. Robust standard errors clustered at prefecture-level cities are in parenthesis.

Table 5.7. Heterogeneous Influences of City Size on the Real Income of Workers: Quantile Regression Results

Dependent variable	(1) 10th	(2) 25th	(3) 50th	(4) 75th	(5) 90th
A. Quantile regressions					
RealInc1	0.0932***	0.123***	0.127***	0.156***	0.165***
	(0.0160)	(0.0128)	(0.00978)	(0.0117)	(0.0150)
RealIncHr1	0.107***	0.125***	0.138***	0.152***	0.155***
	(0.0163)	(0.0118)	(0.0109)	(0.0116)	(0.0174)
RealInc2	0.113***	0.151***	0.165***	0.202***	0.216***
	(0.0182)	(0.0130)	(0.00947)	(0.00938)	(0.0135)
RealIncHr2	0.136***	0.169***	0.176***	0.203***	0.217***
	(0.0150)	(0.0122)	(0.0113)	(0.0130)	(0.0167)
B. Instrumental variable quantile regressions					
RealInc1	0.0833***	0.0855***	0.0871***	0.0923***	0.101***
	(0.0204)	(0.0192)	(0.0142)	(0.0173)	(0.0190)
RealIncHr1	0.0247	0.0812***	0.0949***	0.0727***	0.0772***
	(0.0217)	(0.0182)	(0.0177)	(0.0189)	(0.0243)
RealInc2	0.129***	0.142***	0.139***	0.166***	0.163***
	(0.0193)	(0.0206)	(0.0163)	(0.0184)	(0.0232)
RealIncHr2	0.0839***	0.148***	0.147***	0.152***	0.137***
	(0.0227)	(0.0172)	(0.0170)	(0.0229)	(0.0277)

Note: (1) The result of first stage is from regressions of the endogenous variables (city size) on the instrumental variable and other control variables.
(2) *, **, and *** respectively denote significance at 10%, 5%, and 1%. Robust standard errors clustered at city level are in parenthesis.

deflate the annual income of workers, the positive effect of economic agglomeration on the income of workers at the lowest income level is 0.0833%, which is only 0.018 percentage points lower than the increase of the real income of workers at the highest income level. In Table 5.6, the difference in nominal income growth is 0.082 percentage points. The results are similar as those when nominal income is deflated by housing price index at the city level. This is consistent with the research results of

Moretti (2013) and Diamond (2016). They found that because high-skilled workers are increasingly more concentrated in areas with higher price levels, especially higher housing prices, the real income gap between workers at different skill levels is smaller than the nominal income gap.

Based on the previous analysis, it is believed that low-income workers benefit significantly less from the expansion of city size as their employment is mainly concentrated in low-income consumer service industries. On the one hand, productivity growth in low-income service industries tends to be slow, dimming the effects of city expansions on the income of workers in this sector, despite that total employment in the sector may have increased as a result of higher consumer demand in big cities. On the other hand, low-income service industries are less knowledge-intensive, and so benefit less from knowledge spillover. According to our calculations, employment of workers with incomes lower than the 10th percentile are concentrated in the low-skilled service sectors, accounting for 58.59% of low-skilled manual jobs. Individuals with the lowest income levels (namely those are in the lowest 10%) that work in the manufacturing industry and high-skilled service industry occupy 25.36% and 16.05%, respectively. Although jobs in low-skilled service industries have increased with economic agglomeration (Chapter 4), workers' incomes have increased at a relatively modest pace because of the relatively slow rise in labor productivity and low knowledge intensiveness.

5.4 Summary

Using data from "the Chinese Household Income Project" 2002 and 2007, this chapter examines the impact of city size on workers' incomes. Using urban population growth in the planned economy period as the instrumental variable of the current population, models are estimated using instrumental variable estimates. Regression results show that the expansion of cities will promote the increase income of the workers. On average, every 1% expansion in city size leads to a 0.190% increase in workers' nominal annual income and a 0.189% increase in the nominal hourly income. The chapter also finds that the positive effects of city size on workers' incomes are not completely offset by relatively higher prices in large cities. After considering price differences, the expansion of cities still has a significantly positive effect on workers' real incomes. The positive effect of every 1% increase in city size on the real annual income and real hourly income of workers is 0.084–0.143% and 0.082–0.142%, respectively. This implies that due to various factors that hinder the complete free movement of workers between different cities in China, especially restrictions from the household registration system, labors will gain positive benefits by migrating to big cities.

In addition, quantile regression results for workers at different income levels show that the positive effects of city size on individual incomes is not linear. While workers at all income levels have benefited broadly from the expansion of cities, workers with the lowest income levels have benefited the least. This is mainly results of the concentration of low-income workers in low-skilled service industries. Productivity growth in low-skilled service industries is relatively slow, and knowledge spillover effects are relatively weaker. However, considering price differences across regions and the fact that high-skilled workers are more concentrated in regions with higher living costs, differences in agglomeration effects on real income are smaller than that on nominal income between workers at different skill levels.

Combined with the results from Chapter 4, our study provides an empirical basis for removing restrictions on city sizes and promoting further agglomeration of population from the perspective of employment and income. It is found that in China, economic agglomeration can not only raise employment rate but also enhance labor productivity and increase incomes of workers through agglomeration effect. Moreover, we find that workers at different levels of skills or incomes have benefited broadly from the expansion of cities. Although income growth rate from economic agglomeration is the lowest for low-income workers, and low-income workers are generally low-skilled workers, from the perspective of employment, their benefits from agglomeration are the greatest. In other words, for low-skilled workers, the benefits they get from large cities are mainly job opportunities, while their income benefits are relatively smaller. As employment of low-skilled workers is highly concentrated in the consumer service industry, with the expansion of cities, cities' demands for the manual jobs will also increase, increasing the employment rate of low-skilled workers. But the consumer service sector, with slow productivity growth and limited benefits from knowledge spillovers, has seen the slowest rise in income. For high-skilled workers, their benefits from urban expansion come mainly from higher income levels.

In China, there are still arguments about which pattern of urbanization should be taken, namely, giving priority to the development of large cities, or small and medium-sized cities. The optimal size of a city should be determined by the tradeoff between agglomeration effect and crowding-out effect. However, in practice, the economic agglomeration effect of cities has not been fully understood, and policy-makers often ignore the benefits from agglomeration effect and restrict city expansions through *hukou* system or other measures. The household registration system in China not only strictly limits population growth in big cities but also is biased to high-skilled and high-income migrants while restricting the inflow of low-skilled workers. As a result, the degree of population agglomeration in China is not only lower than the degree of industry agglomerations but also lower than similar levels of economic development in other countries, resulting in a huge loss of efficiency.

The public will benefit broadly from deregulations on city sizes and further agglomeration of labors. In present China, economic agglomeration will not only increase labor productivity and income per capita (Au and Henderson, 2006; Henderson, 2007) but also provide more job opportunities to workers so that more workers could be included in the process of economic growth, and share the benefits from urbanization and economic growth. Policies aiming at limiting urban population, especially those restricting the inflow of low-skilled workers, are neither efficient nor equitable. Urbanization and urban development policies in the future could be improved from the following three aspects.

First, to reduce barriers to labor mobility, reforms of the household registration system should be propelled and restrictions on household registration in big cities should be lifted. At present, obtaining urban *hukou* identities in big cities such as Beijing, Shanghai, and Shenzhen are particularly difficult, especially for low-skilled workers, because education or skill requirements are high for migrants who want to change their *hukou* identity to local. The breakthrough of *hukou* system reform lies in big cities. Restricting the inflow of low-skilled workers is not only unequitable but also will limit supplies of consumer services in large cities, thus reducing the productivity of high-skilled workers and the overall competitiveness of cities. Requirements to obtain urban *hukou* identity should be adjusted, and the misunderstanding that only high-skilled labors should be given priority to should be avoided. In practice, changing *hukou* identity should be based on employment, social security contributions, or other factors, rather than educational background or vocational skills only.

Second, the gap in public services between different regions should be narrowed and the citizenization of migrants should be accelerated. The fundamental difference between people with different *hukou* identities in China lies in differences of public goods and services. Therefore, the most important aspect of reforming the *hukou* system is to narrow the gap of public services between urban and rural areas, and between cities of different sizes. These measures will help guide the flow of labors and encourage relocations of workers for the purpose of employment and career development rather than public services, which is not only in line with the principle of efficiency but also conducive to reducing the influx of population in megacities and releasing the pressure on public finance.

Third, city clusters should be promoted so that coordinated development of large cities and small and medium-sized towns could be achieved. The competitiveness of a city cluster is based on an efficient and reasonable urban hierarchy. At present, improving urban system in China should address the following two misunderstandings: firstly, to equate the coordinated development of cities of different sizes with the synchronous development; secondly, to contradict giving priority to the development of big cities with the development of small and medium-sized towns. In fact, the development of large cities and small and medium-sized towns are not mutually exclusive. The development of small and medium-sized towns should be based on the development of big cities and share the spillover effects from big cities. In the future, coordinated development of city clusters should aim to promote industrial and functional complementarities between cities, strengthening the agglomeration advantages of large cities, and form an efficient urban hierarchical structure.

Chapter 6

Manufacturing Industry Clusters in China: Data, Method, and Spatial Distribution Characteristics

Chapters 4 and 5 analyze the impact of economic agglomeration on the individual's labor market performance, and find that productivity growth and greater labor demand brought by economic agglomeration will significantly improve one's labor market performance. The prosperity of industrial development and the improvement of industrial competitiveness should be the basis for attracting and retaining workers and improving the operation of the labor market. Therefore, considering improving local labor market performance or promoting macroeconomic growth and transformation, industrial development effect of agglomeration should be studied further. In Chapters 6–8, our analysis will focus on impacts of economic agglomeration on industrial development, and on macroeconomic transformation.

We will first study the development of manufacturing industry clusters and their impacts on industry performance. Industrialization and urbanization in many countries are cluster based, and economic development and industrial upgrading are often accompanied by the development of industrial clusters (Bianchi, 1998; Sonobe and Otuska, 2006; Ali *et al.*, 2014). Porter (1990) believed industrial clusters to be the main source of a country's industrial competitiveness which is the key for a country to obtain competitive advantage. In China, cluster-based production adapts to the endowment structure and institutional characteristics in early stages of industrialization, and barriers to investment are lowered and transaction costs are reduced. Therefore, industrial clusters become one important underpinning for the development of the manufacturing industries in China (Zhang Xiaobo and Ruan Jianqing, 2011). However, with continuous rises of labor costs in industrialization, initial advantages of industrial clusters may be weakened. Firms may be stuck at the lower-end of industrial value chain, damaging future industrial development. In addition, in practice, local governments often face the problem of how to promote the development of related industries by facilitating complementarities and spillovers among different industries.

In definition, industrial clusters refer to geographical concentrations of related industries due to connections such as knowledge, technology, input and output, consumer demand, etc. (Delgado *et al.*, 2014; 2016). The industries of a city can often be grouped into multiple clusters according to connections between industries. Cluster development and industrial linkages within or between clusters will affect industrial development and labor market performance of the city. Existing empirical literature on agglomeration effects mainly emphasizes localization or urbanization effects. Localization effect refers to externalities and specialization brought about by the relative concentration of a single industry in a region, while urbanization effect refers to industrial diversification advantages from expansions of the overall economy in a region. The studies in Chapters 4 and 5 provide evidence on urbanization effect. However, studying agglomeration effects from localization effect or urbanization effect may be oversimplified. Externalities in production will neither be confined to one single industry, nor be from all industries in the city. Agglomeration effect mainly comes from various forms of spillover effects among related industries. Therefore, industrial clusters and their influences on industry development will be the focus of Chapters 6 and 7.

Following Delgado *et al.* (2016), this chapter will define clusters of manufacturing industries at the four-digit SIC code level using the 2004 Economic Census data of the People's Republic of China and the input–output data in 2002. Since different algorithms will get different classification results of industrial clusters, advantages and disadvantages of various classifications will be evaluated. Based on cluster definitions, this chapter further describes distribution patterns and characteristics of manufacturing industry clusters in different regions of China.

6.1 Inter-industry Linkages, Agglomeration Effects, and Industrial Clusters

Before starting the analysis of this chapter, we first need to further clarify the definition of industrial cluster, and its differences and connections with inter-industry linkage and agglomeration effect. Porter's definition of industrial cluster emphasizes the concentration of related industries and institutions within a certain geographical area, and industries will benefit from cluster development through mechanisms such as input–output linkages, knowledge spillovers, sharing of consumption market, etc. Agglomeration effect is a broad concept in the literature, and refers to any increase in incomes or productivities resulting from the expansion of local economy (Combes and Gobillon, 2015). Therefore, industrial clusters are formed because of various forms of linkages among industries, and the agglomeration effect is the main mechanism through which industrial clusters may possibly promote industrial development.

Existing studies on industrial clusters are mainly case studies specific to regions or industries. For example, Saxenian (1994) made a detailed comparison between the computer- and software-based cluster development pattern in Silicon Valley and Boston, and believed that the regional institution, culture, industrial structure, and organizational advantages of firms are the main reasons for the success of Silicon Valley. Kerr and Kominers (2015) analyzed the impact of agglomeration on the size and shape of industrial clusters in Silicon Valley based on a firm location model. With regard to industrial clusters in China, Ruan Jianqing *et al.* (2014) constructed a model of industrial cluster development, and divided the development of industrial clusters into three stages, including the period of quantity expansion, the period of quality improvement, and the period of R&D and brand innovation. Based on case studies of industrial clusters such as the cluster of woolen sweaters in Puyuan and the cluster of lamps in Wenzhou, their research confirmed that the provision of public goods with cluster externalities plays an important role in the evolution and upgrading of clusters. Wu Jiebing and Guo Bin (2010) conducted a detailed study on the 30-year history of the textile industry in Shaoxing, Zhejiang province, and investigated the coevolution of enterprise adaptation, networking and cluster development, and confirmed the importance of enterprise adaptation practices and networking in promoting cluster development. Huang *et al.* (2008) took the Wenzhou shoe cluster as an example to illustrate the important role of industrial clusters in deepening the division of labor and promoting industrialization in rural areas. They found that knowledge spillovers in clusters enabled entrepreneurs to improve production technology through imitation to promote firm development. However, conclusions from case studies are specific to industries and regions. To identify effects of industrial clusters, we need systematic studies on clusters of various industries and regions.

In addition to case studies, some scholars use indicators reflecting inter-industry linkages as an alternative to industrial cluster classifications. In different studies, the manufacturing and service industries of the United States are classified into clusters by using such indicators as the industry's disciplinary background, patent citation, input–output relationship, or spatial distribution characteristics. For example, Feldman and Audretsch (1999) classified different industries according to their disciplinary backgrounds based on the Yale Survey of R&D Managers. Porter (2003), based on the geographical distribution characteristics of economic activities, classified all industries in the United States into three sectors, namely the tradable, non-tradable, and natural resource-dependent sector, and further grouped traded industries into 41 clusters according to their spatial concentration characteristics. In China, there were few attempts to classify industrial clusters. Scholars often made use of industrial agglomeration indexes as alternatives to industrial clusters. The only exception is the study of Long Xiaoning *et al.* (2015). In this chapter, they constructed the index of product similarity among different industries based on Hausmann and Klinger (2006). In theory, firms producing similar products tend to use similar inputs in production, so spillover effects are more likely to emerge due to firms' linkages with the same upstream manufacturers or downstream customers. These products also tend to have similar comparative advantages and are therefore more likely to be both exported. Therefore, in theory, researchers can use the probability of two products being exported at the same time to describe similarities between the two products. Based on similarity measures of products, Long Xiaoning *et al.* (2015) studied the influence of cluster development on firm financing and performance by using the average product similarity of all industries in each county in China as the measure of cluster development. They found that industrial clusters would reduce restrictions on corporate financing due to imperfect institutions in early stages of economic development. However, various forms of linkages between industries are only causes of industrial clusters, and reasons for the formation and development of industrial clusters are not limited to product similarities. Factors such as input–output relationships between industries and the sharing of production technologies may also play important roles in the development of clusters. In order to systematically study the effects of industrial clusters on local economic development, we must first construct regionally comparable industrial clusters that comprehensively reflect various forms of linkages among industries.

The input–output relationship, pooling in the labor market, knowledge spillover, and other inter-industry linkages have been studied in literature. For example, Jaffe *et al.* (1993) used patent citation data to depict knowledge spillovers between industries, and found that new patent applications were more likely to cite existing patents in the same state or region (SMSA level), thus illustrating the localization characteristics of knowledge spillover effect. Ellison *et al.* (2010) used the data of 1987 National Industrial Occupation Employment Matrix (NIOEM) of the United States to explore whether pooling in the labor market would promote matching efficiencies between employers and employees.

Apart from studies on inter-industry linkages, some studies focus on the spatial distribution patterns of economic activities. For instance, Ellison and Glaeser (1997) constructed the Industry Localization Index and the Industry Coagglomeration Index based on the model of firm profit maximization. Among them, the Industry Coagglomeration Index depicts the coagglomeration trend of industry pairs. Based on the methods from Ellison and Glaeser (1997), Lu Jiangyong and Tao Zhigang (2006) constructed indexes reflecting the regional agglomeration and coagglomeration trends of manufacturing industries in China, and investigated their trends of development from 1998 to 2003. They found that although manufacturing industries in China were becoming more concentrated, the overall degree of agglomeration was still low compared with other developed countries.

Interactions between economic geographical and new economic geographical factors promote the development of industrial clusters. Classifications of industrial clusters should reflect various types of inter-industry linkages. Delgado *et al.* (2014, 2016) provided an algorithm for generating and evaluating industrial clusters so that various forms of linkages between industries could be captured. Various inter-industry linkages such as input–output relationship, knowledge spillovers, skills, industrial spatial distribution characteristics, and other indicators were integrated into cluster analysis. Besides, since different settings of cluster functions and parameters could result in multiple alternative configurations of industrial clusters, different definitions of industry clusters should be evaluated. The second advantage of Delgado *et al.*'s algorithm is that alternative configurations of industrial clusters could be evaluated and compared based on a common approach that generates consistent scores, so that the optimal definition of industrial clusters could be provided. In addition, the algorithm allows researchers to subjectively adjust abnormal results due to data limitations, and all the adjustments are transparent and can be traced back, thus avoiding the subjective arbitrariness in the adjustment.

Based on the method of Delgado *et al.* (2014, 2016), this chapter will classify China's manufacturing industries at the four-digit SIC code level into different clusters. The data and method used for defining industry clusters are described in Section 6.2. Section 6.3 describes in detail the construction of various industry similarity matrices and conducts a comprehensive evaluation of different cluster configurations. Based on the optimal cluster definition obtained in Section 6.3, Section 6.4 further describes the spatial distribution characteristics of different industrial clusters in China. It is found that although industrial structures among regions in China tend to be highly homogeneous, the strength of industrial clusters in cities in eastern regions is generally smaller than that in central and western regions. This is mainly because, industrial clusters in the central and western regions are not as diversified as are in the eastern regions, and employment there tends to be concentrated in a few industries with obvious endowment advantages. In addition, compared with the eastern region, industrial clusters in the central and western regions are more upstream in the value chain, and employment is more concentrated in the resource-intensive industrial clusters. The last part is the summary of this chapter.

6.2 Data and Method Used in the Chapter

The data used in chapter include the first economic census of the People's Republic of China in 2004, the above-scale industrial firm data from 2004 to 2009, and input–output data in 2002 collected by the National Bureau of Statistics. The economic census data include a survey sample of 5.17 million legal entity units, 6.82 million industrial activity units, and 39.22 million self-employment ventures in China, and comprehensively reflects the development of China's secondary and tertiary industries (National Bureau of Statistics, 2005). Data on above-scale industrial firms are collected annually by the local statistics bureau based on the quarterly and annual financial statements of firms. Before 2011, "above-scale" referred to firms with prime operating revenue higher than 5 million yuan. The threshold was changed to 20 million yuan in 2011. The above-scale industrial firm data are one of the largest enterprise database in China which are available for successive years. In addition, China's 2002 Input–Output Table is also used to depict the input–output relationship between 122 different industrial sectors.

Our research mainly focuses on industrial cluster definitions and their effects on industry development. Existing studies have confirmed that agglomeration effect comes from various mechanisms such as input sharing, labor market pooling, knowledge spillover, etc. It attracts economic activities to concentrate geographically by reducing production costs and improving labor productivity, thus bringing about faster growth and employment expansion in the agglomeration areas. Existing studies on inter-industry linkages generally constructed various indexes measuring inter-industry relatedness, such as input–output relationship, common knowledge and skill background, demand for similar types of skilled workers, patent citation between industries, etc. Some other studies investigated colocation patterns of industries and believed that coagglomeration of industries implies close relatedness of industries. Although indexes constructed by the above two types of research can be compared across regions or industries, limitations exist. First, inter-industry relatedness indexes measure pair-wise industrial linkages only, and linkages among multiple industries and their spatial concentration pattern cannot be studied. Second, the indicators mentioned above only focus on one specific aspect of the inter-industry relationships, while other forms of linkages are ignored. Third, national-level indicators are not able to capture inter-regional heterogeneities. Inter-industry linkages and stages of industrial development may differ across regions. Although some studies analyzed inter-industry relationships and industrial clusters in a certain region through case studies, such as studies on Silicon Valley in the United States, conclusions from case studies are usually specific to regions or industries, and cannot be generalized. The classification method of industrial clusters in this chapter not only integrates various forms of links among industries but also provides a definition of industrial clusters that is comparable among regions. In addition, a comprehensive evaluation of various industrial cluster configurations will be conducted, so that the best cluster definition for China's manufacturing industries could be provided.

The algorithm in this chapter is mainly based on Delgado *et al.* (2014, 2016), and will be conducted in four steps. First of all, a variety of different forms of industry similarity matrices will be constructed to reflect different types of inter-industry linkages. Based on the availability of data, we construct a total of 10 matrices, such as the employment correlation coefficient matrix, the firm number correlation coefficient matrix, the industry coagglomeration index, the input–output matrix and their combinations. Secondly, clustering analysis will be used to group industries into different clusters. We will choose different industry similarity matrices and numbers of clusters as inputs to the cluster function, and use hierarchical clustering or partition clustering in the analysis. Based on different parameters chosen or cluster methods, a total of 500 different cluster configurations will be obtained. Third, different cluster configurations will be evaluated according to their within cluster relatedness, between cluster relatedness, and robustness, so that the best candidate cluster configuration could be found out for further adjustments. Finally, some marginal adjustments will be conducted to rule out abnormal results due to data limitations.

6.3 Defining Clusters of Manufacturing Industries in China

We first construct inter-industry similarity matrix, M^k, and superscript k represents a certain form of relatedness. Each element in the matrix represents relatedness between two specific industries, i.e., element $M^k(i,j)$ in row i and column j represents relatedness between industry pairs i and j. Two types of inter-industry similarity matrix are constructed. The first type shows inter-industry relatedness based on their spatial distribution patterns, and the second type measures direct input–output relationships between industries.

Various forms of linkages between industries will lead to the spatial concentration of employment or firms in related industries. Therefore, industries with stronger spatial correlation in terms of employment or firm number generally have tighter inter-industry linkages, and therefore are more likely to belong to the same cluster. Based on that, we construct matrices *EmpCorr* and *FirmCorr*, elements of which are the correlation coefficient between manufacturing industries. When constructing the correlation coefficient matrices, a city's number of employment or firms are aggregated at the four-digit code level, and pair-wise correlation coefficients of manufacturing industries are calculated according to Equations (6.1) and (6.2)

$$EmpCorr_{ij} = Correlation\left(Emp_{ir}, Emp_{jr}\right) \tag{6.1}$$

$$FirmCorr_{ij} = Correlation\left(Firm_{ir}, Firm_{jr}\right) \tag{6.2}$$

Here, subscripts i, j, and r represent industry i, industry j, and city r, and *Emp* and *Firm* represent city-industry level number of employment or firms.

In addition, we construct industry coagglomeration matrix to depict the co-location tendency of industry pairs, as compared with random distribution of employment or firms. Ellison and Glaeser (1997) believed that the natural advantages of regions and localized industry-specific spillovers are the main forces to promote spatial agglomeration of industries, while firm-level pure random factors become dispersing forces that prevent firms from fully concentrating in a certain region. Based on a firm-level location choice model, they proposed the coagglomeration index of industries, as shown in Equation (6.3):

$$Coagglomeration_{ij} = \sum_{r}\left(s_{ri} - x_r\right)\left(s_{rj} - x_r\right) / \left(1 - \sum_{r} x_r^2\right) \tag{6.3}$$

s_{ri} and s_{rj} represent the employment share of industry i or industry j in city r, and greater values of s means the greater concentration of industries in the city. x_r is the average s_{ri} of all manufacturing industries in city r, which measures the overall size of the city's manufacturing industry. An industry showing no tendency of agglomeration will be distributed randomly across all cities in accordance with city-industry's production size, namely, for any r, $s_{ri} = x_r$. Otherwise, the value of s_{ir} would be far greater than x_r in some cities, and far smaller than x_r in other cities. If there is a tendency for industry i and j to coagglomerate city r, (s_{ri}- x_r) and (s_{rj}- x_r) are more likely to be both positive or negative at the same time. Therefore, the coagglomeration index measures whether two industries are more likely to be concentrated in one place than if their productions were to be randomly distributed. If there is some form of Marshallian externalities promoting the colocation of two industries, the coagglomeration index is positive; otherwise, the coagglomeration index is less than or equal to 0. We calculated the coagglomeration index matrix using both city-industry level number of employment or firms, and denote them respectively as *Emp*COI and *Firm*COI.

The first two types of matrices focus on the spatial distribution pattern of industries. In the following, the input–output matrix is constructed to *s*, capture the direct links between industries. The input–output relationship is one of the most important dimensions of inter-industry linkages. If an industry uses more inputs from another industry, or its products are used more in the production of another industry as inputs, the two industries are relatively more correlated. Industries with close input–output relationships tend to locate with each other to reduce transportation costs and thus are more likely to form clusters. Ellison *et al.* (2010) found that although regional natural endowment, input–output relationship, labor market pooling, and knowledge spillover are all essential for promoting industrial coagglomeration, the impacts from input–output relationship is the most significant. Therefore, we construct the input–output matrix following Ellison *et al.* (2010) and Equation (6.4). The element in row *i* and column *j* measures the input and output relations between industry *i* and *j*.

$$IO_{ij} = Max\left\{input_{i\to j}, input_{j\to i}, output_{i\to j}, output_{j\to i}\right\} \tag{6.4}$$

Here, $input_{i\to j}$ is the share of input from industry *i* in industry *j*'s total value of inputs; $output_{i\to j}$ is the share of output into industry *j* from industry *i*'s total value of outputs; the definitions of $input_{j\to i}$ and $output_{j\to i}$ are *vice versa*. IO_{ij} is the maximum value of the input–output relatedness indicators. It should be noted that the 2002 input–output data in China covers 122 broad sectors, among which only 72 are manufacturing sectors. There are 480 manufacturing industries at the four-digit code level in our study. Therefore, clustering based on input–output data only will lead to the result that cluster configuration being dominated by input–output relationship between industries, so that industries belonging to the same input–output sector would be classified into the same cluster, while inter-industry linkages of other dimensions are ignored. Therefore, we further compute multidimensional similarity matrix by averaging the input–output matrix IO with *EmpCorr* or *FirmCorr*.

$$IO\_EmpCorr_{ij} = \frac{1}{2} IO_{ij} + \frac{1}{2} EmpCorr_{ij} \tag{6.5}$$

$$IO\_FirmCorr_{ij} = \frac{1}{2} IO_{ij} + \frac{1}{2} FirmCorr_{ij} \tag{6.6}$$

Thus, six different kinds of inter-industry similarity matrices are constructed based on different data or methods. In the second step, based on different similarity matrix or different parameters, cluster analysis will be used to obtain preliminary cluster configurations of manufacturing industries.

Cluster analysis is a statistical method to group data objects, so that observations within the same group would have high levels of similarity and observations between different groups would have high degree of dissimilarities. Both hierarchical clustering and partition clustering will be used in our study. In hierarchical clustering, we need to set in advance the number of industrial clusters, cluster linkage and the similarity measure. Since the optimal number of industrial clusters is not pre-determined, at this stage, we explore values for the number of manufacturing clusters from 30 to 79. Theoretically, the number of clusters should not be set too high or too low. On the one hand, too many clusters will increase industry similarity within the same group, between-group distinctions would be reduced. On the other hand, too few clusters may classify industries that are barely related into the same groups. Delgado *et al.* (2014, 2016) classified all tradable goods industries in the United States into 51 clusters, while Feser (2005), based on input–output data, classified all industries in the United States into 45 clusters. As for cluster linkages, we adopt the most commonly used Ward's linkage, which is found to be more efficient in grouping data objects than other linkages such as single linkage, complete linkage and the average linkage, etc. In addition, in hierarchical clustering, we also need to set a similarity matrix to measure distance between industries. We will use alternatively the 6 industry similarity matrices constructed in the first step. Based on different values of possible number of clusters (30–79, a total of 50 possible values), similarity matrices (a total of 6), 300 different configurations of industrial clusters will be obtained using the hierarchical clustering method. In partitioned clustering, we use matrix *EmpCorr* or *FirmCorr* to measure distance between industries. Furthermore, to remove influences from the overall size of industry, not only the raw number of employment or firms at the city-industry level are used but also the standardized number of employment or firms are used to construct the similarity matrices. In this part, we still set the number of possible clusters at 30–79, and thus obtain a total of 200 different cluster configurations.

Given the number of possible clusters, clustering functions and inter-industry similarity matrices that could be chosen, the second step of cluster analysis generates a total of 500 different cluster configurations, among which 300 are from hierarchical clustering and 200 by partition clustering. We denote each cluster configuration as C_S, where $S \in \{1,2,\ldots,500\}$ means one specific form of cluster configuration.

In the third step, we will evaluate the 500 cluster configurations to find out the comparatively better industrial cluster definition. According to the basic principle of clustering analysis, a good cluster definition should satisfy the following two conditions. On the one hand, industries within the same cluster should be more closely related with each other than to industries in another cluster. On the other hand, the optimal cluster configuration should be robust so that they are too different from other cluster configurations with good properties. Therefore, in the third step, different cluster configurations will be evaluated based on three indexes, namely Validation Scores of Clusters (VSC), Validation Scores of Industries (VSI) and Robustness Scores (RS).

First, the Validation Score of Clusters is constructed based on the within cluster relatedness of industries and the between cluster relatedness. A good cluster definition should exhibit relatively higher within cluster relatedness than between cluster relatedness. Therefore, on average, the score of WCR_c should be higher than BCR_c. For any cluster $c \in C_S$, WCR_c is average relatedness of all industry pairs within the cluster. Therefore, WCR measures similarity between industries within a cluster. The between cluster relatedness $BCR_{cc'}$ between cluster c and another cluster $c' \in C_S$ is constructed in two steps. Firstly, for any industry $i \in c$, its relatedness with cluster c' is obtained by calculating its average relatedness with all industries in cluster c'. Secondly, the between cluster relatedness between c and c' is obtained by averaging relatedness of all the industries in cluster with c'. BCR indicates industry similarities between different clusters.

As different inter-industry similarity matrix will lead to different values of WCR_c and $BCR_{cc'}$, we construct an index reflecting the relative within-cluster relatedness of a cluster configurations according to Equations (6.7) and (6.8), in which V_k refers to the similarity matrix we use in constructing VSC.

$$VSC\_AVG_{C_S}^{V_k} = \frac{100}{N_{CS}} \sum_{c \in C_S} I\left[WCR_c\left(V_k\right) - AvgBCR_c\left(V_k\right)\right] \tag{6.7}$$

$$VSC\_P95_{C_S}^{V_k} = \frac{100}{N_{C_S}} \sum_{c \in C_S} I\left[WCR_c\left(V_k\right) - P95BCR_c\left(V_k\right)\right] \tag{6.8}$$

Here, N_{C_S} is the number of clusters of cluster configuration C_s. In Equation (6.7), $AvgBCR_c$ is cluster c's average between cluster relatedness with $\forall c' \in C_S$. $I[\cdot]$ is an indicator function and takes the value of 1 if $WCR_c(V_k) - AvgBCR_c(V_k) > 0$, and 0 otherwise. Therefore, Equation (6.7) measures the proportion of clusters whose within cluster relatedness are greater than the average between cluster relatedness. The definition of $VSC\_P95_{C_S}^{V_k}$ is similar to Equation (6.7) except that WCR_c is compared with the 95th percentile of $BCR_{cc'}$. Cluster validation score VSC_{C_S} is finally obtained by averaging $VSC\_AVG_{C_S}^{V_k}$ and $VSC\_P95_{C_S}^{V_k}$ across all similarity matrices V_k. It is worth noting that to avoid evaluation bias, the similarity matrix V_k used to generate C_s is excluded when calculating VSC_{C_S}.

The validation score of industries of a cluster configuration is constructed similarly, as shown in Equations (6.9) and (6.10). WCR_{ic} represents industry i's within cluster relatedness in cluster c, and it is the average of industry i's relatedness with any other industry in the cluster. In addition, we construct industry i's between cluster relatedness with $c' \in C_S$ $BCR_{ic'}$ by averaging its relatedness with all the industries cluster c'. We compare industry i's within cluster relatedness with the average or 95th percentile of between cluster relatedness $BCR_{ic'}$, so as to show whether an industry is more related to the cluster it belongs to than another cluster. N_i is the number of industries, which in our study is 480 four-digit code level manufacturing industries. Equations (6.9) and

(6.10) measure the share of industries with a higher within cluster relatedness than a between cluster relatedness in cluster configuration C_s. VSI is obtained by averaging all values of $VSC\_AVG_{C_S}^{V_k}$ and $VSC\_P95_{C_S}^{V_k}$ across similarity matrices V_k.

$$VSC\_AVG_{C_S}^{V_k} = \frac{100}{N_i} \sum_i I\left[WCR_{ic}\left(V_k\right) - AvgBCR_i\left(V_k\right)\right] \quad (6.9)$$

$$VSC\_P95_{C_S}^{V_k} = \frac{100}{N_i} \sum_i I\left[WCR_{ic}\left(V_k\right) - P95BCR_i\left(V_k\right)\right] \quad (6.10)$$

After obtaining the VSC_c and VSI_c of all 500 cluster configurations, cluster configurations with top 10% VSC_c and VSI_c scores are chosen as candidate cluster configurations. A total of 31 candidates are obtained and serve as the basis for subsequent analysis. Candidate cluster configurations have properties of strong within cluster relatedness and great between cluster differentiations.

Besides, the optimal cluster configuration should satisfy the criteria of robustness, that is, the optimal cluster configuration should not be too sensitive to model parameter. Therefore, robustness requires the optimal cluster configuration not to differ too much from other candidate cluster configurations. Based on this, we calculate the overlap score between all candidate cluster configurations. The overlap score between cluster configurations c_1 and c_2 are constructed as follows. First, for any $c \in C_1$, the cluster with the highest industry overlap in C_2 is found out and denoted as b. The overlap score between cluster c and b is calculated according to Equation (6.11):

$$Overlap_{bc} = 100 * n_{cb} / \sqrt{n_c n_b} \quad (6.11)$$

where n_c and n_b are the number of industries in cluster c and b, respectively. Therefore, the indicator $Overlap_{bc}$ measures the proportion of industries in common in both clusters. Similar calculations are carried out for all the clusters in C_1, and averages are taken to obtain the overlap index $Overlap_{C_1C_2}$ between cluster configurations C_1 and C_2. The robustness score of C_1 is obtained by averaging the overlap index of C_1 with all the other 30 candidate cluster configurations, and higher robustness score represents similar classifications of industries with other candidate cluster configurations.

Finally, by taking the average of the cluster validation score VSC, the industry validation score VSI and the cluster robustness score RS, the cluster configuration with the highest average score is chosen as the alternative optimal cluster configuration. In our study, the optimal cluster configuration is generated by the similarity matrix *IO_FirmCorr* which is the average of the input–output matrix IO and the locational correlation matrix *FirmCorr* based on the number of firms in a city-industry, and hierarchical clustering is used to divide all 480 manufacturing industries into 46 industrial clusters.

The alternative optimal cluster configuration conveys information on both the spatial distribution pattern and input–output relationships of industries, instead of relying on one single inter-industry relatedness index. More information creates better cluster configurations. On the other hand, cluster configurations based on the number of industrial firms rather than the number of people employed may imply that cluster development and the resulting agglomeration effect may influence the firm locations more. Although the spatial distribution pattern of employment will also be affected by the agglomeration effect, it also involves influences from other factors such as labor intensity of the industry.

In the last step, adjustments will be made to correct anomalies due to data limitations, so that each industry is classified into the cluster with which its relatedness is the highest. All the adjustments are transparent, and are divided into two types: systematic adjustments or marginal adjustments. Systematic adjustments will re-group industries with relatively low cluster relatedness within WCR_i. On the one hand, a favorable cluster configuration requires that industries' WCR_i should not be much lower than their between cluster relatedness with other clusters BCR_{ic}. Therefore, industries with WCR_i lower than the 75th percentile of BCR_{ic} across the clusters will be reassigned to the cluster in which their WCR_i would be the highest. On the other hand, industries whose within cluster relatedness are significantly lower than that of other industries within the same cluster should also be re-assigned. Therefore, an industry's WCR_i is compared to the *WCR*s of other industries in the same cluster. If the WCR_i of an industry is two standard deviations below the average *WCR* of other industries within the cluster, it will be reallocated to another cluster in which it would have the highest WCR_i score. The adjustments mentioned above will be iterated until no further adjustment is made.

Marginal adjustments depend mainly on subjective judgment. In this process, we examine the grouping of all 480 industries one by one, and adjust the classification of industry when necessary. These industries may have relatively high within cluster relatedness, but conceptually are more suitable for another cluster and therefore need to be adjusted. In addition, clusters with industries clearly belong to two or more clusters will be partitioned, and clusters with high between cluster relatedness will be combined. In our study, 70 industries are re-assigned, reducing the number clusters from 46 to 44. The share of adjusted industries in our study is low, as compared with Delgado *et al.* (2016). In Delgado *et al.* (2016), 16.32% of all industries, i.e., 127 out of 778 six-digit code level industries, were reallocated, while the share in our study is 14.58%. In addition, 6 clusters are partitioned, among which 3 clusters are split into 2 clusters each, and the other 3 clusters are split into 3 clusters each. Thus, the number of optimal industrial clusters increased from 44 to 53. Finally, we combine similar clusters and get 41 industrial clusters, which constitute our finalized definition of manufacturing clusters in China. All the marginal adjustments are transparent and can be traced back.

6.4 Spatial Distribution Patterns of Manufacturing Clusters in China

Cluster-based industrialization has been an important driving force for China to become the world's manufacturing center since its reform and opening up. In the previous section, manufacturing industries at the four-digit code level in China has been grouped into different clusters based on various forms of inter-industry linkages. The industrial clusters defined have the properties of strong within cluster inter-relatedness, great between-cluster distinctions, and robustness, which are necessary for good cluster configurations. In this part, we will provide a generally description of spatial distribution patterns of manufacturing industrial clusters in China.

Chapter 3 described the spatial distribution characteristics of manufacturing industries and their changes in China. Reviews of existing literature and China's experience show that the spatial distribution of economic activities is mainly determined by both the agglomeration effect and the dispersing effect. First nature and second nature factors exert different influences on different industries, leading to different distribution patterns of industries. Industries more strongly affected by the agglomeration effect tend to concentrate in the eastern coastal areas with better geographical or economic geographical advantages, while industries more sensitive to dispersing effects tend to leave the agglomeration area. In addition, the spatial distribution pattern of industries is also affected by the region's endowment and economic development policies.

Similar to manufacturing industries, the spatial distribution pattern of industrial clusters is also affected by these factors. To get an intuitive understanding of the spatial distribution pattern of China's 41 industrial clusters, we first provide a description of employment distribution characteristics of industrial clusters in eastern, central, western, and northeastern China. Since the analysis of distribution characteristics of industrial clusters involves city-industry level employment and firm counts data, aggregate data is no longer applicable. In this part, we aggregate the micro-level enterprise data to the city-industry levels based on the above-scale industrial firm data in 2004 and 2009, and construct a strength index of employment for each cluster in each region according to Equation (6.12):

$$Cluster\_Str_{cr} = \frac{Emp_{cr}}{Emp_r} / \frac{Emp_c}{Emp} \tag{6.12}$$

Here, subscripts c and r represent cluster and region respectively, and descriptions for 41 different industrial clusters in 4 regions, including east, central, west, and northeast China, are provided. The four regions are defined in the same way as in Chapter 3. The numerator of Equation (6.12) shows a cluster's employment share in all manufacturing employment in the region, while the denominator is the region's employment share at the national level. Thus, the regional employment strength indicators for clusters reflect the degree of concentration or development of cluster c in region r compared to the national average. Cluster strength values greater than 1 indicate high concentration levels of cluster employment in the regions, while values less than 1 indicates a relatively low degree of local concentration.

Table 6.1 shows the variance of cluster strength in different regions. Results show that in general, the development of industrial clusters in the eastern region is relatively balanced. The standard deviations of cluster

Table 6.1. Standard Deviation of Regional Cluster Strength

	2004	2009
East	0.263	0.256
Central	0.568	0.505
West	0.779	0.859
Northeast	0.805	0.745

strength in the eastern region were 0.263 and 0.256, respectively, in 2004 and 2009. Compared with the eastern region, the development of industrial clusters in other regions is uneven across different clusters. In the central region, industrial clusters have experienced great development in the fields such as coking, smelting and non-ferrous metal processing, tobacco, etc., while the employment strength of other clusters is relatively low. As shown in Table 6.1, the standard deviations of employment strength across different clusters in central China were 0.568 and 0.505 in 2004 and 2009, significantly higher than the standard deviations in eastern China. Employment distribution across different clusters in the western region and the northeast region are more uneven. In 2004, the standard deviation of cluster strength in western region was as high as 0.779, and further increased to 0.859 in 2009, indicating that manufacturing activities in western region are increasingly more concentrated in a few clusters with development advantages. The standard deviations of industrial cluster strength in northeastern China in 2004 and 2009 were 0.805 and 0.745, respectively, which was also higher tendencies of concentration than eastern and central China.

The analysis above on the regional distribution characteristics of industrial clusters is consistent with theoretical predictions based on new economic geography. Different clusters have different spatial distribution patterns due to different impacts from agglomeration effect and dispersing effect. To further study the regional distribution characteristics of China's industrial clusters, we provide a more detailed description of distribution patterns of China's industrial clusters based on prefecture-city level data.

Firstly, we construct a city-level cluster strength in 2004. The calculation of prefecture-city level cluster strength is similar to Equation (6.12), except that subscript r in this part represents cities rather than regions. After obtaining cities' employment strength of clusters, average

Table 6.2. Diversification of Regional Manufacturing Clusters

	Employment proportion of largest clusters (%)	HHI	Number of strong clusters (90th)	Number of strong clusters (75th)
East	21.66	0.110	4.414	12.356
Central	22.83	0.129	3.827	9.938
West	22.92	0.184	3.694	8.412
Northeast	24.40	0.144	4.118	9.294

$Cluster\_Str_{cr}$ in each city r is taken, and the distribution pattern of average employment strength across cities are investigated. Different from the trend that China's overall manufacturing employment is becoming more concentrated in the eastern region, the city-level cluster strength values in the eastern region are generally lower than those in the central, western, and northeastern regions. Results show that average cluster strengths of cities in the eastern, central, western, and northeast regions are 0.997, 0.977, 1.076, and 1.088, respectively, that is, cluster strengths in the western and northeast regions are higher.

The higher employment strengths of clusters in inland areas may be mainly due to their lack of industry diversities. In comparison, cities in the eastern coastal areas have more complete coverage of industries and diversified industrial structures. Therefore, employment is more evenly distributed across different industries or industrial clusters in east China. First, statistics show that manufacturing employment in inland regions tends to be more concentrated in a few largest industrial clusters. We aggregated the employment of each city's largest industrial cluster, and calculated its share in manufacturing employment in each region. As is shown in Table 6.2, the employment proportions of largest clusters in the eastern, central, western, and northeastern regions are 21.663%, 22.830%, 22.918%, and 24.397%, respectively.

The above only shows the employment share of the largest clusters in each city. In order to fully reflect employment diversification across all industrial clusters, we further constructed city-level Herfindahl–Hirschman Index showing employment distribution across clusters according to Equation (6.13), where subscripts c and r represent city and cluster, respectively. Here, Emp_{cr} represents employment of cluster c in city r, and Emp_r is the overall employment of manufacturing industries in city r.

According to the structure, larger HHI values represent higher concentrations of employment, and smaller HHI values imply higher levels of industrial diversification.

$$HHI_r = \sum_c \left(\frac{Emp_{cr}}{Emp_r} \right)^2 \tag{6.13}$$

Results show that cities in east China have lower HHI values than those in central and western regions, implying that manufacturing employment shows more diversity across clusters in the eastern region. We calculate average HHI in each region, and as is shown in Table 6.2, the average HHI in the eastern region is 0.110, lower than 0.129 and 0.144 in the central and northeastern regions. The average Herfindahl–Hirschman Index of cities in the western region is the highest at 0.184, indicating that manufacturing employment in the western region is the least diversified.

In addition, the number of strong clusters in cities also reflects diversification of city industrial clusters. City-clusters with employment strength higher than the 90th or 75th percentile of cluster strengths across all prefecture-level cities in China are defined as strong clusters, indicating corresponding city-clusters have relative higher concentrations of employment. Thus, according to Equations (6.14) and (6.15), we obtain the number of strong clusters in each prefecture-level city. Results show that cities in east China have relatively more strong clusters compared with the central, western, and northeast regions, no matter whether the 90th percentile or 75th percentile is used as the benchmark, confirming employment diversity in the eastern cities. The average numbers of strong clusters in cities of east China are 4.14 and 12.36, when the 90th percentile and 75th percentile are used as benchmarks, respectively, which are higher than those in the inland regions. In comparison, the number of strong clusters in western cities is the lowest, with the average number of strong clusters being 3.69 and 8.41, respectively, under benchmarks of 90th quantile or 75th quantile (Table 6.2).

$$\#StrCluster\_P90_r = \sum_c I(Cluster\_Str_{cr} > P90Cluster\_Str_c) \tag{6.14}$$

$$\#StrCluster\_P75_r = \sum_c I(Cluster\_Str_{cr} > P75Cluster\_Str_c) \qquad (6.15)$$

The analysis above shows that due to influences of agglomeration effect, dispersing effect, and natural endowment advantages, industrial clusters have quite different distribution patterns. Although manufacturing industries are generally highly concentrated in the eastern region, employment strengths of industrial clusters in the eastern region are relatively the smallest compared with other regions. This is mainly because the eastern region has a relatively more complete coverage of industries. Compared with cities in inland regions, eastern cities have more strong clusters and the industrial structure there is highly diversified. Meanwhile, employment of manufacturing industries in inland areas tends to concentrate in only a few clusters, especially the resource-intensive clusters, with a relatively less diversified industrial structure.

A natural corollary of the analysis above is that clusters with different positionings in the industry value chain may have different spatial distribution patterns due to impacts of globalization, new economic geographical factors, as well as regions' resource endowments. As the global value chain is playing essential roles in this round of globalization, we further describe value chain positionings of industrial clusters in different regions of China. First of all, based on the input–output data in 2002 (National Bureau of Statistics, 2006) and Antràs *et al.*'s (2012a) model, we construct the upstreamness index reflecting the position of different sectors in the industry value chain. Upstreamness indexes in the closed economy or open economy settings are constructed.

In a closed economy, the output of an industry can be used for final consumption or as intermediate inputs for the production of other industries. Therefore, output Y_i of industry $i \in \{1, 2, ..., N\}$ can be expressed as Equation (6.16):

$$Y_i = F_i + Z_i \qquad (6.16)$$

where F_i is the part for final consumption, and Z_i is the value of intermediate inputs used in other industries. According to the input–output relationship between different sectors, Z_i can be splitted as shown in Equation (6.17):

$$Z_i = \sum_{j=1}^{N} d_{ij} Y_j \tag{6.17}$$

where d_{ij} is the input value of industry i used by industry j's each unit of output value. Therefore, $d_{ij} Y_j$ represents industry i's value of the products entering the production of industry j in the form of intermediate inputs. At the same time, part of industry j's output will in turn enter the production of industry k in the form of intermediate inputs; the production chain will continue to expand along the industry value chain. By substituting Equation (6.17) into Equation (6.16) iteratively, output of industry i can be expressed as an infinite sequence as Equation (6.18):

$$Y_i = F_i + \sum_{j=1}^{N} d_{ij} F_j + \sum_{j=1}^{N} \sum_{k=1}^{N} d_{ik} d_{kj} F_j + \sum_{j=1}^{N} \sum_{k=1}^{N} \sum_{l=1}^{N} d_{il} d_{lk} d_{kj} F_j + \ldots \tag{6.18}$$

According to Equation (6.18), the output of an industry can be shown as the sum of its values used by other industries at different positions in the industry value chain. According to Alfaro *et al.* (2015), the upstreamness of an industry can be described as Equation (6.19), which is obtained by multiplying each term in Equation (6.18) by their distance from final use plus one and dividing by Y_i:

$$U_{i1} = 1 \times \frac{F_i}{Y_i} + 2 \times \frac{\sum_{j=1}^{N} d_{ij} F_j}{Y_i} + 3 \times \frac{\sum_{j=1}^{N} \sum_{k=1}^{N} d_{ik} d_{kj} F_j}{Y_i} + 4 \times \frac{\sum_{j=1}^{N} \sum_{k=1}^{N} \sum_{l=1}^{N} d_{il} d_{lk} d_{kj} F_j}{Y_i} + \cdots \tag{6.19}$$

Antràs *et al.* (2012a) prove that for any industry j with $\sum_{i=1}^{N} d_{ij} < 1$, the numerator of Equation (6.19) equals to the i-th row of vector $[I - \Delta]^{-2} F$, where Δ is an $N \times N$ matrix whose element in row i and column j is d_{ij}, and F is the column vector of finally use of industries, row i of which is F_i. Higher upstreamness index values indicate that a larger part of the industry's output is used as intermediate inputs in downstream industries, so its position in the value chain is relatively more upstream.

The industry upstreamness index in an open economy can be constructed in a similar way. Different from the closed economy model, output Y_i of industry $i \in \{1,2,\cdots,N\}$ can be divided into three parts, including final use (F_i), intermediate input (Z_i) and net export ($X_i - M_i$). Assuming that input–output relationships in the domestic production, export and import sectors of a country are the same, the upstreamness of industry i can be expressed as Equation (6.20).

$$U_{i2} = 1\times\frac{F_i}{Y_i} + 2\times\frac{\sum_{j=1}^{N}\delta_{ij}F_j}{Y_i} + 3\times\frac{\sum_{j=1}^{N}\sum_{k=1}^{N}\delta_{ik}\delta_{kj}F_j}{Y_i} + 4\times\frac{\sum_{j=1}^{N}\sum_{k=1}^{N}\sum_{l=1}^{N}\delta_{il}\delta_{lk}\delta_{kj}F_j}{Y_i} + \cdots \tag{6.20}$$

Here $\delta_{ij} = d_{ij}Y_i \Big/ \left(Y_i - X_i + M_i\right)$.

Using the input–output data in 2002, the upstreamness indexes of each manufacturing sector in China under both closed or open economy conditions can be obtained according to Equations (6.19) and (6.20). Cluster upstreamness is obtained by averaging upstreamness values of industries in the cluster. Results show that the upstreamness indexes based on the closed economic model or the open economic model are highly correlated, with the correlation coefficient being 0.887. As openness has become one important characteristic of the Chinese economy and manufacturing industries in China are highly export-oriented, in this chapter and the next, we will mainly use the upstreamness index obtained under the open economy model.

Based on the upstreamness index of industrial clusters, we further explore characteristics of clusters' positionings in the industry value chain across different regions in China. When the upstreamness of each city's largest cluster is used to measure city-cluster's positions in the industry value chain, we find that clusters in the central and western regions are generally located in a relatively more upstream position compared with cities in the eastern region. This finding is consistent with our judgment that manufacturing activities in the central and western regions are more concentrated in resource-intensive and upstream industries. The first column of Table 6.3 calculates the average upstreamness of each city's largest clusters in each region. The average upstreamness of the largest clusters in the eastern region is 2.327, lower than the average upstreamness values of 2.835, 2.911, and 2.782 in the central, western, and northeastern regions, respectively. If we further choose industrial clusters with the highest employment strength for each prefecture-level city and analyze their upstreamness, similar conclusions can be reached. Employment strength of the cluster is calculated in the same way as Equation (6.12), indicating the relative concentration or development level of cluster c in city r compared with the national average. Results show that compared with cities in the eastern region, industrial clusters of cities in the inland regions have higher levels of upstreamness (Table 6.3). Finally, we construct an index showing the average upstreamness of each prefecture-level city. As is shown in Equation (6.21), it is the weighted average of upstreamness of all the industries the city has, where the industry's employment share in local manufacturing employment is used as the weight.

$$Upstream_r = \sum_{i=1}^{N} \frac{Emp_{ir}}{Emp_r} U_{i2} \tag{6.21}$$

Here, U_{i2} is industry upstreamness under the open economy assumption, Emp_{ir} is employment of industry i in city r, and Emp_r is total employment of all manufacturing industries in city r. Compared with cities in other regions, industries in east China are located in relatively more downstream positions in the industry value chain and are the closest to the final consumer market. The average upstreamness of manufacturing employment in the eastern region is 2.556, which is the lowest among all regions; lower than 2.850 in the central region and 2.819 in the northeastern region. Comparatively, manufacturing industries in the western region are located in the most upstream positions in the industry value chain, with an average upstreamness index of 2.854 (Table 6.3).

To sum up, the following three conclusions about the spatial distribution pattern of China's manufacturing industrial clusters can be reached. First, although new economic geographical factors promote the concentration of employment in the eastern coastal regions, employment strengths of industrial clusters in the eastern region are relatively lower than those in the inland regions. Second, the relatively lower strength of

Table 6.3. Upstreamness of Manufacturing Industrial Clusters in Different Regions

	Upstreamness of the largest cluster	Upstreamness of the cluster with the highest strength	Average upstreamness
East	2.327	2.307	2.556
Central	2.835	2.605	2.850
West	2.911	2.745	2.854
Northeast	2.782	2.519	2.819

Note: All the above indicators are based on the upstreamness index under the open economy assumption.

clusters in the eastern region is mainly due to the more complete coverage of manufacturing industries there. Compared with other regions, industry structure in the eastern coastal region is relatively more diversified. Third, compared with the eastern coastal areas, manufacturing industries in the inland area are located in more upstream positions in the industry value chain, and are dominated by resource-intensive industries. In other words, outputs of manufacturing industries in the inland region are more likely to be used as intermediate inputs in downstream industries, rather than be used as final consumptions.

6.5 Summary

Based on the 2004 National Economic Census data and the input–output data of the People's Republic of China in 2002, manufacturing industries at the four-digit code level are classified into clusters in this chapter. Clustering analysis is used to group industries and different cluster configurations are evaluated. Our optimal definition of industrial clusters classified 480 four-digit code level manufacturing industries into 41 industrial clusters using hierarchical clustering, and the inter-industry similarity matrix used is the average of the input–output matrix and the locational correlation matrix based on the number of firms in a city-industry. The optimal cluster configuration obtained in this chapter has the advantages of high within-cluster inter-industry relatedness, strong between cluster differentiation and robustness. Compared with the existing literature, our study provides the first systematic cluster definition of manufacturing industries in China, and the cluster configuration generated comprehensively reflects various forms of inter-industry relations, rather than focusing on only one single form of inter-industry relations.

Furthermore, this chapter provides statistical descriptions of spatial distribution patterns of manufacturing clusters in China, and differences of industrial clusters across the eastern, central, western, and northeastern regions are investigated. Consistent with the results from Chapter 3, roles of economic geographical factors, new economic geographical factors, and economic policy in shaping the spatial distribution of manufacturing industrial clusters are confirmed. We find that although employment of manufacturing industries is highly concentrated in the eastern region, the strengths of industrial clusters in the eastern region are lower than those in other regions, which are mainly results of the more complete coverage of industries in the eastern region. Meanwhile, manufacturing productions in the central, western, and northeastern regions tend to be concentrated in a few industrial clusters. We measure diversifications of regional industrial clusters based on cities' employment shares of the largest cluster, the Herfindahl–Hirschman Index of cluster employment, the number of regional strong clusters, etc., and find that industrial clusters in the eastern region are more diversified. In addition, compared with the eastern coastal areas, employment of manufacturing industries in the inland areas is located at more upstream positions in the industry value chain. Larger shares of outputs produced by inland manufacturing industries are used as intermediate inputs in downstream industries.

Chapter 7

Economic Agglomeration and Cluster Effects in Urban China

Chapter 6 provides the optimal configuration of manufacturing industries in China using clustering analysis, and describes development and spatial distribution patterns of industrial clusters in different regions in China. How will industrial clusters affect the development of regional industries? Cluster-based industrial development has played important roles in urbanization and industrialization in various countries around the world. Porter (1990) regarded the development of industrial clusters as the main source of a country's industrial competitive advantage. In accordance with its endowment and institutional contexts in early stages of industrialization, the development of manufacturing industries in China are also cluster-based. However, with further industrialization progress and continuous rises in labor costs, initial advantages of industrial clusters may be weakened, and declines in product quality brought by intensified competition in clusters may lead industries to be stuck at positions with low added values in the industry value chain, impeding further development of industries. In addition, in practice, there are debates about whether local governments should give priority to high-tech and high-value-added industries in development, or should foster complementarities among related industries based on local industrial structure and comparative advantages. The understanding of industrial clusters and their effects will not only provide implications for regional and industrial development policies but also serve as an important basis for enterprises' business strategies.

Economists have been interested in the role of clusters in industry development since Porter (1990). However, due to limitations of data and methods, there are few systematic studies on industrial clusters. Most existing studies are case analysis, which are specific to a certain region or industry. Influences of clusters on industrial development are not predetermined. On the one hand, cluster development may promote labor productivity of industries in the cluster through agglomeration effect, thus fostering industrial development. On the other hand, cluster development may intensify competition among different industries and push the price of lands, labors, and other factors up, and may thus restrain industrial development. In addition, path dependence brought by clusters may lead industries to keep positioning in the low end of industry value chain, impeding sustainable growth of industries and employment (Grabher, 1993; Chen Jiagui and Wang Qin, 2005). Ruan Jianqing *et al.* (2014) construct a three-stage model of industrial cluster transformation and upgrading, and show that though cluster development may promote quantity expansion of industries at early stages of development, intensification of competition among firms and increases in costs may lead to deteriorations in product quality, the resulting quality crisis may undermine further development of clusters. Breakthroughs of clusters require public policies which encourage research and development and brand innovation, so that industries may move to higher positions in the value chain. In this chapter, based on the optimal cluster configuration obtained in Chapter 6, we will comprehensively evaluate the impact of clusters on the development of local industries from both quantity and quality perspectives.

7.1 Why are Clusters of Manufacturing Industries Important?

This chapter focuses on the cluster effect of manufacturing industries. The role of manufacturing sector in promoting economic growth and employment can never be overlooked. Although it is believed that the development of high-end producer services will promote the expansion of domestic demand and strengthen China's international competitiveness, service industry growth without the development of manufacturing industries will not be sustainable. Premature de-industrialization will not only undermine economic growth but also harm employment.

As the most important component of tradable goods sectors, the manufacturing sector in China is essential in creating jobs and trade surpluses. According to the National Bureau of Statistics, by the end of 2016, there were 378,599 above-scale industrial firms in China, of which 355,518 were manufacturing firms, accounting for 93.90%. Total profits created by manufacturing firms reached 6,528.1 billion yuan, accounting for 90.77% of profits created by all above-scale industrial firms. Therefore, manufacturing industries can be regarded as the most important source of profits and industrial development in China.

From the perspective of employment, the manufacturing sector is the most important source of employment in the urban area, especially employment for medium- and low-skilled workers. Cross-country studies on economic growth have found that countries growing faster tend to have relatively larger manufacturing sectors (Rodrik, 2006). As the manufacturing sector absorbs a large number of medium-skilled workers, manufacturing downturns may not only lead to medium-skilled workers losing their jobs but also intensify competition for low-skilled jobs, and thus raise income inequality. In China, the manufacturing sector, which is the most important component of the tradable goods sector, is the key to creating jobs. By the end of 2016, the number of people employed in urban manufacturing firms totaled 48.938 million, accounting for 60.35% of all employment in urban industrial firms. Statistics based on urban household data from Chinese Household Income Project 2002 and 2007 show that the employment of medium- and low-skilled workers is primarily concentrated in manufacturing industries and low-skilled manual sector, and high-skilled abstract jobs such as finance, health care, and software provide limited job opportunities for low-skilled workers, as these industries are highly dependent on technology and innovation. In addition, workers in low-skilled service industries earn relatively less. Workers with incomes at the bottom 10% are mostly employed in low-skilled service industries, accounting for 58.59% of all low-skilled service employment. Shares of the bottom 10% in manufacturing and high-skilled service industries are only 25.36% and 16.05%, respectively. As a result, a shrinking manufacturing sector will not only lead to loss of job opportunities for the low-skilled, but may also lead to widening of the income gap. Furthermore, considering the development of the service sector, growth in employment in the service sector is largely dependent on the development of the manufacturing sector. On the one hand, growth in manufacturing employment will increase the region's overall incomes, leading to larger service consumption demand and enhancing regional equilibrium wages and employment (Clark, 1957; Moretti, 2010, 2011). On the other hand, the development of the manufacturing sector will directly increase the demand for local producer services. Chapter 8 will show that in China, the expansion of urban manufacturing employment will have a multiplier effect on employment in the service sector. On average, every 1% increase in manufacturing employment will lead to a 0.397% increase in service employment, with low-skilled manual industries benefiting the most.

In addition, as for long-term economic growth, manufacturing is critical to innovations and productivity growth. This is mainly because research and development (R&D) investments of a country's business sector come mainly from the manufacturing sector, and positive effects of R&D investment on productivity and innovations have been widely confirmed in literature. Veugelers (2013) found that in Europe, although employment and added values of the manufacturing sector accounted for only 14–15% of the overall economy, about two-thirds investments in R&D came from the manufacturing sector. Rodrik (2016) made similar conclusions on the manufacturing sector in the United States.

In view of manufacturing's essential role in economic development and job creation, industrial policies and place-based policies aimed at promoting the development of manufacturing industries have become a common practice in both developed and developing countries. However, the effectiveness of place-based policies is not predetermined, and more empirical evidence should be provided. In addition, in practice, local governments often face different policy choices. For example, a common debate is whether local governments should give priority to the development of high-tech and high-value-added industries, or should encourage complementarities across related industries and implement policies based on local pre-existing comparative advantages. Whether encouraging the development of manufacturing industries based on clusters or promote the development of high-tech industries which has little pre-existing strength within the region are more effective in local economic development should be empirically tested, which is exactly the focus of this chapter.

There are several mechanisms through which industrial clusters will affect regional industrial development. Industrial clusters will promote economic agglomeration effect in the region, and thus enhance regional productivity. Higher productivities as a demand shock will attract entries of manufacturers from other regions and encourage existing manufacturers to expand productions, thus promoting industrial development and employment expansion. In addition, agglomeration effects will also promote the creation of new firms and create more job opportunities by lowering the entry barriers of industries and encouraging entrepreneurship. However, as employment sizes of industries grow, industries may experience declines in marginal returns to labor, and regional convergence would have negative impacts on the employment and income of workers (Barro and Sala-i-Martin, 1991). For example, Desmet and Rossi-Hansberg (2014) found that county-level initial manufacturing employment and its future employment growth are negatively correlated in the United States from 1970 to 2000, which is evidence of convergence effect. In addition, cluster development and the resulting competition among industries may push up prices of inputs such as land, labor, and other factors. Cluster development may also lead to path dependence, resulting in firms being stuck in lower added-value positions in the industry value chain, undermining sustainable employment growth.

Apart from practical and policy relevance, empirically estimating cluster effects of manufacturing industries will provide new evidence to the literature of new economic geography. Existing studies on agglomeration effect provides evidence either from the perspective of localization effect or from urbanization effect. Localization effect mainly comes from the relative concentration of a single industry in the region, and its positive effects on labor productivity mainly comes from the benefits of specialization. Urbanization effect refers to the advantages of industrial diversification brought by the expansion of the overall economic scale in a region. However, the dichotomy of agglomeration effects is oversimplified. In fact, there is no city which has only one single industry, or has all manufacturing industries. The key for agglomeration effects lies in the spillover effect between related industries. Related industries may have comparatively strong input–output relationship, share labors of similar skills, raw materials or consumer markets, or use similar production techniques to produce similar products (such as Feser and Bergman, 2000; Glaeser and Kerr, 2009; Ellison *et al.*, 2010; etc.). For example, Ellison *et al.* (2010) investigated impacts of regional natural endowment, input—output relationship, labor market sharing, and knowledge spillover on coagglomeration of different industries. The empirical results show that although all factors contribute to industrial coagglomeration, input–output relationships among industries exert the greatest influence. Concentration of industries with weak relatedness will not facilitate labor productivity growth, but furthermore may crowd out other industries by pushing up input prices. Since the concentration of related industries is the main source of agglomeration effect, it is necessary to move beyond the dichotomy of localization effect and urbanization effect, and to distinguish related industries from other industries. Industrial cluster, which is composed of multiple related industries, is a reasonable starting point. Based on the cluster definition provided in Chapter 6, this chapter will study cluster effects on the development of manufacturing industries, so as to provide evidence on agglomeration effects arising among related industries.

The second section of this chapter will construct a city-industry level employment growth model and empirically test industrial cluster effects on employment growth. The third section extends the empirical model, and studies the impact of cluster development on other indicators showing industry performance, and quantity effects and quality effects of clusters will be our research focus. Section 7.4 explores heterogeneous cluster effects across clusters with different industry value chain upstreamness. The last section is the summary.

7.2 Industrial Clusters and Employment Growth

In this section, we will construct a city-industry level employment growth model to empirically test the impact of cluster development on employment growth. The cluster configuration generated in Chapter 6 and above-scale industrial firm data from 2004 to 2009 will be used. Indicators at the city-industry or city-cluster level are aggregated from firm data.

Theoretically, city-industry employment growth will be affected by both the agglomeration effect and the convergence effect. On the one hand, the concentration of related industries in the city will promote the growth of labor productivity and employment through the agglomeration effect. On the other hand, with increases in the city's initial employment size, convergence effect brought by the diminishing returns to scale may inhibit future employment growth (Barro and Salai-Martin, 1992; Delgado *et al.*, 2014). Therefore, we construct a city-industry level conditional convergence model for employment growth, as shown in Equation (7.1).

$$\Delta lnEmp_{icr} = \beta_0 + \beta_1 \ln\left(Industry\_Str_{icr}\right)\beta_2 \ln\left(Cluster\_Str_{(-i)cr}\right) + \alpha'\text{Industry}_i + \gamma'\text{City}_r + \varepsilon_{icr} \quad (7.1)$$

The dependent variable is the difference between natural logarithms of city-industry employment in 2009 and 2004, that is, $lnEmp_{icr,2009} - lnEmp_{icr,2004}$. Here Emp_{icr} is the number of employment of industry i in cluster c and in city r. Using aggregate employment growth of city-industry from 2004 to 2009 rather than yearly employment growth as the dependent variable removes employment fluctuations across years.

The key explanatory variables are the natural logarithms of industry strength and cluster strength in 2004. Here, to reduce two-way causality problems, variable values in the initial year of 2004 are used. The variable of industrial development is constructed following Equation (7.2), in which the numerator is industry's share of employment of in the city's total manufacturing employment, while the denominator is the employment share of industry i in all manufacturing employment of the whole country. The variable of industry strength of a city $Industry\_Str_{icr}$ is a location quotient, measuring the initial concentration or specialization of industry i in city r. Similarly, for each cluster of the city, we construct the cluster strength variable according to Equation (7.3). The employment of industry i is excluded when we build the cluster strength variable, so that influences of industry i's initial development on future employment growth can be excluded. Employment of other industries in the same cluster is denoted with the subscript $-i$. In Equation (7.3), the numerator is cluster c's employment share in the city's total manufacturing employment, with employment in industry i excluded, and the denominator is cluster c's employment share in the whole country. In addition, in order to partial out possible impacts from other industry characteristics and urban characteristics, industry fixed effects Industry_i and city fixed effects City_r are controlled in the regression. ε_{icr} is a city-industry level error term.

$$Industry\_Str_{icr} = \frac{Emp_{icr}}{Emp_r} / \frac{Emp_i}{Emp} \quad \ldots\ldots \tag{7.2}$$

$$Cluster\_Str_{(-i)cr} = \frac{Emp_{(-i)cr}}{Emp_r} / \frac{Emp_{(-i)c}}{Emp} \quad \ldots\ldots \tag{7.3}$$

Our study focuses on the effects of initial industrial and cluster development on future employment growth, namely the sign and significance of β_1 and β_2. Higher initial industry strength means higher concentration of the industry's production activities in the city, which may promote labor productivity and employment growth through the agglomeration effect. This is the localization effect studied in the new economic geography literature. However, initial industrial development may also impede future employment growth due to convergence effect. Therefore, the effect of initial industry strength on future employment growth is not predetermined and should be tested empirically. If the convergence effect is stronger than the agglomeration effect, β_1 would be significantly negative. Otherwise, β_1 would be insignificant or significantly positive. The coefficient β_2 captures the industrial cluster effect which is the focus of this chapter. The development of related industries will influence future employment growth through both agglomeration effect and crowding-out effect. On one hand, the positive effect of agglomeration on labor productivity will increase demand of labor, and thus facilitate employment expansions. On the other hand, cluster development may intensify inter-industry competitions, and higher factor prices may crowd out productions of firms. Furthermore, firms in stronger clusters may profit from input-based growth instead of productivity-based growth. As a result, firms and industries may keep staying at low added-value positions of the industry value chain, which is detrimental to sustainable industry development and job creation. The sign and significance of β_2 depend on the strength of agglomeration effects and crowding-out effects. It is worth noting that the convergence effect brought by initial industry concentration is excluded from cluster effects, since the variable of cluster strength constructed following Equation (7.3) excludes the influence of the industry itself.

Table 7.1 presents baseline regression results of the city-industry employment growth model. Regression 1 studies the impact of initial industry development on future employment growth. As is mentioned above, higher levels of industry development at the initial stage will influence future employment growth through both the agglomeration effect, which promotes employment growth, and the convergence effect, which has negative impacts on employment growth. The regression result show that β_1 is significantly negative, indicating that the convergence effect dominates the agglomeration effect on employment growth in our study. In Regression 2, we estimate the impact of initial cluster strength on employment, and find cluster effects to be significantly positive. This implies that compared with the crowding-out effect, the agglomeration effect brought by cluster development is significantly stronger. Regression 3 includes both initial industry strength and cluster strength in the model, and the main results remain unchanged. However, other city or industry level non-observable characteristics may affect city-industry employment growth and cluster strength simultaneously. Ignoring these factors may lead to biased estimates of cluster effects. Therefore, on the basis of Regression 3, Regression 4 further includes city level and industry level fixed effects in regressions so as to partial out influences from unobservable city or industry characteristics. Regression results show that, even after controlling fixed effects, the positive effect of initial cluster development still exists, and future employment growth of the city-industry is promoted. According to the regression coefficient, we calculate the magnitude of cluster effect. On average, every one standard deviation increase of the cluster strength above the mean will lead to 2.153 percentage points increase in city-industry's expected annual employment growth rate.

Table 7.2 presents robustness checks. Results in Table 7.1 reflect influences of urban industry and cluster strength in 2004 on future industrial employment growth from 2004 to 2009, and are cross-sectional regressions in nature. As a robustness check, Regression 5 in Table 7.2 uses panel data regressions. The dependent variable is the yearly employment growth in industry i of city r, namely, $lnEmp_{icr,t} - lnEmp_{icr,t-1}$. Industry

Table 7.1. Cluster Development and City-Industry Employment Growth: Baseline Regression Results

Explanatory Variables	Regression 1 ΔlnEmp	Regression 2 ΔlnEmp	Regression 3 ΔlnEmp	Regression 4 ΔlnEmp
ln(Industry_Str)	−0.2421***		−0.2646***	−0.3232***
	(0.0084)		(0.0083)	(0.0085)
ln(Cluster_Str)		0.0300***	0.1151***	0.1139***
		(0.0063)	(0.0061)	(0.0064)
City FE	No	No	No	Yes
Industry FE	No	No	No	Yes
Observations	33,678	32,286	32,286	32,286
R^2	0.1166	0.0010	0.1300	0.2775

Note: *, **, and *** respectively denote significance at 10%, 5%, and 1%. Robust standard errors clustered at city level are in parenthesis.

Table 7.2. Cluster Development and City-Industry Employment Growth: Robust Checks

Explanatory Variables	Regression 5 ΔlnEmp	Regression 6 ΔlnEmp	Regression 7 ΔlnEmp	Regression 8 ΔlnEmp	Regression 9 ΔlnEmp
ln(Industry_Str)	−0.6877***	−0. 0649***	−0.3322***	−0.3272***	−0.3504***
	(0.0070)	(0.0017)	(0.0095)	(0.0085)	(0.0083)
ln(Cluster_Str)	0.0227***	0.0335***	0.0896***	0.0772***	0.0900***
	(0.0056)	(0.0036)	(0.0071)	(0.0081)	(0.0064)
HighInd*ln (Cluster_Str)		−0.0118***			
		(0.0036)			
BigCity*ln (Industry_Str)			0.0139		
			(0.0148)		
BigCity*ln (Cluster_Str)			0.0557***		
			(0.0119)		
ln(Industry2d_Str)				0.0599***	
				(0.0083)	
ln(RelatedInd_Str)					0.3557***
					(0.0244)
FE Model	Yes	No	No	No	No
City FE		Yes	Yes	Yes	Yes
Industry FE		Yes	Yes	Yes	Yes
Observations	186,437	32,286	32,286	31,828	31,807
R^2	0.3420	0.2778	0.2784	0.2796	0.2892

Note: *, **, and *** respectively denote significance at 10%, 5%, and 1%. Robust standard errors clustered at city level are in parenthesis.

strength and cluster strength with lags of one year are used as explanatory variables. Fixed effect estimates show that city-industry employment strength significantly inhibits employment growth in the year following, while city-cluster employment strengths significantly promote employment growth. This indicates that even in the short term, clusters can still promote the employment of industries. This chapter focuses on the long-term impacts of industrial clusters on the urban labor market. Therefore, the following analysis will mainly be extensions of Regression 4 in Table 7.1.

As an extension of Regression 4, Regression 6 includes an interaction term of a city's cluster strength and initial industry strength in regression, so as to investigate whether cluster effects are different across industries with different levels of initial development. In theory, the positive effect of clusters on the employment of industries with higher initial concentration levels would be smaller than that of low-concentration industries due to the convergence effect. The dummy variable *HighInd* is used to indicate whether the city-industry is a high-concentration industry or not. If the initial employment strength of a city-industry is higher than the industry's national median, the value of *HighInd* is equal to 1, otherwise it is equal to 0. Regression results show that the introduction of the interaction item does not change results much, and that city-industry level convergence effect and the positive cluster effect on employment still exist. In addition, compared with city-industries with higher initial levels of concentration, other industries benefit more from cluster development. The difference of cluster effects between the two kind of industries is about 0.059 percentage points. In other words, with the development of industrial clusters, industries with lower initial levels of development grow faster in employment.

In addition, we further investigate heterogeneous cluster effects across cities of different sizes. Agglomeration effects in large cities are generally stronger (Glaeser and Resseger, 2009; Chapters 4 and 5). As a result, the positive effect of industrial clusters in big cities may also be greater. We construct the dummy variable *BigCity* showing whether city manufacturing employment size in 2004 was higher than the national median, and include in Regression 7 the interaction term of city size and cluster strength. Regression shows that compared to small cities, cluster effects in big cities are significantly stronger, implying that big cities have stronger aggregation effect. However, influences of initial industry strength are not significant difference among cities with different sizes. We also tried other definitions of big cities such as using different thresholds including the 75th or 90th percentile of employment sizes of all cities across the country, the main results did not change. When city-cluster strength is interacted with the city's initial employment size, regression results still show that cluster effects are stronger in larger cities. To save space, these regression results are not presented.

Finally, in Regressions 8 and 9, we extend the definition of related industries. On the one hand, manufacturing industries with the same two-digit industry code may be clustered together due to similar product characteristics, and thus may capture parts of the cluster effect. In Regression 8, we define related industries as all four-digit code industries within the same two-digit code industry, and construct the strength index *Industry2d_Str* of the two-digit code manufacturing industry to which the industry belongs according to Equation (7.4). The numerator is the employment share of the industry at the two-digit code level in the city's manufacturing employment, with the employment of industry i at the four-digit code level excluded. The subscript d represents the two-digit code industry. The denominator is the national employment share of the two-digit code industry (with employment of industry i excluded). On the other hand, industry employment growth may be affected by the development of all industries within the same city, not just industries within the same cluster. Delgado *et al.* (2014) confirmed that within-city concentration of related industries has significantly positive effects on industry employment growth. Therefore, we construct a more generalized index *RelatedInd_Str* following Equation (7.5). The numerator is the weighted sum of employment of all other manufacturing industries in the city, divided by city manufacturing employment. The weight ω_{ij} is the correlation coefficient of city-industry employment between industries i and j. For industry i in city r, other industries with higher relatedness in the city will have greater impacts on its employment growth, so they should be given higher weights. However, spillover effects between unrelated industries may be very small or even negative, and a negative correlation coefficient indicates substitution or competition effects between the two industries. The denominator of Equation (7.5) is the employment share of related industries at the national level. The results of Regressions 8 and 9 show that city-industry employment growth is significantly affected by the initial development of related industries. However, even after controlling spillover effects among other related industries, clusters still have significantly positive effects on city-industry employment.

$$Industry2d\_Str_{(-i)cr} = \frac{Emp_{(-i)dr}}{Emp_r} \Big/ \frac{Emp_{(-i)d}}{Emp} \quad \ldots\ldots \qquad (7.4)$$

$$RelatedInd\_Str_{ir} = \frac{\sum_{j \neq i}\left(\omega_{ij} \cdot Emp_{jr}\right)}{Emp_r} \Big/ \frac{\sum_{j \neq i}\left(\omega_{ij} \cdot Emp_j\right)}{Emp} \quad \ldots\ldots \qquad (7.5)$$

7.3 Clusters and Industry Development: Quantity Effect vs. Quality Effect

Results in the second section show that, due to the agglomeration effect, cluster development does significantly promote industry employment growth. Furthermore, we hope to analyze how cluster development affects industrial employment. Theoretically, the expansion of industry employment mainly comes from the creation of new firms or the employment expansion of existing firms. Table 7.3 examines the impact of cluster development on the number of urban industrial firms and the growth of firm employment size. Among them, the dependent variable in Regressions 10 and 11 is the increase in city-industry's number of industrial firms from 2004 to 2009.[1] Corresponding to the dependent variable, in Regressions 10 and 11, we construct indexes of initial strength of industries and clusters by using city-industry's number of firms instead of employment following Equations (7.2) and (7.3). Regression results show that, similar to city-industry employment growth, the growth of the number of firms in a city-industry also shows an obvious convergence trend, and the initial development of city-industry significantly inhibits future creation of new firms. Cluster development significantly promotes increases in the number of firms. On average, every one standard deviation increase in initial cluster strength above the mean would raise average annual growth rate of firm number by 2.165 percentage points. Regressions 12 and 13 further examine the impact of cluster development on firm size. We use city-industry level average employment size of firms as the measure of city-industry's firm size, and construct variables of city industry strength and cluster strength using employment data. According to the regression results, the development of industrial clusters significantly promotes the expansion of firm sizes in the future. In addition, the growth of firm size is consistent with the conditional convergence model.

In addition to city-industry employment, city-industry output values or sales can also be considered as quantity measures of industrial development. Therefore, in Regressions 14 and 15 of Table 7.4, we construct the growth model of city-industry output values or sales. The basic structure of the model is similar to Equation (7.1), except that the dependent variable is replaced by the first-order difference of the natural logarithm of

---

[1] We use above-scale industrial firm data in this chapter, so entries and exits of small firms with prime operating revenue lower than 5 million yuan are not included.

Table 7.3. Industrial Cluster and the Development of Urban Industries

Explanatory Variables	Regression 10 ΔlnFirm	Regression 11 ΔlnFirm	Regression 12 ΔlnSize	Regression 13 ΔlnSize
ln(Industry_Str)	−0.1484***	−0.2057***	−0.1851***	−0.2416***
	(0.0082)	(0.0062)	(0.0063)	(0.0083)
ln(Cluster_Str)	0.1087***	0.1288***	0.0593***	0.0522***
	(0.0057)	(0.0058)	(0.0046)	(0.0046)
City FE	No	Yes	No	Yes
Industry FE	No	Yes	No	Yes
Observations	32,314	32,314	32,286	32,286
R^2	0.0545	0.2767	0.1058	0.2212

Note: *, **, and *** respectively denote significance at 10%, 5%, and 1%. Robust standard errors clustered at city level are in parenthesis.

city-industry output values or sales. Regression results show that the development of clusters can still explain city-industry output or sales growth. To sum up, the above results show that from the perspective of quantity performance, industrial clusters, with the agglomeration effect as its main mechanism, do play a significant and robust role in promoting industrial development.

Then, will the quantity effect of clusters come along with quality reductions as a sacrifice? Existing theoretical and case studies on cluster effect found that the successful development of industrial clusters needs to go through three stages including quantity-oriented expansion, quality-oriented improvement, and R&D and brand innovation. Quality crises and the change of regional comparative advantage are the main reasons for industrial clusters' pushing forward along the three stages. Based on the case analysis of industrial clusters such as the woolen sweater cluster in Puyan and the cluster of lamp in Wenzhou, Ruan Jianqing *et al.* (2014) found that race-to-bottom competition among firms in clusters, and the local government's inattention to product quality and brand innovation are mainly responsible for clusters' failures in promoting product quality in China. Quantity expansion without quality improvement will eventually inhibit the further development of industrial clusters or even lead to the extinction of clusters due to crowding-out effects and changes in regional comparative advantages. Therefore, in Table 7.4, variables including

Table 7.4. Clusters and Industry Development: Quantity Effect vs. Quality Effect

Explanatory Variables	Regression 14 ΔlnOutput	Regression 15 ΔlnSales	Regression 16 ΔlnWage	Regression 17 ΔlnOutputPC	Regression 18 ΔlnSalesPC
ln(Industry_Str)	−0.2738***	−0.2757***	0.0188***	0.0148***	0.0130***
	(0.0081)	(0.0082)	(0.0028)	(0.0042)	(0.0043)
ln(Cluster_Str)	0.1027***	0.1005***	−0.0027	−0.0092*	−0.0112
	(0.0077)	(0.0078)	(0.0029)	(0.0050)	(0.0050)
Initial_DepVar			−0.0119***	−0.0008***	−0.0008***
			(0.0037)	(0.0001)	(0.0001)
City FE	Yes	Yes	Yes	Yes	Yes
Industry FE	Yes	Yes	Yes	Yes	Yes
Observations	32,057	32,068	32,723	32,057	32,068
R^2	0.2503	0.2507	0.2205	0.2598	0.2584

Note: *, **, and *** respectively denote significance at 10%, 5%, and 1%. Robust standard errors clustered at city level are in parenthesis.

wages, output per worker, and sales per worker are used as dependent variables measuring the quality of city-industry development, and influences of cluster development are investigated. Regression 16 studies the impact of cluster development on workers' wages. City-industry wage level is calculated by dividing the total amount of wage payables by total employment. As data of wage payables are missing for the years 2008 and 2009, we study the impact of cluster development on wage changes from 2004 to 2007 only. Different from model (7.1), we include in regressions variables showing city-industry initial levels of quality to capture the convergence effect of industrial development concerning quality. In Regression 16, the convergence effect is captured by the coefficient of initial wage level variable, showing that higher initial wages may restrain future wage growth. The influence of city-industry initial employment strength on wages is generally used as a measure of localization effect in literature. The results of Regression 16 show that with higher initial wage levels, city-industry's future wage growth tends to decline, indicating the existence of convergence effect concerning wages. Consistent with existing literature, the increase of initial employment strength in city-industry significantly promotes wage growth, thus providing evidence for the localization effect.

However, cluster effects on industrial wage growth are not significant. Regressions 17 and 18 examine the impact of cluster development on the growth of output per worker and sales per worker, respectively. Cluster effects are found to be significantly negative or insignificant, which indicates that, compared with industries in city-clusters with lower initial levels of development, growth rates of output per worker and sales per worker of industries in strong clusters are relatively lower, and clusters do inhibit firms from moving to higher positions along the industry value chain.

7.4 Industry Value Chain Positions and Heterogeneous Cluster Effects

The division of labor in production along the industry value chain is an important feature of this round of globalization. Economic activities in different regions and industrial clusters are located at different positions in the global value chain, and are affected by globalization and new economic geographical factors differently. The analysis in Section 7.2 focuses on cluster effects on employment growth. In this section, we will further explore heterogeneous cluster effects across industries with different positions in the industry value chain.

In theory, cluster development will have different impacts on industries with different value chain positions due to differences in the forward and backward linkages. Input–output relationships between industries can be classified as forward linkage or backward linkage. Forward linkage means that industrial development will benefit from the concentration of upstream intermediate product providers, while backward linkage reflects the benefits brought by the concentration of downstream firms or consumers (Redding, 2011). Forward linkage promotes labor productivity of manufacturers mainly through availability of intermediate inputs with higher quality and lower cost. Backward linkage can be realized through mechanisms such as direct knowledge spillovers, higher product quality requirements for upstream suppliers, and higher demand for intermediate inputs.

However, there is no conclusive evidence on the existence and magnitude of forward or backward linkages. López and Südekum (2009) found that the spillover effect between industries mainly came from the concentration of upstream intermediate product providers, but they did not find spillover effects from the concentration of downstream industrial firms on the labor productivity of upstream firms. Unlike López and Südekum (2009), Javorcik (2004) found that FDI promoted the labor productivity of domestic firms. On the one hand, local firms could improve labor productivity by learning from FDI firms and employing workers from multinational firms. On the other hand, entries of FDI would intensify market competition, forcing domestic firms to improve labor productivity. In addition, they found that the effect of FDI on the labor productivity of domestic firms was mainly realized through backward linkage, while effects of forward linkage or horizontal spillovers within the same sector were insignificant or even significantly negative. This is mainly because local firms and FDI in the same sector compete in raw materials, consumer markets, and other aspects, and multinational companies have incentives to reduce technology leakage and knowledge spillover. However, for upstream input industries, efficiency improvements of intermediate input suppliers would benefit downstream firms, reducing FDI's incentives to prevent knowledge spillovers. Therefore, cluster effects on the employment growth of industries at different value chain positions might be different.

In Section 6.4, we constructed the upstreamness index reflecting industries' positionings in the industry value chain following Antràs *et al.* (2012), and found that the upstreamness indexes based on closed economy assumption or open economy assumption are not distinctly different. Therefore, in this section, we will mainly use the industrial upstreamness index based on the open economy assumption. After calculating the upstreamness index of the cluster, in order to reflect an industry's relative position in the value chain compared to the upstreamness of the cluster to which it belongs, we calculate the difference between the upstreamness of the industry and the average upstreamness of the cluster, and use it as a measure of the industry's relative upstreamness within the cluster. The higher the value of relative upstreamness, the more upstream the industry is compared with the cluster it belongs to. The significant influence of industrial clusters on the labor market performance of relative downstream industries will provide evidence for the existence of forward linkage. On the contrary, its significant influence on the labor market performance of relative upstream industries confirms the backward linkage effect.

To investigate heterogeneities of cluster effects on employment growth of industries with different relative value chain positions, all industries are divided into three groups according to their relative upstreamness in the cluster. Table 7.5 reports the influence of cluster strength on employment of industries with different relative upstreamness with all the other factors controlled. Regression 19 studies cluster effects on industries with relative downstream positions. The regression results show that the growth of initial cluster strength significantly promotes the employment growth of downstream industries. On average, every 1% increase in initial cluster strength brings a 0.122% increase in employment of downstream industries. The development of industrial clusters also significantly promotes the employment of the upstream industries, with every 1% increase in the cluster strength raising city-industry employment by 0.124%. In addition, regression results show that although cluster effects on industries with similar value chain positions are significantly positive, the magnitudes of influences are relatively smaller. This may be because that input–output relationships between industries with similar value chain positions are weak, thus weakening forward and backward linkages and restraining cluster effects. Moreover, industries with similar value chain positions may compete with each other in the product market and input market, so that increases in initial cluster strength may crowd out employment in other industries by intensifying inter-industry competitions. Javorcik (2004) found that although FDI significantly promotes the labor productivity of domestic firms through backward linkage, due to the

Table 7.5. Heterogeneous Cluster Effects and Employment Growth

Explanatory Variables	Regression 19 Downstream	Regression 20 Horizontal	Regression 21 Upstream
ln(Ind Strength)	−0.3189***	−0.3278***	−0.3257***
	(0.0107)	(0.0141)	(0.0104)
ln(Cluster Strength)	0.1223***	0.0867***	0.1238***
	(0.0102)	(0.0117)	(0.0102)
Observations	12,033	7,279	12,974
R^2	0.3005	0.2905	0.2846
Industry FE	Yes	Yes	Yes
City FE	Yes	Yes	Yes

Note: *, **, and *** respectively denote significance at 10%, 5%, and 1%. Robust standard errors clustered at city level are in parenthesis.

competition for raw materials, consumption market and other aspects between domestic firms and FDI, the horizontal spillover effect of FDI in the same sector is small. Furthermore, we decompose industry employment growth into the creation of new firms and growth in firm employment size, and study cluster effects on industries with different relative upstreamness in Tables 7.6 and 7.7. The results are similar to the employment growth model. With the relative value chain positions of industries changing from more downstream to more upstream, impacts of the initial development of clusters on future firm number growth and firm size growth also presents a U-shaped change.

In order to confirm whether differences of cluster effects on industries with different value chain positions are significant, we introduce the interaction term of cluster strength and the industry's relative value chain position into regression, and interaction term regression results are displayed in Table 7.8. Using industries with medium relative upstreamness values as the benchmark, we construct the dummy variable *Downstream* to show whether the industry's relative upstreamness is in the lowest one-third and the dummy variable *Upstream* to show if it is in the top one-third. Dummy variables *Downstream* and *Upstream* are interacted with cluster strength respectively. The dependent variable in Regression 28 is employment growth of city industries. The regression result shows that the coefficients of the interaction terms are both significantly positive, indicating that

Table 7.6. Heterogeneous Cluster Effects and the Creation of New Firms

Explanatory Variables	Regression 22 Downstream	Regression 23 Horizontal	Regression 24 Upstream
ln(Ind Strength)	−0.2030***	−0.2066***	−0.2123***
	(0.0086)	(0.0110)	(0.0077)
ln(Cluster Strength)	0.1257***	0.1071***	0.1447***
	(0.0090)	(0.0115)	(0.0089)
Observations	12,041	7,289	12,984
R^2	0.2967	0.2616	0.2976
Industry FE	Yes	Yes	Yes
City FE	Yes	Yes	Yes

Note: *, **, and *** respectively denote significance at 10%, 5%, and 1%. Robust standard errors clustered at city level are in parenthesis.

Table 7.7. Heterogeneous Cluster Effects and Firm Employment Size

Explanatory Variables	Regression 25 Downstream	Regression 26 Horizontal	Regression 27 Upstream
ln(Ind Strength)	−0.2351***	−0.2556***	−0.2396***
	(0.0099)	(0.0121)	(0.0099)
ln(Cluster Strength)	0.0613***	0.0366***	0.0548***
	(0.0079)	(0.0092)	(0.0079)
Observations	12,033	7,279	12,974
R^2	0.2389	0.2598	0.2192
Industry FE	Yes	Yes	Yes
City FE	Yes	Yes	Yes

Note: *, **, and *** respectively denote significance at 10%, 5%, and 1%. Robust standard errors clustered at city level are in parenthesis.

Table 7.8. Heterogeneous Cluster Effects: Interactions in Regression

Explanatory Variables	Regression 14 ΔlnEmp	Regression 15 ΔlnFirm	Regression 16 ΔlnSize
ln(Industry_Str)	−0.3235***	−0.2058***	−0.2417***
	(0.0085)	(0.0062)	(0.0083)
ln(Cluster_Str)	0.0925***	0.1180***	0.0363***
	(0.0104)	(0.0104)	(0.0080)
ln(Cluster_Str) * Downstream	0.0310**	0.0215*	0.0201*
	(0.0135)	(0.0126)	(0.0110)
ln(Cluster_Str)* Upstream	0.0286**	0.0077	0.0245**
	(0.0131)	(0.0119)	(0.0110)
City FE	Yes	Yes	Yes
Industry FE	Yes	Yes	Yes
Observations	32,286	32,314	32,286
R^2	0.2777	0.2768	0.2214

Note: *, **, and *** respectively denote significance at 10%, 5%, and 1%. Robust standard errors clustered at city level are in parenthesis.

compared with industries with similar value chain positions, cluster development has stronger effects on the employment growth of more upstream or downstream industries. Similarly, Regressions 29 and 30, respectively, examine the heterogeneous effects of industrial clusters on city-industry's number of firms and firm employment size. The results show that stronger positive effects of cluster development on employment growth of downstream industries come from both higher growth rates of firm number and employment size. However, compared with industries at similar value chain positions, cluster effects on the growth of firm number in more upstream industries are not significantly different. The heterogeneous cluster effects on employment growth mainly come from stronger cluster effects on firm size in the more upstream industries.

7.5 Summary

This chapter constructs city level cluster strength index, and investigates the influence of clusters on industrial development from perspectives of quantity and quality. In addition, heterogeneous influences of clusters on industries with different industry value chain positions are explored. It is found that there is a significant convergence effect in the growth of city-industry employment, and with the increase of initial industrial concentration, future employment growth of the industry will decline significantly. The development of urban industrial clusters will significantly promote employment growth through agglomeration effect. Every one standard deviation increase in initial cluster strength above the mean will raise average annual growth rate of industrial employment by 2.153 percentage points. Cluster effects on city-industry employment growth mainly come from the creation of new firms and employment expansion of existing firms. In addition, we also find that cluster development significantly promotes city-industry production sizes, no matter city-industry output values or total sales are used as measures. However, cluster effects on quality aspects of industry development are found to be insignificant or even significantly negative, "race to the bottom" competition among firms in clusters and the local government's inattention to goods quality might be reasons. In addition, this chapter explores heterogeneous cluster effects on employment growth of industries with different industry value chain positions. By constructing interaction effects between city-industry's relative upstreamness in the value chain and cluster development, we find that although employment promotion effects of clusters exist for industries with different value chain positionings, compared to relative upstream or downstream industries, industries with similar positions in the industry value chain as other industries in the same cluster benefit the least.

The results from this chapter show that the development of industrial clusters in China are still in the stage of quantity expansion at present, and the development of clusters has not yet brought improvement of industrial quality. However, with the intensification of competition and the reversal of regional comparative advantage, quantitative growth without quality improvements cannot be sustained. Possible quality crises may lead to the extinction of clusters. Therefore, based on the results of this chapter, to maintain long-term sustainable development of manufacturing industries and to promote industrial upgrading, industry and regional development policy of local government should aim at promoting agglomeration effect and quality-oriented industrial cluster growth.

First, place-based policies should be based on local industrial structures and comparative advantages to encourage complementarities between industries, and promote the development of key industries with strong spillover effects. One of the debates on place-based policies is whether local governments should prioritize the development of high-tech and high-value-added industries or develop industries that are closely related to the local economy based on the local industrial structure and comparative advantages. Our results show that the latter might be more effective. Cluster-based industrial policies which encourage the development of industries with stronger externalities may benefit all related industries through various forms of linkages, leading to the "big push" development of local industries.

Second, public policies which encourage research and development and brand innovation would promote the transition of industrial clusters from quantitative growth to quality-oriented growth and enhance regional industrial competitiveness. Cluster development may lower entry barriers of firms, leading to "race-to-bottom" competition among firms in the cluster. Potential quality crises may not only undermine sustainable growth of industries but also endanger cluster survivals. The empirical results of this chapter show that at present, China's development of industrial clusters is still in the stage of quantitative growth, and quality improvement has not been achieved. Case studies of Ruan Jianqing *et al.* (2014) on clusters in China show that local governments could support the development of clusters by improving public services and encouraging brand innovation so that competitive advantages of clusters could be fostered. In addition, the government can encourage technical training and motivate firms to improve product quality and promote the overall transition and upgrading of industrial clusters.

Third, regional development policies should complement place-based policies to improve inter-regional allocation efficiency of resources and strengthen the agglomeration effect. Agglomeration effect is a main driving force for the development of local industries, and its strength largely depends on the size of local economy or population. The empirical results in Table 7.2 show that stronger agglomeration effects in large cities would enhance cluster effects. However, current regional and labor market policies strictly limit the population growth of large cities, thus may reduce agglomeration effect. In the future, by reforms of household registration system and equalizing public services among regions, regional policies should be adjusted so that inter-regional flows of population could be promoted and resource allocation efficiency could be improved.

Chapter 8

Urbanization, Urban Development, and Structural Transformation

Chapter 7 examines the development of manufacturing industries in China from the perspective of industrial clusters. It is found that the development of industrial clusters will promote employment and output expansions of manufacturing industries through agglomeration effect. However, cluster effects on quality-based growth of industries are little. Then, what is the effect of economic agglomeration on the development of service industry? Results in Chapters 4 and 5 show that economic agglomeration effect will not only enhance employment probability of workers but also raise nominal income and real income of individuals. In particular, for low-skilled workers, their employment benefits from city expansions are the largest, and better development of consumer service industries in big cities is its main mechanism. To study economic agglomeration effect comprehensively, it is necessary to explore its impacts on city-industry structures. Based on city-level employment data, this chapter investigates employment multiplier effect of urban manufacturing jobs, and studies industrial structure transformation influenced by economic agglomeration in cities.

This chapter focuses on employment expansions in the service sector. Service economy is a typical characteristic of modern economy, and its development plays an important role in modern economic growth. Since the reform and opening up, thanks to the low labor cost and the resulting product competitiveness in the international market, China has adopted an export-oriented economic growth pattern. However, the unbalanced growth pattern results in both internal imbalances and external imbalances, undermining sustainable economic growth (Lu and Ou, 2011). The internal imbalance is mainly manifested as continuous increases in domestic income inequality. Widening income gaps lead to declines in GDP's consumption share, and investment and export then become the most important driving forces of economic growth. The external imbalance is reflected as China's rising exports and huge foreign currency reserves. On the one hand, under the law of diminishing marginal propensity to consume, high-income workers tend to save more. On the other hand, low-income workers also have strong incentives to save due to higher income risks, resulting in a higher household savings rate in China than in other countries with similar levels of development. Ravallion (1998) found that wealth inequality had significantly negative impacts on household consumption growth. Yang and Zhu (2007) also provided evidence that widening income gaps would inhibit consumption. The widening income gaps and the continuous decline of household consumption in China have led to weak domestic demand. Although investment can promote aggregate demand in the short term, in the medium and long term, the expansion of investment will lead to excess capacity. Together with weak domestic demand, excess capacity must be absorbed by external demand, leading to rising international trade dependence in China. The external imbalance can be a natural result of the internal imbalance of the economy.

Economic growth based on investment and export is not sustainable. In the long run, economic growth is mainly determined by capital accumulation, labor supply, and TFP growth. Thanks to China's high savings rate, capital accumulation contributed 85.4% to economic growth over the four decades since reform and opening up. However, savings rate in China has exceeded the golden rule level, and dynamic inefficiency of the macroeconomy would inhibit further rises of savings rate and reduce future capital accumulation rate. An aging population will reduce savings rate, reducing the rate of capital formation and investment. However, investment dominated by the government is unsustainable in the long run due to its lack of efficiency (Yuan Zhigang and Yu Yuxin, 2012). In particular, accumulation of local government debt restrains local governments' ability to invest. Therefore, long-run economic growth driven by capital accumulation cannot be sustained. As for labor force, with the aging of population and fading out of dividends from labor market reforms, labor cost tends to rise in the future. The gradual fading of demographic dividend increases China's labor costs, impairing the cost advantage of manufacturing industries in China, which may further lead to declines in exports (Wan Guanghua and Cai Fang, 2012). TFP, which is essential for endogenous economic growth, has also performed poorly since 2000. Dong Minjie and Liang Yongmei (2013) found that from 1978 to 1991, the contribution rate of TFP to economic growth was as high as 28.9% due to the institutional dividends brought by the land system reform in rural China and the establishment of a market-oriented economy. Thanks to a series of major reforms in China's labor market, foreign exchange market, financial system, fiscal system, and real estate market, the contribution rate of TFP further increased to 30.5% during 1991–2001. However, after 2001, TFP's contribution to economic growth declined significantly, with an average contribution rate being as low as only 1.9%. By studying TFP's contribution to economic growth rate in years from 2001 to 2010, Dong Minjie and Liang Yongmei (2013) found that TFP's contribution was significantly positive only at the early stage of China's entry into WTO, and then the contribution was close to 0, and even turned negative after 2008.

Changes in a series of fundamental structural factors such as capital, labor, and TFP lead to declines in long-term potential economic growth rate. Although the macroeconomy is challenged by long-term structural problems, the absence of new economic growth engines, obstacles to further structural adjustments, and great short-term growth and employment pressures make short-term stimulus economic policies the inevitable choice of the government. The Chinese economy has been increasingly more dependent on capital inputs rather than the forces of marketization and globalization, leading to rapid assets and liabilities expansions at the macro level. Especially after the 2008 financial crisis, challenged by shrinking external demand and weak domestic demand, the Chinese government launched the four-trillion-yuan stimulus plan to boost economic growth. Statistics show that since 2000, investment in infrastructure and real estate has become an essential driving force for economic growth, and aggregate investment in infrastructure and real estate and their shares in GDP have kept rising. In 2003, infrastructure investment and fixed asset investment in real estate and construction accounted for 6.06% and 10.24% of GDP respectively. By 2015, these shares reached 11.96% and 20.21%, respectively. The added value of the construction industry accounted for 6.9% of GDP in 2013, absorbing 16% of urban employment. Glaeser *et al.* (2017) found that in China, the growth rate of per capita housing stock was negatively correlated with regional initial income from 2000 to 2010, with the correlation coefficient reaching −0.45, while the correlation coefficient in the United States was only −0.29 in the same period. Housing stock grew faster in regions with lower initial levels of development, indicating that local governments with the worst economic performance are becoming more aggressive in using debt financing investment as tools to promote economic growth. It is urgent for China to find new growth engines, and shift from an investment- and export-led growth pattern to that driven by domestic demand. To boost domestic demand, the development of the service sector is the key.

The phase of investment and export-driven economic growth in China has ended. The Chinese economy is now entering the phase of growth based on economic efficiency, and urbanization and the development of service industry are important drivers. Service economy is a typical post-industrialization economic characteristic, which plays a vital role in the economic growth and employment in most industrialized countries. Schettkat and Yocarini (2003) found that all the developed countries in the world have entered the era of service economy, and the vast majority of new jobs in industrialized countries come from the development of the service industry. The service sector is becoming increasingly more important for economic growth and job creation in China. However, compared with other countries, the development of the service sector in China is significantly slower. Cheng Dazhong (2004) found that, compared with other countries with similar levels of development, the service sector in China has lower share of added values, lower employment share, and lower added value per worker. How to promote the development of the service sector further is an urgent and important issue for China.

However, encouraging the development of the service sector does not mean that we should sacrifice the development of manufacturing industries. In fact, in early stages of development, the service sector cannot grow without manufacturing industries. Manufacturing industries will directly produce the demand for producer services and promote their development. As the manufacturing sector grows, urban income rises, raising the demand for service consumptions, especially those can be regarded as market-substitutes for home production activities. Manufacturing spillovers to manual service industries would be stronger in areas with high concentrations of high-skilled workers. Studies have found that high-skilled workers have a relatively higher demand for low-skilled service products, and the resulting "consumption spillover" will create jobs in low-skilled service industries (Mazzolari and Ragusa, 2013). Our study in Chapter 4 also shows that economic agglomeration will bring job expansions in manual industries. To promote the development of service industries while maintaining prosperity in the manufacturing sector, influences of manufacturing employment on service employment need to be empirically investigated.

8.1 Place-Based Policies and Employment Multiplier Effect

The expansion of manufacturing employment will affect service employment through a variety of mechanisms. According to Moretti (2010) and Moretti and Thulin (2013), when the tradable sector of a city experiences a permanent increase in labor demand, wages and employment of the city will increase, resulting in a higher level of total income in the city. Increases in total income will lead to the expansion of demand for the non-tradable goods, increasing wages or employment in the non-tradable goods sector at equilibrium. Influences of manufacturing employment growth on service employment are regarded as the "employment multiplier effect". In addition, the development of manufacturing industries will directly generate demand for local producer services in cities. However, the employment multiplier effect of manufacturing industries is not necessarily positive. Employment growth in the manufacturing sector due to exogenous demand shocks will increase the overall wage level in cities, while higher wages may crowd out employment in other industries. The crowding-out effect is especially serious when local labor supply is inelastic. Moreover, distortions in resource allocations may offset the spillover effects of place-based policies across industries. Therefore, whether changes in manufacturing employment will promote or inhibit the expansion of service employment should be empirically investigated.

Apart from policy relevance, studies on how manufacturing employment affects service employment will contribute to the literature on place-based policies. Existing studies on place-based policies found that local government's efforts to attract manufacturing firms by implementing various preferential policies will not necessarily bring about the development of local economy, and effectiveness of place-based policies depend on the strength of agglomeration effect to a large extent. Kline's (2010) theoretical model confirmed that strong economic agglomeration effect is the necessary condition for place-based policies being effective at promoting local economy takeoffs and turning the local economy from a low-level equilibrium with low employment and low wages to a high-level equilibrium with relatively higher wage levels and larger employment sizes. In addition, measures taken by local governments to attract firms and investment tend to distort allocations of factors, resulting in inefficiency and deadweight loss of residents' welfare (Wilson, 1999; Glaeser, 2001). Empirical evidence on the effects of place-based policies are also mixed. However, place-based policies are common ways for local governments to promote local economic growth. "Competition for growth" among local governments in China is considered to be an important driver of economic growth for China after the tax reform in 1994. Therefore, more empirical evidence on the influences of place-based policies and their determinants should be provided.

The reason why existing evidence on the effects of place-based policies is mixed might be that heterogeneities in policy effects in different regions or under different economic structures are ignored. The effect of place-based policies will not only be influenced by agglomeration effects but might also be weakened by market inefficiencies and distortions in allocations of factors. In China, one of the important institutional distortions is the household registration (*hukou*) system, which hinders urbanization and economic agglomeration in China. Au and Henderson (2006) found that the *hukou* system in China hinders rural–urban mobility of labors, and has led to insufficient agglomeration of Chinese cities, resulting in huge efficiency losses. If the economic agglomeration effect is not given full play, local economy will always be stuck in a low-level equilibrium with low wages and employment, resulting in a large waste of resources. Therefore, to promote the effects of place-based policies, policy distortions must be reduced and economic agglomeration effects should be strengthened. This chapter not only investigates the average manufacturing employment multiplier effect but also further examines its heterogeneities across regions with different levels of urbanization or population sizes, so as to provide a more complete analysis of employment multiplier effect and a reference for the structural transformation in China.

This chapter studies the employment multiplier effect of manufacturing industries on service employment in urban labor market, and examines the heterogeneity of the multiplier effect among regions with different urbanization levels and city sizes. Regression results show that increases in urban manufacturing employment will promote the increase of local service employment. On average, for every 1% increase in urban manufacturing employment, the service employment increases by 0.397% on average, with the consumer service sector benefiting the most. In addition, we find that further urbanization and agglomeration in cities would promote the multiplier effect of manufacturing employment. However, in regions with low urbanization levels or small population sizes, manufacturing employment does not promote the expansion of services employment, but instead crowds out local service employment and inhibits the development of service industries.

Section 8.2 describes the data and models used. Section 8.3 empirically examines the impact of urban manufacturing employment on the employment of the service sector. Section 8.4 expands the model to study the impact of urbanization and changes in city size on the multiplier effect. The last section is conclusions and policy implications.

8.2 Data and Model Specification

In order to investigate employment multiplier effect, we constructed an industry-level employment panel data covering 286 prefecture level cities in China from 2003 to 2009 based the *China City Statistical Yearbook* from 2004 to 2010. The four municipalities that are directly under the administration of central government, including Beijing, Tianjin, Shanghai, and Chongqing, are not included in our regressions due to their particularity. Service industries in our study include transportation, warehousing and postal service, information transmission, computer services and software industry, wholesale and retail sales, accommodation, catering, finance, real estate, leasing and business services, scientific research, technical services and geological survey, water conservation, environment and public facilities management, education, health, social security and social welfare, culture, sports and entertainment, residents service and other services, as well as the public administration and social organization industries. These industries mainly serve the local needs of cities and are therefore determined by local economic conditions to a large extent. It should be noted that products of some service industries are often used as intermediate inputs, so can be classified as tradable goods and is not completely determined by the local demand of cities. In China, such tradable service industries are mainly concentrated in producer services (Lu and Xiang, 2012). However, since the development of producer services in

China is relatively low in levels, producer services are still localized and mainly serve the local demand of cities. Labor demand of producer services in China is also mainly determined by the development of manufacturing industries. Our core explanatory variable is manufacturing employment in cities.

In the first part of our empirical test, we will test whether changes in city manufacturing employment will have any impact on local service employment in cities, so as to provide empirical evidence from China for the effectiveness of place-based policies. According to the previous analysis, increases in manufacturing employment will increase employment and wages of the city. Higher wages and employment imply higher total incomes of the city, thus raising consumption demand for local services. At the same time, the development of manufacturing industry will generate demand for local producer services in cities directly, and thus the employment of producer services may also grow. However, when city labor supply is inelastic and economic agglomeration effect is not strong enough, growth in manufacturing employment may crowd out the employment of the service sector, thus offsetting the multiplier effect. In addition, the employment multiplier effect of manufacturing industries may be weakened by efficiency losses caused by policy distortions. Based city-industry level panel data, Equation (8.1) is estimated:

$$lnEMP_{sct} = \beta_0 + \beta_1 lnEMP_{mct} + \delta_t + (\eta_c + \varepsilon_{ct}) \tag{8.1}$$

Here, the dependent variable is the natural logarithm of employment in the service sector, subscript s means employment of the service data, and subscripts c and t represent city and year, respectively. On the right-hand side of the equation, $lnEMP_{mct}$ is the natural logarithm of city manufacturing employment, with the subscript m representing the manufacturing sector. Our study will focus on the sign and significance of β_1. If increases in manufacturing employment will lead to the expansion of service employment, β_1 would be significantly positive; otherwise, β_1 is insignificant or significantly negative. In addition, in all regressions, year fixed effects δ_t are controlled to remove national level service employment shocks. We also assume that employment in the service sector is affected by the unobservable city fixed effect η_c and the error term ε_{ct}.

8.3 Employment Multiplier Effect in the Local Labor Market: Empirical Results

Table 8.1 reports baseline regression results of the impact manufacturing employment growth on local service employment. Regression 1 is the ordinary least squares estimates. Results show that increases in city manufacturing employment have a significantly positive effect on local service employment, with an average increase of 0.445% in service employment for every 1% increase in manufacturing employment. Regressions 2 and 3 are random effects and fixed effects estimates respectively. Since city fixed effects may be correlated with local employment of manufacturing and service industries, random effects estimate of the model may be biased. Hausman test, with the Hausman statistic being 90.92, rejects the random effects estimates. In addition, in order to reduce the potential two-way causality problem between manufacturing employment and service employment, manufacturing employment with the lag of one year is used as the key explanatory variable in Regressions 4–6, and the estimates of ordinary least squares, random effects model, and fixed effects model are repeated. Regression results show that manufacturing employment growth still contributes significantly to the growth of service employment in the local labor market. Hausman test results also indicate that fixed effects estimates are more desirable in our study. Therefore, in all the subsequent regressions, fixed effects estimates will be used.

Table 8.1. Employment Multiplier Effect: Baseline Regression Results

Explanatory Variables	(1) Regression 1 OLS	(2) Regression 2 RE	(3) Regression 3 FE	(4) Regression 4 OLS	(5) Regression 5 RE	(6) Regression 6 FE
$lnEMP_{mct}$	0.445***	0.218***	0.183***			
	(0.00974)	(0.00942)	(0.00987)			
L1. $lnEMP_{mct}$				0.454***	0.155***	0.101***
				(0.0107)	(0.0106)	(0.0110)
Year FE	Yes	Yes	Yes	Yes	Yes	Yes
Observations	1,974	1,974	1,974	1,690	1,690	1,690

Note: *, **, and *** respectively denote significance at 10%, 5%, and 1%. Standard errors are in parenthesis.

Despite the use of fixed effects models, the results in Table 8.1 are likely to be biased. This is mainly because in estimating the multiplier effect of local manufacturing employment, not only manufacturing employment will promote the expansion of local service employment but also development of the service sector may in turn enhance labor productivity in the manufacturing sector, bringing about increases in manufacturing employment. Jiang Jing *et al.* (2007) found that in China, the development of producer services promoted manufacturing productivity. Every 1 percentage point increase in employment share of producer service industries will lead to an average 0.927% increase in labor productivity in the manufacturing sector. In addition, there may also be other factors of cities which may change over time and affect both manufacturing and service employment in the city, leading to omitted variable bias. Therefore, we further estimate the model using instrumental variables estimator. The instrumental variable we use is the export shock of a city in a given year, which is related to the city's level of manufacturing development in the initial year, its geographical location and export changes of the whole country. The instrumental variable is constructed as follows:

$$Export\ Shock_{ct} =$$

$$Exports_t * \frac{Employment\ Share\ of\ Manufacturing\ Industries\ in\ 2003}{Shorter\ Distance\ from\ Shanghai\ or\ Hongkong} \tag{8.2}$$

where, subscripts c and t stand for city and year, respectively. To be specific, since the performance of manufacturing industries in China is largely dependent on changes in external demand, city manufacturing employment will be affected by exports in the same year. The expansion of exports of the whole country will lead to increases in manufacturing employment across the country; conversely, a contraction in exports would reduce manufacturing employment. However, manufacturing employment in different cities is affected differently when national exports change. The influence of export change on a city's manufacturing industry will be influenced by the following two factors. On the one hand, if a city's manufacturing sector occupies a relatively more important position in the country, influences of export shock will be stronger. Many studies have confirmed the influence of a city's initial industrial development on its future labor demand (Bartik, 1991; Blanchard and Karz, 1992). Therefore, in this chapter, we take a city's share of manufacturing employment in national manufacturing employment in the initial year (2003) to measure its level of manufacturing development. On the other hand, coastal areas have geographic advantages of low transportation costs and industrial agglomeration (Jin Yu *et al.*, 2006), therefore changes in national exports will have greater impacts on areas close to seaport cities. Increases in exports will lead to increases in manufacturing output and employment, which can be realized through the expansion of productions by existing firms or the establishment of new firms. Agglomeration of manufacturing firms in coastal areas will reduce the production cost and improve labor productivity. To maximize profit, existing firms tend to expand production in coastal areas, while new firms also tend to locate in coastal areas. As a result, manufacturing employment in coastal areas will rise more significantly as exports increase. Jin Yu *et al.* (2006) found that China's industrial agglomeration mainly centered on the Yangtze River Delta and the Pearl River Delta. Here, we take a city's shorter distance from two major ports in China, Shanghai, and Hong Kong, as the measurement of the city's geographical advantage. Based on the analysis above, we construct the export shock variable as the instrument variable of city manufacturing employment according to Equation (8.2), which is positively correlated with country level total exports in year t and city c's national share of manufacturing employment in year 2003, but negatively correlated with the city's distance to the nearest major port.

Table 8.2 shows instrumental variable estimates for the fixed-effects model. Columns (1) and (3) are the first stage regression results, and Columns (2) and (4) are the instrumental variable regression results. In Regression 7, we obtain IV estimates of the multiplier effect of manufacturing employment on service employment in the same year. In Regression 8, both manufacturing employment and its instrumental variable with the lag of one year are used to partially reduce the estimation bias caused by reverse causality. First stage regression results show that city-level export shock has significantly positive effects on city manufacturing employment, with F-statistics values being 56.88 and 52.35, respectively, in Regressions 7 and 8, implying that the problem of weak instrumental variables is not obvious in our regressions.

The instrumental variable estimates in Table 8.2 identify the causal effects of city manufacturing employment growth on increases of local service employment. The expansion of manufacturing employment in cities will not only directly promote employment in producer service industries but also raise city residents' demand for local services, increasing

Table 8.2. Employment Multiplier Effect: Instrumental Variable Regression Results

	Regression 7		Regression 8	
	(1)	(2)	(3)	(4)
Explanatory Variables	First Stage	IV	First Stage	IV
Export Shock	0.241*** (0.0319)			
L1.Export Shock			0.224*** (0.0309)	
$lnEMP_{mct}$		0.494*** (0.0693)		
L1. $lnEMP_{mct}$				0.397*** (0.0718)
Year FE	Yes	Yes	Yes	Yes
Observations	1,952	1,952	1,673	1,673

Note: *, **, and *** respectively denote significance at 10%, 5%, and 1%. Standard errors are in parenthesis.

employment in the service sector. Moreover, rapid urbanization in China has led to large-scale rural-to-urban migrants, providing sufficient labor supply for cities. Therefore, crowding-out effects from increases in manufacturing employment are relatively small. The result of Regression 8 shows that every 1% increase in city manufacturing employment will bring about an increase of about 0.397% in services employment.

In Table 8.3, a series of robustness tests are performed. On the one hand, in order to avoid the possible non-stationarity in city employment data, we take the first-order difference for both the dependent variable and independent variables, and obtain instrumental variable estimates based on the differenced variables. The regression results are shown in Regression 9 of Table 8.3. Accordingly, the instrumental variable for changes in city manufacturing employment is obtained by dividing changes in national exports by the city's shorter from the two major ports, Shanghai and Hong Kong. Regression results show that estimates obtained by using first-order difference variables are similar to those obtained by using the instrumental variable fixed effects method.

Table 8.3. Employment Multiplier Effect: Robustness Test

	Regression 9	Regression 10	Regression 11	Regression 12
	(1)	(2)	(3)	(4)
Explanatory Variables	t	t	$t-1$	$t-1$
First stage#				
ΔExport Shock	0.00235***	0.00225***	0.00247***	0.00234***
	(0.000508)	(0.000522)	(0.000520)	(0.000534)
Second Stage				
$\Delta\, lnEMP_{mct}$	0.476***	0.513***	0.367***	0.435***
	(0.148)	(0.162)	(0.105)	(0.126)
Government Expenditure / GDP		0.0632		0.0597
		(0.0428)		(0.0378)
Invest / GDP		−40.19		163.5
		(161.2)		(176.5)
Year FE	Yes	Yes	Yes	Yes
Observations	2,529	2,494	2,247	2,212

Note: (1) # — The result of first stage is from regressions of the endogenous variables (changes in city manufacturing employment) on the instrumental variable and other control variables.
(2) *, **, and *** respectively denote significance at 10%, 5%, and 1%. Standard errors are in parenthesis.

Furthermore, we control in regressions city's GDP share of government expenditures and GDP share of fixed asset investment. Government expenditure is used as a proxy for government intervention. In theory, government intervention will promote local economic growth through the multiplier effect, and rises in city income will increase demand for service goods, thus leading to the expansion of employment in service industries. However, government intervention may also crowd out private investment and distort market mechanisms, thus reducing employment, especially employment in the service sector. Lu and Ou (2011) found that in China, local governments often prioritize the development of capital-intensive industries for tax considerations, weakening city's ability to create jobs. Similarly, fixed asset investment in cities could create more manufacturing jobs in cities. But cities with higher investment-to-GDP ratios are likely to have lower demand for services than cities where growth is more dependent on consumption, which in turn will hinder employment growth in the service sector. The results are shown in Regression 10 in Table 8.3, and our main conclusions remain unchanged. Moreover, the regression results show that neither government expenditure nor fixed asset investment has significant influences on service employment.

In Regressions 11 and 12, all explanatory variables are lagged one year. Results show that increases in manufacturing employment with the lag of one year will still have significantly positive effects on the employment of service industries, but the effect is smaller. Influences of government expenditure or fixed asset investment with the lag of one year is still insignificant.

The above analysis confirms the positive effect of manufacturing employment growth on local services employment, implying that local governments in China may implement place-based policies to promote local service industry employment growth through the development of manufacturing industries. So, are there any differences in the extent to which different types of service industries benefit from regional expansion of manufacturing employment? Moretti (2010, 2011) believed that the multiplier effect of manufacturing employment would be affected by the labor intensity of non-tradable goods sector. The more labor-intensive non-tradable goods sector has a greater spillover effect from employment growth. This is mainly because similar demand growth in cities requires more labor input in high labor-intensive sectors. In addition, the spillover effect of manufacturing employment on different service industries will also be influenced by market efficiency and labor mobility in that sector. Industries with higher market efficiency and greater mobility of labor will have more elastic labor supply, and are therefore easier to adjust employment in face of demand changes. In Tables 8.4 and 8.5, we divide service employment into three categories, including producer service, consumer service, and public service employment, and investigate the impact of manufacturing employment growth on the employment of different types of service industries. Among them, producer service industries mainly include transportation, warehousing and postal services, information transmission, computer services and software, financial services, leasing and commercial services, as well as scientific research, technical services, and geological survey. Consumer-service industries include wholesale and retail industry, accommodation, catering, real estate, residential services, and other services. Industries of water conservation, environment and public facilities management, education, health, social security and social

Table 8.4. Heterogeneous Employment Multiplier Effect (Fixed Effect Regression Results)

	(1)	(2)	(3)	(4)	(5)	(6)
	R13	R14	R15	R16	R17	R18
Explanatory Variables	Producer Service	Consumer Service	Public Service	Producer Service	Consumer Service	Public Service
$lnEMP_{mct}$	0.239***	0.548***	0.0359***			
	(0.0183)	(0.0271)	(0.00609)			
L1. $lnEMP_{mct}$				0.137***	0.344***	0.0259***
				(0.0201)	(0.0315)	(0.00646)
Year FE	Yes	Yes	Yes	Yes	Yes	Yes
Observations	1,974	1,974	1,974	1,690	1,690	1,690

Note: *, **, and *** respectively denote significance at 10%, 5%, and 1%. Standard errors are in parenthesis.

welfare, culture, sports and entertainment, and public administration and social organization departments are classified as public service.

Tables 8.4 and 8.5, respectively, report the fixed effect regression results and the instrumental variable regression results of the multiplier effect of manufacturing employment on employment of different types of service industries. Among them, first stage regressions of Table 8.5 are the same as Regression 8 in Table 8.2, both of which investigate the impacts of export shocks on city manufacturing employment. To save space, only second-stage regression results are reported. Instrumental variable estimates show increases in manufacturing employment significantly promotes the employment of all types of service industries, and the multiplier effect is smaller when manufacturing employment with the lag of one year is used. The multiplier effect is the largest in consumer service industries, while the multiplier effect in public service industries is the smallest. Larger benefits in consumer service industries are mainly results of higher labor-intensities there, and similar demand expansions in urban service industries will lead to greater employment growth in more labor-intensive industries. Chapter 4 confirmed that employment of low-skilled workers is highly concentrated in consumer service industries. We further investigate skill levels of different service sectors, and find that the education level of workers in the consumer service industry is relatively the lowest, with an average of 11.15 years of education,

Table 8.5. Heterogeneous Employment Multiplier Effect (Instrumental Variable Regression Results)

	(1)	(2)	(3)	(4)	(5)	(6)
	R19	R20	R21	R22	R23	R24
Explanatory Variables	Producer Service	Consumer Service	Public Service	Producer Service	Consumer Service	Public Service
$lnEMP_{mct}$	0.566***	0.891***	0.313***			
	(0.110)	(0.157)	(0.0507)			
L1. $lnEMP_{mct}$				0.418***	0.716***	0.254***
				(0.113)	(0.176)	(0.0471)
Year FE	Yes	Yes	Yes	Yes	Yes	Yes
Observations	1,952	1,952	1,952	1,673	1,673	1,673

Note: *, **, and *** respectively denote significance at 10%, 5%, and 1%. Standard errors are in parenthesis.

which is lower than the average of 12.58 years in producer service industries and 13.53 years in public service industries. As a result, low-skilled workers would benefit most from manufacturing development in cities. As for public service industries, compared with other types of service industries, with lower levels of marketization and labor mobility, the expansion of employment would be more difficult. Restrictions on employment expansion in the public service sector restrains supply growth of public services, resulting in the supply shortages and rising prices of public services.

8.4 Model Extensions: Urbanization, Economic Agglomeration and Heterogeneous Employment Multiplier Effect

In the previous regressions, we mainly examine the average effect of changes in manufacturing employment on employment in the service sector. As the effects of place-based policies can be influenced by economic agglomeration, labor supply elasticities, and other factors, we need to further investigate heterogeneities brought by structural characteristics of cities. Urbanization and city size might be important factors affecting the multiplier effect of manufacturing employment in China.

In theory, urbanization and city size will influence the employment multiplier effect through the following four channels. First of all, urbanization and the expansion of city sizes will promote economic agglomeration, enhancing labor productivity. As we have pointed out in Chapter 2, economic agglomeration will raise labor productivity and wages in cities through greater input sharing, better factor market matching, and more learning opportunities. Therefore, similar manufacturing employment growth will bring more substantial increases in wages and income levels in the regions with strong economic agglomeration effect, which in turn will bring higher demand for service consumption. Secondly, urbanization and city size also partly reflect differences in labor supply elasticities among cities. Low levels of urbanization or small city sizes may lead to a relative shortage of labor supply. In the case of inelastic labor supply, the expansion of city labor demand brought by manufacturing employment growth will lead to greater rises in city wage levels, partially crowding-out employment in other industries and offsetting the multiplier effect of manufacturing employment on service employment. When the crowding-out effect is strong enough, increases in manufacturing employment may even reduce service employment. Existing studies on industrial parks or defense industries have provided evidence for the existence of crowding-out effects (Bondonio and Engberg, 2000; Hooker and Knetter, 1999). Therefore, the development of the service industry is more likely to be restricted by labor supply shortages in cities with lower levels of urbanization or smaller sizes. Thirdly, as the development of the service sector relies on local consumer demand much, and minimum consumption is a prerequisite, increases in demand for service consumption do not necessarily imply supply expansions in cities with low levels of urbanization or population sizes. Finally, due to differences in consumption structures among urban residents, migrants, and rural residents, the progresses in urbanization will also influence the income elasticity of service demand, and thus affect the employment multiplier effect. According to Cheng Dazhong (2009), expenditures on services account for a relatively higher proportion in total income for urban residents compared with rural residents.

In the first panel of Table 8.6, based on the fifth national census data in 2000, all cities are divided into three groups according to their urbanization rates, and the multiplier effect of manufacturing employment on service employment in cities with different levels of urbanization is investigated. Urbanization is measured as the proportion of permanent urban population in the total population. To save space, we report only the coefficient and the standard error of manufacturing employment with the lag of one year. Each entry in Table 8.6 is a separate regression showing the employment multiplier effect of manufacturing industries at a given level of urbanization. The regression results show that only in the group with the highest urbanization rates, manufacturing employment has a significantly positive effect on service employment growth. In the most urbanized cities, a 1% increase in manufacturing employment leads to an average 0.345% increase in service employment. However, in cities with medium levels of urbanization, the influence of manufacturing employment on service employment is not significant. In cities with the lowest urbanization rate, the expansion of manufacturing employment does not promote the growth of local service employment, but exerts a significantly negative impact on service employment, which is mainly caused by reductions in public service employment. This is mainly because agglomeration effects in cities with lower levels of urbanization are generally weak. In addition, labor supply in low urbanized cities is insufficient. With constrained labor supply, increases in manufacturing employment will crowd out service employment.

In addition, we report the impact of urban manufacturing employment growth on changes of employment in different types of service industries, including producer service, consumer service, and public service. Results show that manufacturing employment has a significantly positive effect on employments of all types of service industries in cities with the highest urbanization rates. Changes in employment in consumer service industries is the greatest, mainly because consumer service industries are more labor-intensive and have lower entry barriers for labors. On average, every 1% increase in manufacturing employment leads to 0.496% employment growth in the consumer service sector. The impact of manufacturing employment growth on public service employment is relatively the smallest. This is mainly because employment in the public service sector is more influenced by local government policies and fiscal revenues, and its level of marketization is relatively low. Therefore, in face of increases in labor demand, growth in labor supply is slower. In cities with medium levels of urbanization rates, the influence of manufacturing employment on the employment in different types of service sectors is not significant. In cities with the lowest urbanization rates, the multiplier effect of manufacturing employment on service employment is significantly negative. On average, for every 1% increase in manufacturing

Table 8.6. Urbanization, Economic Agglomeration, and Heterogeneous Employment Multiplier Effect

Urbanization	Dependent Variable	Low	Medium	High
	Service Employment	−0.497**	0.114	0.345***
		(0.251)	(0.0989)	(0.0852)
	Producer Service	−0.443	0.194	0.456***
		(0.363)	(0.169)	(0.130)
	Consumer Service	−0.515	0.251	0.496***
		(0.507)	(0.301)	(0.183)
	Public Service	−0.316*	0.0424	0.216***
		(0.170)	(0.0464)	(0.0570)
Population	Dependent Variable	Small	Medium	Large
	Service Employment	−0.529**	0.475***	0.488***
		(0.218)	(0.131)	(0.0994)
	Producer Service	−0.384	0.554***	0.474***
		(0.276)	(0.201)	(0.153)
	Consumer Service	−0.951*	0.783***	0.652***
		(0.518)	(0.296)	(0.215)
	Public Service	−0.0775	0.351***	0.349***
		(0.0779)	(0.0908)	(0.0735)
Immigrants	Dependent Variable	Small	Medium	Large
	Service Employment	−0.803***	−0.00721	0.642***
		(0.302)	(0.114)	(0.137)
	Producer Service	−0.698*	−0.397*	0.570***
		(0.364)	(0.239)	(0.179)
	Consumer Service	−1.384**	0.0238	0.827***
		(0.642)	(0.340)	(0.265)
	Public Service	−0.226**	0.0893	0.492***
		(0.103)	(0.0607)	(0.109)

Note: *, **, and *** denote significance at 10%, 5%, and 1%, respectively. Each entry is a separate regression studying the employment multiplier effect of manufacturing industries on employment of the corresponding type of service industries, with city characteristics and year fixed effects controlled.

employment, public service employment in cities with the lowest urbanization rates is likely to fall by 0.316%.

So what effect does city size have on the manufacturing employment multiplier effect? In the regressions in the second and third panel in Table 8.6, we grouped all cities according to city population size or the number of immigrants, respectively, to investigate employment multiplier effect across cities of different sizes. It is found that it is only in regions with the largest populations that the expansion of manufacturing employment contributes significantly to local service employment growth. On average, every 1% increase in manufacturing employment leads to a 0.488% increase in services employment in these regions. However, in cities with the smallest population sizes, manufacturing employment has a significantly negative impact on local service employment. A 1% increase in manufacturing employment squeezes out an average of 0.529% service jobs. This indicates that the expansion of cities is indeed a prerequisite for manufacturing employment to promote employment in the service sector. In the absence of significant increases in urban population, the expansion of manufacturing employment will not promote employment growth in service industries due to lacks of economic agglomeration effect and labor supply, and may even crowd out service job opportunities and inhibit its development. When comparing the multiplier effect across cities of different sizes, we find that the multiplier effect of cities with medium-size population is similar to that of the cities with the largest populations.

Similarly, we separately examine the manufacturing employment multiplier effect on different types of service industries in cities with different population sizes. Regression results show that in cities with medium population sizes and in large cities, increases in manufacturing employment contribute significantly to the increase in services employment. The multiplier effect of manufacturing employment on service employment is the largest in medium-sized cities. This may be because larger cities adopt more strict measures to restrain the inflow of labor. In China, due to the stricter household registration restrictions in big cities, the proportion of people born in rural areas in big cities is significantly lower than that in small or medium-sized cities (Lu Ming, 2010). In addition, higher housing prices and living costs in big cities also discourage labor inflows. Therefore, the elasticity of labor supply in large cities is relatively lower, and the greater crowding-out effect offsets the benefits that may be brought by stronger economic agglomeration effects in large cities, reducing the manufacturing employment multiplier effect in large cities. Comparatively, the number of immigrants in cities may better reflect labor supply elasticity and economic agglomeration in cities.

Therefore, in the third panel of Table 8.6, we group all cities according to their immigrant numbers and repeat the analysis in Regression 8 of

Table 8.2. It is found that the multiplier effect of manufacturing employment on service employment is indeed the greatest in cities with the largest immigrant population. The influence of manufacturing employment on service employment is not significant in cities with medium-sized immigrant population. In cities with the fewest immigrants, manufacturing employment has a significantly negative impact on local service employment. When the heterogeneous employment multiplier effect on different types of service industries in cities with different migrant population are investigated, we find that, the expansion of manufacturing employment significantly promotes the increase of all types of service employment in cities with the largest immigrant sizes. However, in cities with medium immigrant population, the manufacturing multiplier effect on both consumer service and public service industries is not significant, and the employment of producer service industries is squeezed out marginally. In the cities with the smallest sizes of immigrants, manufacturing employment crowds out employment of all types of service industries.

8.5 Summary

Using the data from the *China City Statistical Yearbook* from 2004 to 2010 and the fifth national census of the People's Republic of China in 2000, this chapter examines the impact of urban manufacturing employment on local service employment and heterogeneous employment multiplier effect among cities with different urbanization rates and city sizes. The instrumental variable estimates of fixed-effects model show that increases in urban manufacturing employment will promote the increase of local service employment. On average, every 1% increase in urban manufacturing employment will lead to a 0.397% increase in service employment, among which the consumer service sector benefits the most. In addition, we also find that urbanization and city size have influences on the multiplier effect. Only in regions where urbanization and the size of cities reach a certain level, manufacturing employment will promote the growth of local service employment. Otherwise, employment growth in manufacturing industries will crowd out service employment.

The Chinese economy is going through a structural transformation from growth based on investment and export to a growth pattern more dependent on domestic demand, and the development of the service sector is the key to boosting domestic demand. Results in this chapter show that in China, although local government can promote the development of local service industry by developing manufacturing industries, the effect of place-based policies depends largely on the government's urbanization and urban development policies. The key to the effectiveness of place-based policies is whether urban economy can make full use of the benefits brought by economic agglomeration. Policies encouraging the development of manufacturing industries must be complemented by other regional development policies. However, the urbanization process in China is hindered by restrictions from the household registration system, which not only leads to cross-region inequalities in public services but also inhibits agglomeration effects, impairing economic growth efficiency.

The research in this chapter shows that low urbanization rate and insufficient economic agglomeration in cities restrain the spillover effect of manufacturing employment on service employment, impeding the development of service industries. To promote the transition of economic growth pattern in China, restrictions on the development of large and medium-sized cities should be restricted, so that the concentration of economic activities and population in big cities can be promoted. Only in this way will the development of service industries in China will benefit from the development of manufacturing industries to the greatest extent, and the growth in domestic demand will become a sustainable driving force for economic growth.

Chapter 9

Conclusions

9.1 Main Conclusions

The book systematically studies the effects of economic agglomeration on urban labor market performance and industrial development. Not only are the characteristics of the spatial distribution pattern of China's manufacturing industries and its determinants clarified, but the theoretical mechanisms through which economic agglomeration may affect the performance of urban labor market and industrial development are also explored. We find that economic agglomeration will promote labor productivity through the mechanisms of sharing, matching, and learning, leading to higher employment probabilities and incomes for workers in the agglomeration areas and promoting the development of manufacturing and service industries. However, we have not found evidence of economic agglomeration improving the quality of industrial development. Based on theoretical analysis and empirical test, the main findings of this book can be summarized in the following six aspects.

First, from the perspective of spatial distribution, factors including economic geography, new economic geography, and economic policies jointly shape the spatial distribution of China's manufacturing industry. The distribution map of China's manufacturing industry both as a whole and from the perspective of industrial clusters are depicted. In general, manufacturing industries in China are highly concentrated in the eastern coastal areas, but the trend of inward relocation has begun to emerge in recent years. Globalization and the geographical advantages in coastal areas have led to the initial concentration of manufacturing activities in the eastern region, and the spatial concentration of economic activities will promote labor productivity growth through the agglomeration effect. The concentration of manufacturing industry has been continuously strengthened under influences of new economic geography factors. However, with growing crowding-out effect and policies aiming at reducing inter-regional disparities, manufacturing industries are relocating to inland areas in recent years. The trends of dispersion vary among industries with different skill levels. Low-skilled industries are more sensitive to input costs of land, labor, and other factors, and benefit less from knowledge spillover, so have stronger incentives to move to inland areas. On the contrary, the concentration of high-skilled industries in the east has been strengthened because knowledge spillover effects are becoming increasingly more important in these industries. From the perspective of regional industrial clusters, we find that compared with the eastern coastal areas, the strength of industrial clusters in inland areas is relatively greater. The Eastern region has a more complete coverage of industries and a more diversified industry structure. Based on the 2004 economic census data and the 2002 input–output data, 480 four-digit code manufacturing industries in China are classified into 41 industrial clusters. Indicators such as city's employment share of the largest cluster, the Herfindahl–Hirschman Index of cluster employment, and the number of regional strong clusters are used to measure the diversification of regional manufacturing clusters. The results show that industrial clusters in the eastern region are more diversified. In addition, by studying the upstreamness of industrial clusters in different regions, we find that industrial clusters in the central and western regions have relatively higher levels of upstreamness, and local strong clusters are mainly concentrated in resource-intensive upstream industries.

Second, the book provides micro evidence for the fact that the expansion of cities helps improve labor market performance. With the expansion of cities, increases in labor supply will certainly intensify labor market competition. However, the economic agglomeration effect brought by urban development will also increase the labor demand of firms. When economic agglomeration effect is strong enough, rises in labor demand will offset the adverse effect from a more competitive labor market, promoting employment probabilities and incomes of workers. Using city population growth from 1953 to 1982 as the instrumental variable for current city size, individual-level employment and wage determination models are estimated. Instrumental variable regression results show that every 1% increase in city size will bring an average increase of 0.017–0.023 percentage points in individual employment probability, and an increase of 0.190% in nominal annual income and 0.189% in nominal hourly income of workers, respectively. Moreover, we find that the positive effects of city size on workers' incomes are not entirely offset by relatively higher prices in big cities. When nominal incomes are deflated by different price indexes, estimates show that every 1% increase in city sizes will raise real annual income and hourly income of workers by 0.084–0.143% and 0.083–0.142%, respectively.

Thirdly, having confirmed that economic agglomeration will promote the employment and income of workers, heterogeneous agglomeration effects on laborers with different incomes or skill levels are investigated. Regression results based on different skill groups show that growth in city sizes broadly promotes employment probabilities of workers with various skill levels. As laborers with different skills are employed in different industries, they are affected differently by city expansions. In general, those with the lowest skills benefit the most, while those with the highest skill levels benefit the least. This is mainly because employment of the least-educated workers tends to be concentrated in low-skilled consumer service industries, and rapid employment growth in consumer service industries is a significant feature in city expansions. In addition, quantile regression is used to investigate heterogeneous influences of city size on individual income. Similar to employment, we also see the general positive effect of city expansion on incomes of workers with different income levels. However, workers with the lowest income levels have benefited the least. This is mainly because that employment of low-income workers is highly concentrated in low-skilled consumer service industries, whose productivity growth are slower and benefits from human capital externalities in large cities are smaller. Combining the empirical results of heterogeneous economic agglomeration effect on employment and income of workers, we find that all workers benefit broadly from the economic agglomeration effect; the greatest benefit that city expansion brings for low-skilled and low-income workers is mainly more job opportunities, while the high-skilled and high-income workers in big cities will get greater income growth.

Fourthly, industrial clusters have significantly positive effects on the expansion of manufacturing industries, while their influences on quality aspects of industry development are insignificant. The book provides a definition of manufacturing clusters in China, and classifies 480 four-digit code level manufacturing industries into 41 clusters, which has the advantages of high within-cluster inter-industry relatedness, strong between-cluster differentiation and robustness. Based on the industrial cluster configuration, a city-industry level employment growth model is constructed, and influences of the initial development of city industries clusters on future employment growth are investigated. Regression results show that the cluster effect significantly promotes industrial employment growth, and this employment expansion comes simultaneously from the creation of new firms and employment growth of the existing firms. However, due to race-to-bottom competition among firms and the local government's inattention to goods quality and brand building, influences of clusters on the growth of city-industry wage levels or output per worker are insignificant or even significantly negative.

Fifthly, heterogeneous cluster effects are investigated. By introducing interaction terms between cluster strength and city size or industry upstreamness into regressions, we find that the positive effect of clusters on employment growth is significantly higher in large cities than in medium-sized or small cities due to the stronger agglomeration effect. However, influences of city-industry's initial strength on future employment growth are not significantly different across cities of different sizes. From the perspective of industry value chain positions, we find that initial cluster development significantly promotes the employment growth of all industries at different value chain positions. However, compared with relative upstream or downstream industries, industries at similar value chain positions as other industries within the same cluster benefit significantly less from cluster development. This is mainly because the forward and backward linkages between industries at similar value chain positions are relatively weaker, and competitions in the product and input markets are more intense.

Finally, the multiplier effect of urban manufacturing employment on the employment growth of service industries and the role of agglomeration effect are studied. Since the expansion of manufacturing employment will lead to increases in local income, city service demand will thus be expanded and more job opportunities will be created. Regression results showing increase in city manufacturing employment will significantly promote the increase of local service employment. On average, every 1% increase in manufacturing employment will lead to 0.397% increase in service employment. By comparing the employment multiplier effect of manufacturing industries across different types of service industries, we find that compared with industries of producer services and public services, the consumer service sector with relatively higher labor intensity gains the greatest benefit. In addition, we focus on the role of economic agglomeration in the employment multiplier effect, and find it to be significantly affected by urbanization rate and population of the city. Only in cities with high urbanization rates or large city sizes will manufacturing employment significantly promote the growth of local service employment. Otherwise, increases in manufacturing employment will crowd out service employment.

9.2 Inclusive Growth and Coordinated Development among Regions

Improving allocation efficiency of economic resources and giving full play to the agglomeration effect will become important driving forces for China's sustained economic growth. How to promote the inclusiveness of economic growth so that the public will benefit broadly from economic prosperity is a major strategic issue challenging China, and labor market performance will be an important perspective. Economic growth of a country is "inclusive" and meaningful only if it actually enhances welfares of individuals by improving their labor market performance.

The book provides references for urbanization and regional development policies from the perspectives of labor market performance and industrial development. The Chinese economy is challenged by a series of structural factors, such as population aging and declining capital accumulation rate, and long-term potential growth rate tends to decline. In the short term, declines in exports, inefficiencies in local government-led investment and the resulting local government debt risk, all require transition of economic growth model in China from the one based mainly on investment and exports to the one more dependent on domestic demand expansion and improvement of total factor productivity. Urbanization has become a pivotal stimulus for domestic demand in China. However, urbanization based on extensive urban construction and expanding land area is inefficient, and urbanization without concentration of labors and industries cannot promote the structural transformation and upgrading of the local economy. Large-scale constructions of new towns are inefficient, leading to a huge waste of resources and heavy debt burdens of local governments (Chang Chen and Lu Ming, 2017). Efficient urbanization should come from the concentration of labors and industries, and the concentration of economic activities in cities will greatly increase labor productivity through the agglomeration effect, thus providing sustainable impetuses for economic growth in China. In addition, since TFP contributes more to economic growth in the eastern region than in the central and western regions (Liu Ruixiang, 2013), structural reallocation of production factors among regions will also be a feasible way to restart TFP growth (Perkins and Rawski, 2008).

A common misunderstanding about urban and regional development is to equate "coordinated development between regions" with "synchronized development between regions" and to further contrast "economic agglomeration" with "coordinated development between regions". In terms of policies, the government has endeavored to narrow the development gap between different regions and cities of different sizes, so as to balance the welfare of residents in different regions and cities. By studying the impact of economic agglomeration on individual's labor market performance and urban industrial development, this book provides support for urbanization patterns that promote economic agglomeration and encourage the development of large cities. We believe that the urbanization pattern aimed at promoting agglomeration effect will not only contribute to the improvement of labor productivity and provide a sustainable impetus for economic growth but also enable workers to actually benefit from urbanization through better job opportunities and higher income levels in agglomeration areas. In addition, our study provides empirical evidence for the existence of economic agglomeration effect in China, indicating that economic growth in China will enjoy again the dividend of TFP growth by improving allocation efficiency of production factors across regions and encouraging the further concentration of population and economic activities in big cities, so that the benefits brought by economic agglomeration effect can be fully reaped.

In addition, the book provides implications for regional economic development and the formulation of place-based policies in China from the perspective of industrial development. The development of the manufacturing sector is critical to sustaining China's economic growth and promoting employment expansion. In the short term, the manufacturing sector is the most important source of employment. Premature deindustrialization may not only lead to declining economic growth rate and the loss of jobs but also increase income inequality. Furthermore, manufacturing employment growth plays essential roles in the development and employment expansion of the service sector. In the long run, as R&D investment of a country's business sector mainly comes from the manufacturing sector, a shrinking manufacturing sector may lead to declines in R&D investment, which will further weaken labor productivity and innovation capability of the country (Veugelers, 2013; Rodrik, 2016; and others). Therefore, how to give full play to the agglomeration effect and to promote the rapid and high-quality development of manufacturing industry through raising spatial allocation efficiency of economic activities is a strategic problem that needs to be solved in China. By investigating the role of industrial clusters in the development of manufacturing industries, the book confirms the effectiveness of policies based on local industry structures to encourage the development of industries with stronger local relatedness and to strengthen the role of complementary effects between industries. The research shows that the spatial distribution of industries and the implementation of place-based policies should aim at promoting economic agglomeration effect, which is a prerequisite for the effectiveness of place-based policies. In terms of specific policy operations, the book identifies the role of industrial clusters in promoting job growth in manufacturing industries, implying that regional and place-based policies should be based on the understanding of local industrial structure and inter-industry linkages of the city.

For service industry development considerations, strengthening employment multiplier effect of manufacturing industries requires appropriate urbanization and regional development policies, the key of which is to enhance economic and population agglomeration. At present, China is in a stage of gradual transformation from an industrialized society to a post-industrialized society, and the economy of a post-industrialized society will be dominated by service industries. Population aging and rising labor costs will weaken the competitiveness of the manufacturing industry, enhancing the importance of service industries in future economic growth and employment expansion. In recent years, a general trend in developed countries is the concentration of employment in the service sector. Not only jobs in the high-skilled service industries such as finance, lawyers, and medical care have expanded, but jobs in low-skilled consumer service industries such as security and catering have also increased significantly. This book provides implications for promoting economic structural transformation and creating jobs in the service sector from the perspective of economic agglomeration. The multiplier effect of manufacturing employment on service employment is positive only when the economic agglomeration effect is strong enough. Moreover, service industries with stronger elasticities of labor supply and higher degrees of marketization will benefit more from the expansion of manufacturing employment. Therefore, regional development policies should endeavor to reduce barriers of labor mobility among regions and industries, increasing the elasticity of labor supply and the concentration of population.

Choosing the right pattern of urbanization is a challenge facing all countries in the process of economic development. In China, there are debates about whether the development of large cities or small and medium-sized towns should be given priority in development. Local governments and urban residents always tend to support policies restraining population growth in large cities, resulting in insufficient population concentration and loss of efficiency. This book emphasizes the role of economic agglomeration in labor market performance and industrial development. Measures hindering economic agglomeration will not only be detrimental to economic efficiency but also harm the welfare of workers due to their negative impacts on worker incomes and employment, and restrain industrial development. In fact, the development of large cities and that of small and medium-sized towns are not contradictory against each other. In development, small towns can fully enjoy the benefits of spillover effects from large cities (Xu Zheng *et al.*, 2010). Economic agglomeration does not necessarily lead to enlarging inter-regional disparities. By encouraging the free flow of production factors across regions, China can achieve the goal of "balance in agglomeration" (Lu Ming and Chen Zhao, 2007) and realize coordinated development among regions.

9.3 Prospects for Future Researches

This book theoretically and empirically clarifies mechanisms through which economic agglomeration may affect urban labor market performance and industrial development, enriches the existing literature on new economic geography and labor economics, and provides implications for the improvement of future urban and regional development policies. However, there are still many unsolved problems concerning agglomeration effect and industrial clusters, which deserve more studies in the future.

First, the book focuses on possible benefits that economic agglomeration effect can bring about from the viewpoints of labor market performance and industry development. However, the influences of economic agglomeration in such aspects as traffic congestion, environmental pollution, and crimes which are directly related to the welfare of urban residents are not taken into account. In future studies, welfare consequences and crowding-out effect of agglomeration effect can be further investigated.

Second, the book only studies the impact of cluster development on the quantity and quality perspectives of industry development, determinants of the evolution of urban industrial clusters are not explored. The first nature advantage of a city, the input–output linkages between industries, the sharing of labor market and knowledge spillover effect will lead to the spatial concentration of related industries and the formation of industrial clusters. However, these factors' roles in the formation and development of China's industrial clusters are not clear empirically. Investigating the determinants of industrial cluster development should be a promising direction for future studies of both theoretical and policy importance.

Third, this book only examines the impact of economic agglomeration on local labor markets in cities, rather than the spillover effects between different cities. As urbanization rate reaches a high level, the development of city clusters and the optimization of urban system will become a new growth engine for China. How to coordinate urban development and build city clusters with efficiency and international competitiveness will largely determine China's growth potential. In fact, the spillover effect between cities is an important reason for the existence of city clusters. The three metropolitan areas, including the Yangtze River Delta, the Pearl River Delta, and Beijing–Tianjin–Hebei, are playing increasingly more important roles in urban and regional development in China. Our study highlights the benefits of economic agglomeration from the development of large cities. However, we also point out that the development of large cities and the development of small and medium-sized towns are not contradictory with each other but are mutually dependent. However, issues such as the spatial structure of industries and the coordinated development of industries among cities within the same city cluster are not covered in our book.

References

English

Acemoglu, D., 1996, "A Microfoundation for Social Increasing Returns in Human Capital Accumulation," *Quarterly Journal of Economics*, Vol. 111, No. 3: 779–804.

Acemoglu, D., 1998, "Why Do New Technologies Complement Skills? Directed Technical Change and Wage Inequality," *Quarterly Journal of Economics*, Vol. 113, No. 4: 1055–1089.

Acemoglu, D. and D. Autor, 2010, "Skills, Tasks and Technologies: Implications for Employments and Earnings," in *Handbook of Labor Economics* (O. Ashenfelter and D. E. Card eds.), Amsterdam-Elsevier, 4.

Ades, A. and E. Glaeser, 1995, "Trade and Circuses: Explaining Urban Giants," *Quarterly Journal of Economics*, Vol. 110, No. 1: 195–227.

Alfaro, L., P. Antràs, D. Chor, and P. Conconi, 2019, "Internalizing Global Value Chains: A Firm Level Analysis," *Journal of Political Economy*, Vol. 127, No. 2.

Ali, M., J. Peerlings, and X. Zhang, 2014, "Clustering as an Organizational Response to Capital Market Inefficiency: Evidence from Microenterprises in Ethiopia," *Small Business Economics*, Vol. 43, No. 3: 697–709.

Antràs, P., D. Chor, T. Fally, and R. Hillberry, 2012a, "Measuring the Upstreamness of Production and Trade Flows," *American Economic Review: Papers and Proceedings*, Vol. 102, No. 3: 412–416.

Au, C. and V. Henderson, 2006, "Are Chinese Cities Too Small?" *Review of Economic Studies*, Vol. 73, No. 3: 549–576.

Audretsch, D. and M. Feldman, 2004, "Knowledge Spillovers and the Geography of Innovation," in *Handbook of Regional and Urban Economics* (J. Henderson and J. Thisse eds.), North Holland, 4.

Autor, D. H. and D. Dorn, 2013, "The Growth of Low Skill Service Jobs and the Polarization of the U.S. Labor Market," *American Economic Review*, Vol. 103, No. 5: 1553–1597.

Autor, D., H. Levy, and R. Murnane, 2003, "The Skill Content of Recent Technological Change: An Empirical Exploration," *Quarterly Journal of Economics*, Vol. 118, No. 4: 1279–1333.

Barbieri, E., M. Tommaso, and S. Bonnini, 2012, "Industrial Development Policies and Performances in Southern China: Beyond the Specialised Industrial Cluster Program," *China Economic Review*, Vol. 23, No. 3: 613–625.

Barro, R. and X. Sala-i-Martin, 1991, "Convergence across States and Regions," *Brookings Papers on Economic Activity*, Vol. 22, No. 1: 107–182.

Bartik, T. J., 1991, "Who Benefits from State and Local Economic Development Policies?" MI: W.E. Upjohn Institute for Employment Research.

Bianchi, G., 1998, "Requiem for the Third Italy? Rise and Fall of a Too Successful Concept," *Entrepreneurship and Regional Development*, Vol. 10, No. 2: 93–116.

Blanchard, O. and L. Katz, 1992, "Regional Evolutions," *Brookings Papers on Economic Activity*, Vol. 23, No. 1: 1–75.

Bleakly, H. and J. Lin, 2012, "Thick-Market Effects and Churning in the Labor Market: Evidence from U.S. Cities," *Journal of Urban Economics*, Vol. 72, No. 2–3: 87–103.

Bondonio, D. and J. Engberg, 2000, "Enterprise Zones and Local Employment: Evidence from the States' Programs," *Regional Science and Urban Economics*, Vol. 30, No. 5: 519–549.

Brandt, L. and C. A. Holz, 2006, "Spatial Price Differences in China: Estimates and Implications," *Economic Development and Cultural Change*, Vol. 55, No. 1: 43–86.

Buchanan, J. M., 1965, "An Economic Theory of Clubs," *Economica*, Vol. 32, No. 125: 1–14.

Chamberlin, E. H., 1933, *The Theory of Monopolistic Competition*, Cambridge: Harvard University Press.

Charles, K., E. Hurst, and M. Notowidigdo, 2013, "Manufacturing Decline, Housing Booms, and Non-Employment," NBER Working Paper No. 18949.

Ciccone, A. and R. Hall, 1996, "Productivity and the Density of Economic Activity," *American Economic Review*, Vol. 86, No. 1: 54–70.

Clark, C., 1957, *The Conditions of Economic Progress*, London: Macmillan & Co.

Coles, M., 1994, "Understanding the Matching Function: The Role of Newspapers and Job Agencies," Center for Economic Policy Research Discussion Paper No. 939.

Coles, M. and E. Smith, 1998, "Marketplaces and Matching," *International Economic Review*, Vol. 39, No. 1: 239–255.

Combes, P., 2004, "The Spatial Distribution of Economic Activities in the European Union," in *Handbook of Regional and Urban Economics* (J. V. Henderson and J. F. Thisse eds.), North Holland-Elsevier, 4.

Combes, P. and L. Gobillon, 2015, "The Empirics of Agglomeration Economics," in *Handbook of Regional and Urban Economics* (G. Duranton, V. Henderson, and W. Strange eds.), North Holland-Elsevier, 5.

Davis, D. and D. Weinstein, 1996, "Does Economic Geography Matter for International Specialization?" NBER Working Papers 5706.

Davis, D. and D. Weinstein, 1999, "Economic Geography and Regional Production Structure: An Empirical Investigation," *European Economic Review*, Vol. 43, No. 2: 379–407.

Delgado, M., M. Porter and S. Stern, 2014, "Defining Clusters of Related Industries," NBER Working Paper No. 20375.

Delgado, M., M. Porter, and S. Stern, 2016, "Defining Clusters of Related Industries," *Journal of Economic Geography*, Vol. 16, No. 1: 1–38.

Desmet, K. and J. Henderson, 2014, "The Geography of Development within Countries," in *Handbook of Regional and Urban Economics* (G. Duranton, V. Henderson, and W. Strange eds.), North Holland-Elsevier, 5.

Desmet, K. and E. Rossi-Hansberg, 2014, "Spatial Development," *American Economic Review*, Vol. 104, No. 4: 1211–1243.

Diamond, R., 2016, "The Determinants and Welfare Implications of US Workers' Diverging Location Choices by Skill: 1980–2000," *American Economic Review*, Vol. 106, No. 3: 479–524.

Dixit, A. and J. Stiglitz, 1977, "Monopolistic Competition and Optimum Product Diversity," *American Economic Review*, Vol. 67, No. 3: 297–308.

Duranton, G. and D. Puga, 2004, "Micro-Foundations of Urban Agglomeration Economies," in *Handbook of Regional and Urban Economics* (J. V. Henderson and J.-F. Thisse eds.), North Holland, 4.

Ellison, G. and E. Glaeser, 1997, "Geographic Concentration in U.S. Manufacturing Industries: A Dartboard Approach," *Journal of Political Economy*, Vol. 105, No. 5: 889–927.

Ellison, G., E. Glaeser and W. Kerr, 2010, "What Causes Industry Agglomeration? Evidence from Coagglomeration Patterns," *American Economic Review*, Vol. 100, No. 3: 1195–1213.

Ethier, W., 1982, "National and International Returns to Scale in the Modern Theory of International Trade," *American Economic Review*, Vol. 72, No. 3: 389–405.

Feldman, M., and D. Audretsch, 1999, "Innovation in Cities: Science-Based Diversity, Specialization and Localized Competition," *European Economic Review*, Vol. 43, No. 2: 409–429.

Feser, E. and E. Bergman, 2000, "National Industry Cluster Templates: A Framework for Applied Regional Cluster Analysis," *Regional Studies*, Vol. 34, No. 1: 1–19.

Fuchs, V., 1968, *The Service Economy*, New York and London: Columbia University Press.

Fujita, M., P. Krugman and A. Venables, 2001, *The Spatial Economy: Cities, Regions, and International Trade*, Cambridge: MIT Press.

Fujita, M. and T. Mori, 1996, "The Role of Ports in the Making of Major Cities: Self-Agglomeration and Hub-Effect," *Journal of Development Economics*, Vol. 49, No. 1: 93–120.

Fujita, M. and T. Mori, 1997, "Structural Stability and Evolution of Urban Systems," *Regional Science and Urban Economics*, Vol. 27, No. 4–5: 399–442.

Fujita, M., T. Mori, V. Henderson, and Y. Kanemoto, 2004, "Spatial Distribution of Economic Activities in Japan and China," in *Handbook of Regional and Urban Economics* (J. V. Henderson and J. F. Thisse eds.), North Holland-Elsevier, 4.

Garnsey, E., 1998, "A Theory of the Early Growth of the Firm," *Industrial and Corporate Change*, Vol. 7, No. 3: 523–556.

Gill, I. and H. Kharas, 2007, *An East Asian Renaissance: Ideas for Economic Growth*, the World Bank.

Glaeser, E., 1999, "Learning in Cities," *Journal of Urban Economics*, Vol. 46, No. 2: 254–277.

Glaeser, E., 2001, "The Economics of Location-Based Tax Incentives," Harvard Institute of Economic Research Discussion Paper No. 1932.

Glaeser, E., 2007a, "Entrepreneurship and the City," NBER Working Paper No. 13551.

Glaeser, E., 2007b, "The Economics Approach to Cities," NBER Working Paper No. 13696.

Glaeser, E. L. and J. D. Gottlieb, 2009, "The Wealth of Cities: Agglomeration Economies and Spatial Equilibrium in the United States," NBER Working Paper No. 14806.

Glaeser E., W. Huang, Y. Ma, and A. Shleifer, 2017, "A Real Estate Boom with Chinese Characteristics," *Journal of Economic Perspectives*, Vol. 31, No. 1: 93–116.

Glaeser, E. and W. Kerr, 2009, "Local Industrial Conditions and Entrepreneurship: How Much of the Spatial Distribution Can We Explain?" *Journal of Economics & Management Strategy*, Vol. 18, No. 3.

Glaeser, E. and M. Lu, 2018, "Human-Capital Externalities in China," NBER Working Paper No. 24925.

Glaeser, E. and M. Resseger, 2009, "The Complementarity between Cities and Skills," NBER Working Papers No. 15103.

Glaeser, E., J. Scheinkman, and A. Shleifer, 1995, "Economic Growth in a Cross-Section of Cities," *Journal of Monetary Economics*, Vol. 36, No. 1: 117–143.

Goos, M. and A. Manning, 2007, "Lousy and Lovely Jobs: The Rising Polarization of Work in Britain," *Review of Economics and Statistics*, Vol. 89, No. 1: 118–133.

Grabher, G., 1993, *The Embedded Firm: On the Socioeconomics of Industrial Networks*, Oxfordshire: Routledge.

Granovetter, M., 1973, "The Strength of Weak Ties," *American Journal of Sociology*, Vol. 78, No. 6: 1360–1380.

Greenstone, M., R. Hornbeck, and E. Moretti, 2010, "Identifying Agglomeration Spillovers: Evidence from Winners and Losers of Large Plant Openings," *Journal of Political Economy*, Vol. 118, No. 3: 536–598.

Hanson, G., 2005, "Market Potential, Increasing Returns and Geographic Concentration," *Journal of International Economics*, Vol. 67, No. 1: 1–24.

Hart, O., 1995, *Firms, Contracts, and Financial Structure*, Oxford: Oxford University Press.

Hausmann, R. and B. Klinger, 2006, "Structural Transformation and Patterns of Comparative Advantage in the Product Space," Harvard University CID Working Paper No. 128.

He, C. and J. Wang, 2012, "Regional and Sectoral Differences in the Spatial Restructuring of Chinese Manufacturing Industries during the Post-WTO Period," *Geo Journal*, Vol. 77, No. 3: 361–381.

Helsley, R. and W. Strange, 2014, "Coagglomeration, Clusters, and the Scale and Composition of Cities," *Journal of Political Economy*, Vol. 122, No. 5: 189–212.

Henderson, V., 2007, "Urbanization in China: Policy Issues and Options," China Economic Research and Advisory Programme Working Paper.

Holmes, T. and J. Stevens, 2004, "Spatial Distribution of Economic Activities in North America," in *Handbook of Regional and Urban Economics* (J. V. Henderson and J. F. Thisse eds.), North Holland-Elsevier, 4.

Hooker, M. and M. Knetter, 1999, "Measuring the Economic Effects of Military Base Closures," NBER Working Paper No. 6941.

Hoover, E. and R. Vernon, 1962, *Anatomy of a Metropolis: The Changing Distribution of People and Jobs within the New York Metropolitan Region*, New York: Anchor/Doubleday.

Huang, Z., X. Zhang, and Y. Zhu, 2008, "The Role of Clustering in Rural Industrialization: A Case Study of Wenzhou's Footwear Industry," *China Economic Review*, Vol. 19, No. 3: 409–420.

Humphrey, J. and H. Schmitz, 1996, "The Triple C Approach to Local Industrial Policy," *World Development*, Vol. 24, No. 12: 1859–1877.

Jaffe, A., M. Trajtenberg, and R. Henderson, 1993, "Geographic Localization of Knowledge Spillovers as Evidenced by Patent Citations," *Quarterly Journal of Economics*, Vol. 108, No. 3: 577–598.

Jovanovic, B., 1997, "Learning and Growth," in *Advances in Economics and Econometrics: Theory and Applications, 2* (D. M. Keps and K. F. Wallis eds.), Cambridge: Cambridge University Press.

Jovanovic, B. and R. Rob, 1989, "The Growth and Diffusion of Knowledge," *Review of Economic Studies*, Vol. 56, No. 4: 569–582.

Javorcik, B., 2004, "Does Foreign Direct Investment Increase the Productivity of Domestic Firms? In Search of Spillovers Through Backward Linkages," *American Economic Review*, Vol. 94, No. 3: 605–627.

Kerr, W., and S. Kominers, 2015, "Agglomerative Forces and Cluster Shapes," *Review of Economics and Statistics*, Vol. 97, No. 4: 877–899.

Kline, P., 2010, "Place Based Policies, Heterogeneity, and Agglomeration," *American Economic Review: Papers and Proceedings*, Vol. 100, No. 2: 383–387.

Koenker, R. and G. Bassett, 1978, "Regression Quantiles," *Econometrica*, Vol. 46, No. 1: 33–50: 143–156.

Kravis, I. and R. Lipsey, 1988, "National Price Levels and the Prices of Tradables and Nontradables," *American Economic Review*, Vol. 78, No. 2: 474–478.

Krugman, P., 1980, "Scale Economies, Product Differentiation, and the Pattern of Trade," *American Economic Review*, Vol. 70, No. 5: 950–959.

Krugman, P., 1991a, "Increasing Returns and Economic Geography," *Journal of Political Economy*, Vol. 99, No. 3: 483–499.

Krugman, P., 1991b, *Geography and Trade*, Cambridge: MIT Press.

Krugman, P. and A. Venables, 1995, "The Seamless World: A Spatial Model of International Specialization," CEPR Discussion Papers 1230.

Lemieux, T., 2006, "The 'Mincer Equation' Thirty Years after Schooling, Experience and Earnings," in *Jacob Mincer: A Pioneer of Modern Labor Economics* (S. Grossbard ed.), Springer.

Li, H., L. Li, B. Wu, and Y. Xiong, 2012, "The End of Cheap Chinese Labor," *Journal of Economic Perspectives*, Vol. 26, No. 4: 57–74.

Li, H., P. Liu, and J. Zhang, 2012, "Estimating Returns to Education Using Twins in Urban China," *Journal of Development Economics*, Vol. 97, No. 2: 494–504.

Li, H., P. Liu, J. Zhang, and N. Ma, 2007, "Economic Returns to Communist Party Membership: Evidence from Urban Chinese Twins," *The Economic Journal*, Vol. 117, No. 523: 1504–1520.

Liu, Z., 2007, "The External Returns to Education: Evidence from Chinese Cites," *Journal of Urban Economics*, Vol. 61, No. 3: 542–564.

López, R. and J. Südekum, 2009, "Vertical Industry Relations, Spillovers, and Productivity: Evidence from Chilean Plants," *Journal of Regional Science*, Vol. 49, No. 4: 721–747.

Lu, M. and H. Gao, 2011, "Labor Market Transition, Income Inequality and Economic Growth in China," *International Labour Review*, Vol. 150, No. 1–2: 101–126.

Lucas, R., 1988, "On the Mechanics of Economic Development," *Journal of Monetary Economics*, Vol. 22, No. 1: 3–42.

Manning, A., 2004, "We Can Work It Out: The Impact of Technological Change on the Demand for Low-Skill Workers," *Scottish Journal of Political Economy*, Vol. 51, No. 5: 581–608.

Marshall, A., 1890, *Principles of Economics*, London: Macmillan.

Mazzolari, F. and G. Ragusa, 2013, "Spillovers from High-Skill Consumption to Low-Skill Labor Markets," *The Review of Economics and Statistics*, Vol. 95, No. 1: 74–86.

Mincer, J., 1974, *Schooling, Experience, and Earnings*, New York: Columbia University Press.

Montgomery, J., 1991, "Social Networks and Labor-Market Outcomes: Toward an Economic Analysis," *American Economic Review*, Vol. 81, No. 5: 1407–1418.

Moretti, E., 2004a, "Human Capital Externalities in Cities," in *Handbook of Regional and Urban Economics* (J. V. Henderson and J. F. Thisse eds.), North Holland-Elsevier, 4.

Moretti, E., 2004b, "Workers' Education, Spillovers, and Productivity: Evidence from Plant-Level Production Functions," *American Economic Review*, Vol. 94, No. 3: 656–690.

Moretti, E., 2004c, "Estimating the Social Return to Higher Education: Evidence from Longitudinal and Repeated Cross-Sectional Data," *Journal of Econometrics*, Vol. 121, No. 1–2: 175–212.

Moretti, E., 2010, "Local Multipliers," *American Economic Review: Papers and Proceedings*, Vol. 100, No. 2: 373–377.

Moretti, E., 2011, "Local Labor Markets," in *Handbook of Labor Economics* (D. Card and O. Ashenfelter eds.), North Holland, 4.

Moretti, E., 2013, "Real Wage Inequality," *American Economic Journal: Applied Economics*, Vol. 5, No. 1: 65–103.

Moretti, E. and P. Thulin, 2013, "Local Multipliers and Human Capital in the United States and Sweden," *Industrial and Corporate Change*, Vol. 22, No. 1: 339–362.

Oort, F. and E. Stam, 2006, "Agglomeration Economies and Entrepreneurship in the ICT Industry," ERIM Report Series No. ERS-2006-016-ORG.

Perkins, D. and T. Rawski, 2008, "Forecasting China's Economic Growth to 2025," in *China's Great Economic Transformation* (D. Perkins and T. Rawski eds.), Cambridge: Cambridge University Press.

Porter, M., 1990, *The Competitive Advantage of Nations*, New York: Free Press.

Porter, M., 2003, "The Economic Performance of Regions," *Regional Studies*, Vol. 37, No. 6–7: 549–578.

Rauch, J., 1993, "Productivity Gains from Geographic Concentration of Human Capital: Evidence from the Cities," *Journal of Urban Economics*, Vol. 34, No. 3: 380–400.

Ravallion, M., 1998, "Does Aggregation Hide the Harmful Effects of Inequality on Growth?" *Economics Letters*, Vol. 61: 73–77.

Ravallion, M. and S. Chen, 2007, "China's (Uneven) Progress against Poverty," *Journal of Development Economics*, Vol. 82, No. 1: 1–42.

Redding, S., 2009, "The Empirics of New Economic Geography," Working Paper.

Redding, S., 2011, "Economic Geography: A Review of the Theoretical and Empirical Literature," Working Paper.

Roback, J., 1982, "Wages, Rents, and the Quality of Life," *Journal of Political Economy*, Vol. 90, No. 6: 1257–1278.

Rodrik, D., 2006, "Industrial Development: Stylized Facts and Policies," Working Paper.

Rodrik, D., 2016, "Premature Deindustrialization," *Journal of Economic Growth*, Vol. 21: 1–33.

Rosenthal, S. and W. Strange, 2004, "Evidence on the Nature and Sources of Agglomeration Economies," in *Handbook of Regional and Urban Economics* (V. Henderson and J. Thisse eds.), North-Holland, 4.

Saxenian, A., 1994, *Regional Advantage: Culture and Competition in Silicon Valley and Route 128*, Harvard: Harvard University Press.

Schettkat, R. and L. Yocarini, 2003, "The Shift to Services: A Review of the Literature," IZA Working Paper No. 964.

Shen, K. Y. and J. H. Chen, 2014, "Analysis on the Sustainability of the Balanced Development Trend of the Regional Economy in China," *Academic Monthly*, Vol. 8: 97–105.

Sonobe, T., D. Hu, and K. Otsuka, 2002, "Process of Cluster Formation in China: A Case Study of a Garment Town," *Journal of Development Studies*, Vol. 39, No. 1: 118–139.

Sonobe, T. and K. Otsuka, 2006, *Cluster-Based Industrial Development: An East Asia Model*, London: Palgrave MacMillan.

Spence, M., 1973, "Job Market Signaling," *The Quarterly Journal of Economics*, Vol. 87, No. 3: 355–374.

Sveikauskas, L., 1975, "The Productivity of Cities," *Quarterly Journal of Economics*, Vol. 89, No. 3: 393–413.

United Nations, Department of Economic and Social Affairs, Population Division, 2015, *World Urbanization Prospects: The 2014 Revision*, (ST/ESA/SER.A/366).

United Nations, Department of Economic and Social Affairs, Population Division, 2018, *World Urbanization Prospects: The 2018 Revision*.

Veugelers, R., 2013, *Manufacturing Europe's Future*, Brussels: Bruegel.

Wei, S. J., Z. Xie, and X. B. Zhang, 2017, "From 'Made in China' to 'Innovated in China': Necessity, Prospect, and Challenges," *Journal of Economic Perspectives*, Vol. 31, No. 1: 49–70.

Wen, Y. and J. Wu, 2014, "Withstanding Great Recession like China," Federal Reserve Bank of St. Louis Working Paper Series No. 2014-007A.

Williamson, O., 1985, *The Economic Institutions of Capitalism: Firms, Markets, Relational Contracting*, New York: Free Press.

Wilson, J., 1999, "Theories of Tax Competition," *National Tax Journal*, Vol. 52, No. 2: 269–304.

World Bank, 2006, *World Development Report 2006: Equity and Development.*

World Bank, 2008, *World Development Report 2009: Reshaping Economic Geography.*

Yao, Z. Q. and J. C. Xia, 2005, "Capital Deepening, Technology Progress, and Their Effects on China's Employment," *The Journal of World Economy*, Vol. 1: 58–67.

Chinese

Cai, Y. F. and C. W. Zhang, 2012, "A New Perspective of Regional Disparities: Research on the Mismatch of Population and Industrial Distribution," *China Industrial Economics*, Vol. 5: 31–43.

Chang, C. and M. Lu, 2017, "Misery of New Town — Density, Distance and Debt," *China Economic Quarterly*, Vol. 4: 1621–1642.

Chen, J. G. and Q. Wang, 2005, "The Sustainable Development of China's Industrial Clusters and Public Policy Choices," *China Industrial Economics*, Vol. 9: 5–10.

Chen, J. J., G. L. Chen, and J. Huang, 2009, "A Study on the Agglomeration of Producer Services and its Influencing Factors from the Perspective of New Economic Geography: Empirical Evidence from 222 Cities in China," *Management World*, Vol. 4: 83–95.

Chen, Z. and M. Lu, 2009, *Balancing in Agglomeration: An Empirical Study on Coordinated Development between Urban and Rural Areas and Regions in China*, Peking: Peking University Press.

Cheng, D. Z., 2004, "Features, Causes and Effects of Service Industry Growth: Baumol-Fuchs Hypothesis and an Empirical Study," *Social Sciences in China*, Vol. 2: 18–32.

Dong, M. J. and Y. M. Liang, 2013, "The Sources of China's Economic Growth from 1978 to 2010: A Non-parameter Framework," *Economic Research Journal*, Vol. 5: 17–32.

Fan, J. Y., 2006, "Industrial Agglomeration and Difference of Regional Labor Productivity: Chinese Evidence with International Comparison," *Economic Research Journal*, Vol. 11: 72–81.

Fan, J. Y. and B. J. Yang, 2002, "Concentration Transmission of Manufacturing Industry in Early America and Its Enlightenment for China's Western Development," *Economic Research Journal*, Vol. 8: 66–73.

Fu, S. H. and J. J. Hong, 2008, "Firm Size, City Size, and Agglomeration Economics: Evidence from China Manufacturing Census," *Economic Research Journal*, Vol. 11: 112–125.

Ge, J. X. and J. S. An, 2010, "Periodical Characters in History of Chinese Migrants in the 20th Century," *Exploration and Free Views*, Vol. 2: 71–75.

Gu, N. H., D. D. Bi, and W. B. Ren, 2006, "Relationship between Producer Services' Development and Manufacturing's Competence in China During Transition Period: An Empirical Research Based on Panel Data," *China Industrial Economics*, Vol. 9: 14–21.

Jiang, J., Z. B. Liu, and M. C. Yu, 2007, "The Development of Producer Services and Manufacturing Efficiency Growth: An Empirical Analysis Based on Regional and Industry Panel Data," *The Journal of World Economy*, Vol. 8: 52–62.

Jin, Y., Z. Chen, and M. Lu, 2006, "Industry Agglomeration in China: Economic Geography, New Economic Geography and Policy," *Economic Research Journal*, Vol. 4: 79–89.

Li, G. P. and H. Z. Fan, 2003, "The Distribution of Production, Population and Regional Inequality," *Economic Research Journal*, Vol. 11: 79–86.

Liu, R. X., 2013, "Exploring the Sources of China's Economic Growth: Factor Inputs, Productivity and Environmental Consumption," *The Journal of World Economy*, Vol. 10: 123–141.

Liu, X. J. and Y. H. Zhao, 2009, "The Impact of Labor Migration on Urban Labor Markets in China," *China Economic Quarterly*, Vol. 2: 693–710.

Long, X. N., J. Zhang, and X. B. Zhang, 2015, "Impact of Industrial Clusters on Contract Protection and Financing," *China Economics Quarterly*, Vol. 4: 1563–1590.

Lu, J. Y. and Z. G. Tao, 2006, "Industrial Agglomeration and Coagglomeration in China's Manufacturing Industries: with International Comparison," *Economic Research Journal*, Vol. 3: 103–114.

Lu, M., 2010, "Reconstruction of Urban System: On the Strategy of Regional and Urban Sustainable Development in China," *Journal of Nanjing University (Philosophy, Humanities and Social Sciences)*, Vol. 5: 15–26.

Lu, M. and Z. Chen, 2007, "Balancing in Agglomeration: The Third Way of Coordinated Urban-rural and Regional Development," *The Journal of World Economy*, Vol. 8: 57–61.

Lu, M. and H. J. Ou, 2011, "High Economic Growth and Low Job Creation: An Empirical Study of Government Intervention and Employment Elasticity," *The Journal of World Economy*, Vol. 12: 5–33.

Lu, M. and K. H. Xiang, 2012, "Geography and Service: Does Domestic Demand Disperse China's Urban System?" *China Economic Quarterly*, Vol. 3: 1079–1096.

Ma, G. X., M. J. Shi, and N. Li, 2007, "The Degree of Coagglomeration and the Mechanism of Spatial Agglomeration in China's Manufacturing Industries," *Management World*, Vol. 8: 58–65.

Meng, K. Q. and M. Lu, 2011, "Three Major City Clusters in China: Scopes and Differences," *South China Journal of Economics*, Vol. 2: 3–15.

National Bureau of Statistics, 2005, *China Economic Census Yearbook 2004*, China Statistics Press.

National Bureau of Statistics, 2006, *Input-Output Table of China 2002*, China Statistics Press.

Qian, A. M., C. Y. Zhang, and D. L. Bu, 2015, "Macroeconomic Shock, Industrial Policy and Government Subsidy," *Industrial Economics Research*, Vol. 5: 73–82.

Qin, D. J., 2008, "Small City Development and Urbanization with Chinese Characteristics", *Studies on the Socialism with Chinese Characteristics*, Vol. 3: 96–99.

Ruan, J. Q., Q. Shi, and X. B. Zhang, 2014, "The Regular Pattern of Dynamic Evolution of the Industrial Clusters, and the Policies of the Local Government," *Journal of Management World*, Vol. 12: 79–91.

Shen, K. Y. And J. H. Chen, 2014, "Analysis on the Sustainability of the Balanced Development Trend of the Regional Economy in China," *Academic Monthly*, Vol. 8: 97–105.

Wan, G. H. and F. Cai, 2012, "Challenges in China's Economy and the Urbanization," in *Urbanization and Development in China: Challenges, Prospects and Policies* (G. Wan, F. Cai *et al.*, eds.), Economic Science Press.

Wang, X. L., 2010, "Urbanization Path and City Scale in China: An Economic Analysis," *Economic Research Journal*, Vol. 10: 20–32.

Wu, J. B. and B. Guo, 2010, "The Coevolution of Firm's Adaptation, Networking and Industrial Clusters: A Longitudinal Case Study on the Growth of the Textile Industrial Cluster in Shaoxing County," *Management World*, Vol. 2: 141–155.

Xu, Z., Z. Chen, and M. Lu, 2010, "Core–Periphery Model of Urban Economic Growth: Empirical Evidence from Chinese City-Level Data 1990–2006," *The Journal of World Economy*, Vol. 7: 144–160.

Yang, R. D. and S. E. Zhu, 2007, "Can Equity and Efficiency Coexist: Study on the Marginal Propensity to Consume in China," *Economic Research Journal*, Vol. 12: 46–58.

Yao, Z. Q. and J. C. Xia, 2005, "Capital Deepening, Technology Progress, and Their Effects on China's Employment," *The Journal of World Economy*, Vol. 1: 58–67.

Yuan, F. H. and Y. X. Li, 2008, "Capital Deepening and Employment Adjustment in China's Manufacturing Sector," *China Economic Quarterly*, Vol. 1: 197–210.

Yuan, Z. G. and Y. X. Yu, 2012, "Long-term Growth and Short-term Fluctuations of the Chinese Economy," *Academic Monthly*, Vol. 7: 62–72.

Zhang, X. B. and J. Q. Ruan, 2011, *The Evolution and Development of Industrial Clusters in China*, Zhejiang University Press.

Zhao, W. and C. Zhang, 2007, "FDI and Manufacturing Agglomeration in China: Evidence of 20 Industries," *Economic Research Journal*, Vol. 11: 82–90.

Zhao, Z., 2004, "Rural–Urban Migration in China: What Do We Know and What Do We Need to Know?" *China Economic Quarterly*, Vol. 3: 517–536.

Zhong, N. H., 2011, "Can Rural Industrialization Keep Working in China," *Economic Research Journal*, Vol. 4: 18–27.

Zhu, X. G., 2000, "Urbanization and Small Town Construction: An Analysis of the Advantages and Disadvantages," *Journal of Socialist Theory Guide*, Vol. 4: 29–32.

Index

A

abstract jobs, 47, 95, 157
agglomeration, 159
agglomeration effect, 6–21, 25, 27, 31–32, 34–35, 37–40, 42–45, 51–53, 55–58, 61, 70, 74–75, 80–81, 91–92, 107, 111, 117–119, 126–127, 130–131, 135, 143–146, 149, 156, 158–160, 162, 165, 167–168, 175–177, 179, 183–184, 186, 195–196, 198, 200, 202–209

B

backward linkage, 18, 170–172, 204

C

capital-intensive industries, 56, 83, 91, 191
centrifugal force, 25, 53–54
Chinese Household Income Project, 36, 77, 104, 106, 109, 125, 157
Clark's Law, 35, 46, 48, 78
cluster strength, 145–148, 161–165, 167, 172–173, 175, 204
coagglomeration, 133, 135–138, 159
collectively owned enterprises, 58
comparative advantages, 5, 11, 21, 40, 42–43, 45, 47–48, 56, 132, 155, 158, 168, 175–176
complementarity, 80
complementary effect, 10, 21, 43, 120, 207
consumer service, 121, 125–127, 179, 185, 192–193, 196, 199, 203, 205, 207
convergence effect, 159–160, 162, 165, 169, 175
core–periphery model, 54
crowding-out effect, 7, 8, 12, 14, 26, 32, 40–41, 51, 53, 62, 65–66, 69–70, 74–75, 97–98, 127, 162, 168, 183, 190, 195, 198, 202, 209

D

dispersing effect, 53, 55, 56, 63, 145, 146, 149
double imbalance, 5

E

employment multiplier effect, 18, 36, 48–49, 76, 179, 183–186, 195–199, 204–205, 207

employment polarization, 47, 48
employment rate, 9, 75, 81, 95, 104, 126
export-oriented development strategy, 5
external imbalance, 5, 180

F
first nature geography, 25
fixed effects, 49, 161, 163, 186, 187, 188, 190
forward linkage, 170–171

H
Herfindahl–Hirschman Index, 148, 154, 202
heterogeneity, 16, 18, 20, 34, 38, 45, 69, 91, 106, 184
hierarchical clustering, 136, 139, 140, 143, 153
high-level equilibrium, 11, 18, 40, 184
human capital externality, 29

I
inclusive economic growth, 3, 10, 32
income disparities, 55
increasing returns to scale, 8, 11, 25, 26–29, 38, 75, 108
industry strength, 161, 163, 165, 167
input–output relationship, 51, 53, 132–133, 135–136, 138, 143, 149, 151, 159, 170, 172
instrumental variable, 15, 18, 31–32, 77, 82, 85, 87, 92, 104, 106, 112, 114, 122, 125, 188–190, 202
interaction term, 165, 173, 204
inter-industry linkage, 16, 131–133, 135–136, 138–139, 144, 207
inter-industry similarity matrices, 136, 139–141, 153
internal imbalance, 5, 180
inter-regional coordinated development, 7

K
knowledge-intensive, 100, 121, 125
knowledge spillover, 14, 20, 24, 29–30, 44, 51, 53, 66, 69, 76–77, 91, 100, 121, 125–126, 131, 133, 135, 138, 159, 170–171, 202, 209

L
labor demand, 9, 11, 14, 35, 49, 75, 78, 80–81, 90–91, 112, 129, 183, 186, 188, 195–196, 202
labor economics, 13, 19, 27, 33, 34, 208
labor market pooling, 24, 51, 53, 135, 138
labor supply, 4–5, 9, 14, 18, 35, 38, 40, 58, 70, 75, 90, 108–109, 117, 121, 180, 183, 186, 190, 192, 194–196, 198, 202, 208
land-intensive, 62, 98
localization effect, 42, 43, 130, 159, 160, 162, 169
low-level equilibrium, 11, 18, 40, 184

M
manual jobs, 18, 20, 47, 95–96, 100–101, 121, 125–126
marketization, 49, 58, 64, 181, 194, 196, 208
matching, 8–9, 13, 26–28, 31, 35, 53, 75, 195, 201
Mincer equation, 33, 106, 110
monopolistic competition model, 27, 49

N
new economic geography, 8, 13, 14, 19, 25, 34, 43, 45, 51, 55, 105, 146, 159, 162, 201, 208
nominal income, 15, 19, 37–39, 105–106, 108–111, 114, 117–118, 122–126, 179, 203
nominal value, 109
non-tradable good, 15, 35–39, 41, 46, 47, 48, 49, 62, 76, 78, 105, 108–111, 117–118, 121–122, 183, 192
non-wage income, 9, 15, 19, 31, 36, 105, 108–109

O
output relationship, 159

P
partition clustering, 136, 139, 140
place-based policies, 10–11, 14, 18, 21, 39–42, 50, 158, 176–177, 183–184, 186, 192, 194, 200, 206, 207
planned economy, 3–4, 56, 85, 112, 125
post-industrialization, 12, 46, 182
Probit model, 15, 36, 78, 81, 89
producer service, 10, 49, 156, 158, 182–183, 185–186, 188–189, 192, 194, 196, 199, 205
public service, 6, 127, 176, 177, 192–194, 196–197, 199, 205

Q
quantile regression, 16, 122, 126, 203

R
real income, 15, 19, 32, 37–39, 73–74, 105–106, 108–111, 117–118, 122–126, 179
regional price disparities, 37, 105
research and development, 156, 158, 176
Robustness Scores (RS), 140
robustness test, 190

S
second nature geography, 25
service economy, 12, 46, 179, 182
sharing, 9, 13, 26–27, 31, 107, 131, 133, 201, 209
social capital, 33, 90
spatial general equilibrium, 11, 15–16, 20, 38–40, 81, 108
spillover effect, 11–12, 21, 41–42, 44, 48, 74, 128, 130, 132, 159, 166, 170–171, 176, 183, 192, 200, 208, 209
state-owned enterprises, 56
structural transformation, 4, 14, 18, 39, 50, 62, 73, 98, 184, 205, 207

T
the Gini coefficient, 65
the hukou system, 6, 7, 15, 128, 184
the Newey's two-step method, 90
the Pearl River Delta, 24, 51, 55, 63–64, 189, 209
the reform and opening up, 2–5, 23, 51–52, 55–57, 62, 70, 144, 179
the spatial Kuznets curve, 62
the Third Front Construction program, 84
the Yangtze River Delta, 24, 51, 54, 63, 64, 189, 209
thick labor market, 27
total factor productivity, 29
township and village enterprises, 57
tradable goods, 10, 35, 41, 48, 52, 76, 139, 157, 185

U

upstreamness, 149–152, 160, 171–173, 175, 202, 204
urbanization effect, 42–43, 79, 130, 159–160
urban system, 6, 15, 53, 73, 128, 209

V

Validation Scores of Clusters (VSC), 140
Validation Scores of Industries (VSI), 140